THE DESERT PILGRIM

En Route to Mysticism and Miracles

MARY SWANDER

Ice Cube Press
North Liberty, Iowa

The Desert Pilgraim: En Route to Mysticism and Miracles

Isbn 9781888160338

Afterword © 2008 Mary Swander

Ice Cube Press Edition
copyright © 2008 Mary Swander

First published with Viking 2003
Published in Penquin Compass 2004

Library of Congress Control Number: 2008921928

Ice Cube Press (est 1993)
205 N Front Street
North Liberty, Iowa 52317
www.icecubepress.com
steve@icecubepress.com

Manufactured in the United States of America

The paper used in this publication meets the minimum requirements of the American National Standard for Information Sciences—Permanence of Paper for Printed Library Materials, ANSI Z39.48-1992

Cover art is an icon entitled, *Out Lady of the Sandia* and was a gift to author.

Also by Mary Swander

Nonfiction
Out of This World: A Journey of Healing

Parsnips in the Snow
(with Jane Staw)

Poetry
Heaven-and-Earth House

Driving the Body Back

Succession

Edited collections
The Healing Circle: Authors on Recovery
(with Patricia Foster)

Bloom and Blossom:
The Reader's Guide to Gardening

Land of the Fragile Giants
(with Cornelia Mutel)

For Maclovia and Clemente

The person who seeks the connecting threads in the history of his life has already ... created a coherence in that life.

—Wilhelm Dilthey,

*Pattern and Meaning in History:
Thoughts on History and Society*

Prologue

I stand near the back of the nave of Father Sergei's church, my eyes fixed on the two nuns bowing and chanting at a lectern near the wall, their black veils drawn down to their eyebrows, the room dark and hazy from the incense rising up in the air. "*Kyri-e e-le-ison*" the three Russian Orthodox monks in the next room sing. "*Kyri-e e-le-ison*" the tiny congregation of about a dozen parishioners answers. In unison, they bow and cross themselves according to the Eastern rite—from right shoulder to left. I follow suit, standing there barefoot, our shoes all piled in a clump near the door of this converted garage in Albuquerque, New Mexico.

"*Christ-e e-le-ison*," the monks chant. Father Sergei—or *Papa*, as he is called by his followers—passes by the sanctuary door, his bright gold-and-white vestments rustling and glittering, the flames from the candelabra stationed near the altar flickering in the dimness. A large votive candle encased in red glass hangs down from the ceiling in our room, casting eerie shadows on the walls, every square inch filled with brightly painted icons, statues of saints, skulls of animals, photographs of dead monks in their caskets. Even the ceiling is covered with icons: long-haired men staring down at me from slightly crazed-looking eyes. My feet dig into the old oriental carpet, its threads worn and dusty. I am a white, middle-aged, middle-class university professor from Iowa. What am I doing here? I ask myself.

"*Christ-e e-le-ison*," I chant back with the congregants and cross myself again. Even though I can't understand the sprinkling of

Russian prayers that enter into the worship, I remember enough Latin from my old Catholic school days to get the drift of the service. The format is following that of an old pre–Vatican II Mass. The congregants bow, and I bow with them. A single wooden pew graces the back wall, but we all stay on our feet and sway to and fro, gracefully, rhythmically, hypnotically, knees bent, heads bobbing from side to side. An old Hispanic woman in a long, lacy black veil. A suburban-looking couple in their late fifties with their grown Down's syndrome son who sings out the responses in a strong, hearty voice. A younger couple with three small children, one crawling across the floor, weaving in and out around our feet. Over my left shoulder, mounted on a waist-high platform, is a shrine of the Blessed Mother, her eyes open, serene, less psychotic-appearing than the male icons. The odor of roses wafts toward me.

"*Kyri-e e-le-ison*" the monks continue. The suburban woman cracks the door, the incense so thick now that we can barely see across the room. A streak of warm, bright desert light beams into the church. Outside, Sunday morning traffic passes by, first one car, then a full five minutes later, another. Once, this had been a busy thoroughfare in Albuquerque, part of Route 66, a street that ran through the heart of the city, through the flesh and blood of an old working-class section of town that sprang up around the railroad. Once, the street had been teeming with shops, cafés, tortilla factories, the Jewish and Hispanic owners sweeping the dust off the sidewalk together in the early morning hours. Then freeways outclassed two-lane roads, and urban renewal severed the area from the flow of traffic. Slowly, over the course of several decades, businesses began to die, and by the mid-1990s, the neighborhood had given way to crack houses and drive-by shootings.

Yet some businesses withstood the changes in the barrio. Across the street, the drugstore and oldest pharmacy in New Mexico, established by a man who had ridden with Pancho Villa, is still open for business. Its walls are lined with herbs—boxes, crates, and gallon jugs of dried leaves, bark, and flowers. Luisa, part-owner and manager, stations herself at a card table near the front counter. "Lu," as her people call her, keeps track of her clients on little white index cards, filing them by their first names in a small recipe box. There, she records your symptoms and her recommendations: yerba del manzo, echinacea, red clover. One after another, people find their way to her store, her door decorated with an icon painted by Father Sergei, an icon of St. Francis of Assisi, the light from the saint's stigmata shooting out from his hands. The ill approach Lu with stomach problems, Bell's palsy, migraine headaches. One by one the people find themselves cured of their suffering, cured by the herbs Lu gathers along the Rio Grande.

The Rio Grande flows south through Albuquerque, winding past the Isleta Pueblo and casino. The stark white walls of St. Augustine's, the mission church built around 1629, stand in contrast to the flashing neon casino signs advertising blackjack and slot machines. The river pushes beyond Albuquerque's sprawl into the open countryside, where the sky and desert slice the horizon into two equal halves. The Manzano Mountains provide a backdrop for Tome, where just beyond the small town three crosses sit on top of a sacred hill to commemorate the death of Christ. Farther south, the fertile farming valley near Belen with its green irrigated fields gives way to a drier, crustier topography near Socorro. The marshlands of the Bosque del Apache National Wildlife Refuge, with its great blue herons and migrating flocks of snow geese and sandhill cranes, provide a cool oasis in the midst of blowing sand and tumbleweed.

The Rio Grande proceeds north out of Albuquerque on an ear-popping ascent into the high desert country. Rolling hills punctuated with piñon and juniper trees fold into the feet of mountains jutting their peaks up into the clear, bright blue sky. The vistas of the high desert narrow, the focal point shifting from an outward to an upward perspective. The Rocky Mountains humble humans, their presence large, looming, and encompassing. Past Santa Fe, the river carves out another fertile valley, a valley filled with red chili pepper plants, with grazing sheep, and with shops containing woolen rugs handwoven by fifth-generation weavers using Old World Spanish techniques and natural dyes. The region is also rich with healing sites. The best known is the Santuario de Chimayo, a Roman Catholic shrine built on the site of an old Tewa Indian hot spring.

The desert is at once inviting and threatening. Its landscape is varied with geological formations from plainslike terrain to rock cairns to ancient cliff cave dwellings. Its people are as multidimensional as the landscape, with a dominant blend of Native American and Spanish cultures. Its vast open ranges produce a leveling effect, its mountain passes a passage through adversity. Here, I am awed by the sweep of the desert's panorama, the absolute envelopment of its reach. Here, I can feel secure in a land that takes such command of its space. Here, I can also sense the danger of the hard, rocky mountain outcroppings and cliffs, and of the beds of volcanic rock and ash. I can grasp my own insignificance in the grand scheme of the earth and the universe. In that realization, in that sheer expanse of emptiness, I am forced to confront my deepest fears, my aloneness and individuality, and my relationship to the

Divine. I am forced to intone my own chants of penitence, forgiveness, and gratitude.

"Kyri-e e-le-ison" Father Sergei intones, and the monks fade from view again into the privacy of the sanctuary. The nave is ours now, the babe at our feet finding our shoes and scattering them across the carpet, the Down's syndrome man wiping his nose with his sleeve, the old woman in the lacy veil lowering her head and kissing the crucifix on her rosary, crossing herself again and again. The mid-May sun shines through the bars of the one window on the door. The bright desert sun forces you to squint even here in this dim room. Light spreads out from the window. Light spreads toward me like St. Francis's hands. The smell of roses encircles me: roses in bloom along the boulevard in front of this church, rosewater mixed into the Virgin's tears, rose hips sealed in a gallon Mason jar in the drugstore across the street. My hands warm. My feet warm. My whole body feels transported to another time and place, a place suspended in time. What is unsealing inside me? From where have I journeyed?

1.

The year before my participation in Father Sergei's services, I'd awoken on an early February Saturday morning in Iowa, the temperature thirty-five degrees below zero and a howling wind driving snow against my windowpanes. I'd opened my eyes but was unable to move my limbs. Pain shot down my neck, through every vertebra in my back, and out my tailbone. Pain pulsated through my shoulders, elbows, and hips. My knees, swollen twice their size, throbbed with an excruciating rhythm of their own, and the nerves running down my calves to my big toes felt like piano wires tightening tauter and tauter. I tried to raise my legs, but couldn't. I tried to twist my torso, but couldn't. I'd been ill and alone before but had always been able to hop, stagger, or crawl to the bathroom. This was different. Overnight, I'd become a Kafkaesque cockroach, stuck on my back, incapable of righting myself.

The previous day I had felt a stabbing pain in my right knee. But what was new? I'd walked around in pain since age fifteen when I had suffered a severe neck injury in an automobile accident. During the next twenty years, I had been whiplashed three more times. I had tried various forms of physical therapy with varied results. When the injury finally manifested itself as post-traumatic fibromyalgia, a neuro-endrocrine condition, the doctors simply advised: Learn to live with it. A midwesterner to the core, I masked my daily discomfort, bullying my way through the days, trying to focus on other things, trying not to complain. The pain finally suppressed my immune system, and a reaction to an overdose of a vaccine sent me spinning into a world of multiple chemical and food sensitivities. In response to that illness, my life became restricted, controlled, and isolated.

Then when I was forty-five years old, I was in a fifth accident. On a cold December night, I was hit near the university campus. The driver, who had been drinking, had run a stop sign, the wheels of his pickup truck streaming across the ice.

I was taken to the hospital and released with a neck brace, an all-too-familiar appendage, and the diagnosis of "cervical strain." I remained in severe pain for weeks. Then I got the flu, coughing and sneezing into the night. Then I thought I was getting over the flu, my head and chest clearing, when suddenly I became a character in a Kafka story.

There I was at 6 A.M., unable to turn my head, wiggle my toes, or even reach up and scratch my nose. I was living in rural Iowa, fifteen miles from town, in the heart of the heart of the country, on the coldest night of the coldest month of the year, of the decade, of my lifetime. I lay in the darkness and tried to think, the pitch of the pain rising higher and higher. One hour passed, then another, the pain becoming more and more intense, hammering my spine, the keys rising up and falling down, resounding through my whole body with long, low, sustained notes, the piano wire underscoring a whole symphony orchestra.

Fortunately, the phone was right beside my bed, and I could bend my elbow just enough to get it up to my ear. I considered whom to call. Years before, through death and divorce, my family of origin had disintegrated. Both my parents were only children, so I had no aunts, uncles, or cousins. I had no spouse, no children of my own. I had my friends and neighbors, thank God, and good ones, too, but I didn't want to impose on anyone. With the extreme cold, many cars were dead. For some reason it didn't occur to me to call an ambulance.

Finally, I got hold of a couple of friends who jumped their car and drove me to the local emergency room, where I lay on a gurney and my socks were cut off my legs. I received a diagnosis of "gout" and was sent home to my own devices. (Over the course of the next four months, the diagnosis progressed from gout to an exacerbation of my fibromyalgia, to rheumatoid arthritis or lupus. A full ten months later I would find out just how wrong these diagnoses were.) Home from the ER, I was bed-bound and forced again to turn to my neighbors and friends.

So in they came. Thirty-nine different people. Three or four a day for three weeks. From my closest chums to my students and colleagues. Even my electrician signed up for a shift. "It looks like all your circuits blew," he joked, sitting beside my bed. Every four or five hours a new pair of hands opened my kitchen drawers, rummaging for utensils. They opened my closet, hunting for clean clothes. Some steady, some hesitant, some downright shaky, they opened my robe and lifted my neck to change hot packs.

Whish, boom. When they first opened the door, each one of these men and women—old and new friends alike—entered wide-eyed, willing but unaccustomed to their new caretaker roles. Shedding their coats and hats, they stepped into my bedroom and no longer were just acquaintances and pals. Suddenly, they were my nurses, my guardians. I was their patient, their child.

"Welcome to the funhouse," I quipped, trying to ease my nervousness.

To ease theirs, the women chopped onions and carrots, and stirred big pots of stew. They sat beside my bed and read me stories. They helped me hobble to the bathroom and turned away their faces until it was time to wipe. *Whish, boom.* Most of the men were back out the door as soon as they came in, feeding the cats and dog, running after groceries, renting a walker, a commode. Inside, they sat at the kitchen table and sharpened my knives.

"Hey, Mom," I whispered to my friend Sarah who slept beside me on the sofa one morning. It was 7:30 A.M. I'd been awake since six, needing to urinate. Ashamed of my problem, I hadn't wanted to wake Sarah. I lay there in the darkness, the tick of the clock growing louder and louder, until I finally murmured, "Can you get me up?"

Sarah roused herself and stood beside my bed, swallowing hard.

Tentatively, she put one hand under my neck and wrapped the other around my waist, as I had coached her. Then, cradling me in her arms, she pulled my body upward, and we abandoned ourselves to the primitive intimacy of the moment. Awkward though we were in our newfound tie, we were kin.

A few minutes later, she sat me down at the kitchen table. Immobile, I was like a child in a high chair, a voyeur at my own feeding. I directed her to the freezer compartment of the refrigerator in search of a bag of cherries. She pawed through cold packs and hunks of frozen meat until she found the fruit, which she began warming in a pan on the stove. My stomach growling, mouth watering, I watched her slowly stir the fruit, steam rising from the pan. Sarah tied a napkin around my chin. I opened my mouth wide.

"Coming in for a landing," she said, buzzing the spoon through the air and dishing up a bright red cherry.

The fruit lodged on my tongue, the juice warm and sweet, pooling in my cheeks, trickling down my throat. Sarah reloaded the spoon, and I chewed again and again, one cherry at a time, my teeth breaking through each membrane, sinking down into the flesh. We had both given in.

Shortly, Sarah left for work. I thanked her, wished her a pleasant day, and held back my tears until I heard her car pull out of my drive. Then I let myself cry. I realized I forgot to ask her to put me back in bed, and I was stuck in the kitchen chair until early afternoon when someone else was due to arrive. Now, I was the baby in her crib, left with a sitter, bawling her head off when her mother steps out the door. Except there was no baby-sitter. Now, in the midst of the parade of these genuine caregivers, I'd never felt more alone.

Solitude had always been an important factor in my life. As a child, I was constantly thankful that I had two older brothers who had to share a room and that I was privileged enough to have my own. I would enter my space, an enclosed sleeping porch, shut the door, and play by myself for hours, the wind blowing the elm trees back and forth past my windows, the breeze cooling and slightly raising the hairs at the nape of my neck. Or I would curl up with a book in my bed and read while the squabbles and oversights of the rest of the family brewed all around me.

I devoured such books as *The Secret Garden, Treasure Island*, and *Jane Eyre*. Oliver Twist's orphanage made the household tensions around me seem manageable. I was the child who abhorred the thought of going away to summer camp, even if we had been able to afford it. Camp seemed like the ultimate orphanage, lacking any kind of privacy. Although I loved sports and the outdoors, the thought of sharing a cabin with ten or twelve other girls terrified me. That was way too much noise and togetherness.

At the same time, I sincerely liked people, liked to laugh, joke, and play team games with them. But at the end of the day, I craved alone time, to gather my thoughts, to be quiet and feel safe emotionally. I was extremely shy. People, although fascinating and fun, were scary, saying and doing unpredictable things that I found difficult to comprehend. I needed the time and space to regroup and reorganize before launching off on another morning.

In my adult life I have mostly lived alone, again happy to have my own space and time at the end of the day. Self-sufficient, I've always supported myself financially and grown almost all my own food. Self-entertaining, I have existed without a TV or a VCR. From this single lifestyle has come a paradoxical connection to a large number of people as well as an unblocked passionate outpouring of artistic work.

For several winters in a row I had been in the habit of getting up early every morning, pulling on my boots, hat, and down coat, and taking a walk to the local Amish General Store. On the way back I usually passed Gracie, an Amish girl of about fifteen who clerked behind the counter and stocked the shelves with flannel work gloves and wool socks. Babushka tied under her chin, Gracie walked to my house every morning, and when we crossed paths, the sky streaked magenta with the dawn, we often stopped for a few seconds and exchanged bits of information about the weather or our lives. Some days Gracie was the only other human being with whom I interacted, and that small exchange was enough to sustain me.

Yes, living alone, I did have my spooky nights and frustrations with having to cope with every event and decision myself. I did sometimes feel outside of "normal" social circles, but it wasn't until I became chronically ill that the spooky nights became the "dark nights of the soul." It wasn't until I became chronically ill that I felt my cherished solitude slip away into the chill of loneliness.

I sat in the kitchen chair that day, and loneliness pushed all my "stuff" to the surface as if I were clicking through the slide show of my life. Tray after tray of images beamed on my interior screen—the good, the bad, the ugly—from the thrill of my first airplane ride and the way the wings dipped and dived over the rolling green Loess Hills near my home, to the fright of my last car accident and the way the automobile spun uncontrollably on the winter ice. From the gift of my first pair of ice skates one Christmas morning, and later that afternoon my attempts to maneuver their blades across the lagoon, to my wiggling and wobbling attempts to maneuver in and out of relationships in my adult life. From my first splash in academe in second grade with a thoroughly researched A paper on milk, to my first failure and fall from grace weeks later when the teacher hung my artwork upside down.

Months, seasons, and years juxtaposed with one another, reversing and fast-forwarding, blurring and focusing and blurring again. Suddenly, I had to look at myself on the screen, with all my strengths and imperfections—the little lines that had formed around my eyes, the extra pounds I'd gained. I could not back away. My own image was blown up larger than life in front of my face. The carousel clicked to my face at four years old, beaming, tongue out, licking the frosting from my fork, one big bite of birthday cake about to go into my mouth. The carousel whirled to the grimace on my lips, tongue out, when I was facing down my playground tormentors when I was eight. The carousel clicked to the powerful arms of the neighbor boy who tried to choke me when I was ten, then the arms of the college boy holding me down on the bed, trying to date-rape me when I was twenty. The carousel clicked to my mother's arms securing the sides of my crib when I was two, then my arms lifting the sides of her hospital bed when I was twenty-two. The carousel clicked and whirled. The carousel spun uncontrollably on thin ice.

2

I sat in a wheelchair—the fold-up variety—and emotionally
everything collapsed around me. On late Wednesday afternoons
the county handicapped bus arrived in my lane. The friendly
driver greeted my dog and then tried to maneuver me in my
wheelchair down the front steps, over the ice and snow, up onto the
lift, and into the van. Once I was belted in place, we bounced along
in the frigid weather, the driver making conversation, shouting back
to me about the songs he had written to perform on his guitar, his
voice echoing in the cavernous empty van.

I had been trying to keep teaching my graduate class one night a
week from seven until ten o'clock. We were only two weeks into a
fifteen-week semester when I woke unable to move. I needed the
money from teaching and knew that my absence would cause the
department nightmarish hassles. So each week I crawled out of bed,
dressed, and got myself to the university. There I threw myself into
the professorial role, taught with cheer and confidence, and then
returned home, in too much pain to even step out of my clothes, and
crawled back under the covers for another week.

And the weeks stretched into a month, with only slight marks of
improvement. The parade was long gone, my family of whish-
boomers having returned to their extremely active lives. I coped with
two hired helpers who each came in four hours a week and a loyal
friend who made a weekly pot of soup. Most of the time I was alone.
Bare, bald alone. This state was different from the self-imposed exile

of my youth. This condition was superimposed, so at first I fought it. I thought about cross-country skiing, about the concerts and plays I was missing. I railed against myself for having to cancel readings and writing assignments from major newspapers. And I longed for company, some steady, quiet, reassuring presence.

I thought about my mother and my grandmother, remembering both of them in their final days. I'd stood beside their separate bedsides, spooning a few slivers of ice chips into their mouths, smoothing an extra blanket on top of their frail bodies, holding their hands. Finally, their days turned into one long twilight, their eyes closing, their minds drifting into the never-never land between life on earth and the existence in the beyond. "Mother," they had both called, as if inviting the spirits of their ancestors into the room. "Mother," they had both called over and over again. "Let me go." They had both been ready to embark on the pilgrimage to the other world.

I had not been ready for this great transition. Instead, I had lain in the darkness and begged them to come to my aid. "Mother, grandmother," I called, yearning for their actual physical presence beside my bed: the rustle of their dresses, the touch of their palms on my forehead. I could smell the faint scent of their soap and perfume. I could see the sheen of their dark hair in contrast to my lighter strands. I could recapture the twinkle of their eyes and the sense of fun, play, comfort, and security that each face engendered in me. Still, I knew that their existence remained only in my memory. I asked them to be my spirit guides and help me in my recovery.

Finally, I tried not to think about what could be happening but instead noticed what was happening. First, the ceiling fan became interesting, and I learned to meditate to the tilt and twirl of its blades. Then I began to notice more nuances, how the shape of the clouds could predict the brushstrokes of the sunset, how as we headed toward spring the days became longer and longer, and the geese began to venture farther and farther from the neighbor's coop.

I was finally home long enough to peer out the window long enough to figure out how Scruff, one of the pygmy goats, could escape from the pen while Mac and Shenanigan couldn't. At last I saw Scruff take a running jump from the top of the shed, plant his hoof on the five-foot-high cattle panel, twist and spin in the air, doing a back flip and landing with grace on all fours on the other side of the fence. I was finally home long enough to spot the red fox slinking back toward the ditch in the early morning. As if in one breath, its whole body disappeared into its den, the den I'd never before been able to find.

Above ground, the Hyakutake comet streaked through the sky. While others traveled to observatories and strained to locate the celestial body, its presence filled my window. Its tail, millions of miles long, trailed across my vision through the night and led my thoughts back down to earth where the ground lay frozen and bare. In its dormancy, my garden plot readied itself for spring, for the arrival of my hoe and spade, an expectation I was becoming more and more worried I could not meet.

I was home long enough to meet every UPS delivery and began to recognize the sound of the home health aide's car, its low throaty voice, almost like that of a heavy smoker, when it pulled into the lane. I learned the growl of the mail carrier's jeep, its wheels spinning in the mud near my box. I learned the whine of the poacher's light pickup truck parked on top of the hill, a rifle poking out the window in hopes of popping off deer running down by Picayune Creek.

When I watched the deer dash through the trees unharmed, when my neighbor appeared at the door with the first six goose eggs of the new year, when Scruff wiggled his way back into the pen, this time through the tiny crack in the gate, I learned to sit back in that wheelchair and do what those doctors had told me to do years ago: I learned to live with the pain.

But the pain went on. And the months began marching right toward spring break, a week when many in the university take off for more exotic places for exercise and fun. I skied down my own slippery slopes, my mobility improving during the sunlight hours. I was now able to bend over to pull on my socks, to reach up and blow-dry my hair. But when darkness descended, my limbs locked into place like the brakes of the wheelchair. My pleasure in the nuances of the sunsets disappeared as they began to mark the transition into fitful nights when I was unable to raise my arms or kick my feet to remove my down comforter. I lay there like a stone until morning, staring into the night.

"Is there anything I can do for you?" a friend from Alabama finally asked one night on the phone. "I feel so frustrated being so far away. Is there anyone I can call?"

"Yes," I said. "Do you have a pen and paper?"

"Shoot. Who is it?"

"Well, I don't know the number, but you can get it from Pontiac, Michigan, information."

"Okay. First name?"

"Jack."

"Jack ... Last name?"

"It's spelled K-e ..."

"K-e ..."

"V-o-r ..."

"V-o-r ... No, no, I'm not calling him."

Suicide is actually not in my ethical code. Although I have had suicidal thoughts during bouts of other severe illnesses, I've fought too long and hard to stay alive to prematurely put an end to my existence. Yet this time the 3 A.M. darkness became a literal state of mind, a black mood I couldn't shake. I thought about staying forever in the underworld, and then I thought again. No, I didn't really want to call Jack. I just wanted to get drunk, to alter my reality for an hour or two. But since medical restrictions had eliminated alcohol from my diet for the last twenty-five years, booze was out. And wisely so. But what's a good Irish Catholic girl to do? One night, almost as reflex, my lips began moving in prayer. "Hail, Mary," I began.

Raised a strict Catholic during my youth, but disillusioned by both the structure and strictures of the Church, I have been a "recovering" Catholic most of my adult life. As I lay awake one night, drifting in and out of sleep, the sky dark and all-enveloping outside my windows, I searched for any remnant of my former religion that would bring solace. I flashed back to the lives of the saints, that other parade of characters who whish-boomed their stories through my early life.

The martyrs might provide the easiest answers. They at once fascinated and horrified me as a child with their boilings, beatings, and beheadings. Yet in my present state it wasn't the martyrs and their gory ends that gave me solace. Rather, the mystics came to mind, with their kinder, gentler acceptance of suffering. The mystics seemed more accessible to me, more like the presences of my mother and grandmother—the Zen saints, as I liked to think of them:

Hildegard, St. Teresa of Avila, St. John of the Cross, Sts. Francis and Clare of Assisi. These men and women had chosen a path of deprivation to reach some higher state of consciousness.

I had studied these mystics in college, but there under the ceiling fan I strained to remember the details of their lives. The tilt and twirl of the fan's blades led me to a meditation on how the mystics had gone through their own kinds of hell. I knew that St. John had been in solitary confinement for years, that St. Francis had received the stigmata, that St. Teresa had been so ill she'd been given up for dead. I remembered how these mystics had allowed their solitude to take them down a different path, where they found an interconnection with all beings, a life of love and giving.

I stopped answering e-mail and the phone. I stopped playing the radio and the stereo. I let the silence fill my room. I couldn't reconstruct the specifics of the mystics' biographies, but I knew that all of them understood the same basic truth: that suffering can either pull you inward, turning you guarded and bitter, or it can push you up out of the underworld, out of the "dark night of the soul," to another level of consciousness where, as the Buddhists say, we can find the jewel in the lotus of the heart. At its best, suffering opens the heart to others' suffering and produces love and compassion—what we all long for from each other but find so hard to both give and find. The love for our fellow humans seems inevitably to work its way "down" toward all other living creatures and "up" to find its full force in the love of God or a higher power.

"What does this mean?" asked Hildegard of Bingen. "No creature is so dull in its nature that it does not know the completeness of its case. What does this mean? The sky has light, the light air, and the air winged creatures. The earth nourishes greenness, the greenness fruit, and the fruit animals. All things bear witness to this order because the strongest of all possible hands ordered these things."

Hildegard as well as the other mystics knew that the spiritual was not found in the grandiose but in the small growing things and the ordinary moments that previously you may have overlooked or found mundane—the antics of a pygmy goat, the sound of a car in the lane.

I fixated on the small things, the tiny seeds. In my case, the literal seeds of my literal garden. Lying awake in bed at night, I had worried how I would ever prepare the soil, plant, weed, dig, and harvest. I was on a medically prescribed organic diet and needed to grow my own food. Buying produce—even when available—was prohibitively expensive. I contemplated making raised beds. I contemplated making trellises. I contemplated not having a garden at all. The covers up to my chin, I stared out at the comet and remembered reading Viktor Frankl's classic *Man's Search for Meaning* my freshman year in college. The book's message flooded back to me. Those who survived the Holocaust held on to a faith in something spiritual, no matter how large or small, be it their God, their memory of family, or the fulfillment of a special talent.

Finally, I got up one morning, clomped down to the basement with my walker, and started my garden seedlings. Two little seeds in each pot. Then back up the steps, one slow foot in front of the other. Four trays in front of the window, the sun streaming in through the glass. I put all my faith in those living plants—tomatoes, peppers, cabbages, brussels sprouts, and broccoli—even though I had no faith in my ability to garden ever again. I fussed over their temperature, their watering. I misted them with organic fertilizer. I labeled their pots, switched their positions in their trays, and watched their tiny necks struggle up through the soil. "The Ground of God and the Ground of the soul are one and the same," Meister Eckhart had said, and I was getting ready to transplant my seedlings into the ground.

The spring began, the grass turning green, the pink buds unfurling on the maple tree. I still lay awake at night, and the fan went round and round, but my mind was at rest. Lawrence LaShan, the research and clinical psychologist who works with cancer patients to help them rally their weakened immune systems, asks his clients, "If your whole life were designed to carefully and lovingly teach you a lesson, what would that be?" *Two little seeds in each pot. Stripped of all connections, it was only then that I could experience the inner connectiveness of all things.*

No trumpets sounded, no locusts or horses swept across the land, but now the air was crisp and clear, the stars so bright that I had to pull down the window shades that night to sleep. Despite the hardships, or because of them, I had carved out a pleasurable life. I began talking to people again and enjoying their company, wanting nothing more than that.

From there I got up and learned to use a cane, learned when and where to lean. The comet disappeared from the sky. I hobbled down the road again each morning, where I met Gracie.

"Nice morning," she said when we passed, not mentioning my new appearance or long absence. "I don't know why, but I feel so much better when I walk this road."

"So do I," I said.

I had worked my way through stages of recovery, but I knew that in the coming months I'd have to work them through again and again. I knew that nothing was static, but I longed for a state of higher consciousness that felt stable and solid in its affirmation of life. I clung to the thought of the mystics and vowed to study them anew. Recovery from chronic illness is similar to recovery from the devastation of a flood, for you don't know exactly when crisis begins and when it ends. The only certainty is that it will surely flood again. Many nights I lay awake in the dark with only one thought: Tomorrow the ceiling fan will still be there above me, spinning around and around.

3

By mid-May I stood out in my garden, leaning against my cane, the ground warm enough to receive my seedlings, the leaves on the cabbage, broccoli, and brussels sprouts plants round and full, spilling their bright green color over the edges of the small peat pots. I rested my cane against the garden gate, and the goats poked their noses through the mesh, nibbling on the dandelions growing near the fence posts. I live in an old Amish one-room schoolhouse, the building perched on top of a hill, the Picayune Creek winding through the valley below. My garden is just a few feet from my front door, and when I stand in the middle of my plot, a vista of patchwork fields, farmsteads, and wide open sky stretches out in front of me for a good ten miles.

The day was bright and clear, the blue sky filled with puffy white clouds. The early morning fog had burned off the land, and the soil was soft and pliable. I shuffled along the ground with a large hoe, creating a furrow. I took three or four steps, using the hoe as a walking stick, letting it bear my weight, dragging it behind me. I stopped and rested, took another couple of steps, then stopped and rested. The pain pooled in my biceps and triceps, making it difficult to raise my arms above my chest. The pain shot down my thighs and stabbed me in my knees, making it difficult to walk. But I was determined to start my garden. I bent down as far as I could—my hand reaching just above my knee—and let the carrot seeds slip through my fingers into the furrow. Most landed in the right spot, but some of the seeds drifted on either side of the row. Others were carried away by the wind. I didn't care. Something would come up.

I spent five days planting my garden. Usually I spend one. I inched along, thinking that this pain in my limbs was still just a temporary problem, that it might wax and wane but I wouldn't be in this state the rest of my life. After all, hadn't things slowly gotten better over the course of the last four months? By harvest time I would be waltzing through the garden gate, basket on my hip, to pick my beautiful ripe tomatoes.

But by late July when the tomatoes were red and juicy, I was still on the cane. I finally realized that I had plateaued, that my condition wasn't changing. The pain remained a steady, constant voltage, zinging up and down my legs when resting, attacking my muscles and nerves whenever I tried to move. I started researching lupus and rheumatoid arthritis. Neither of those illnesses seemed to act like mine. Throughout the months, I had had so many different kinds of diagnoses that I didn't know which one, if any, to believe. Finally, I called a chiropractor. I knew he wouldn't be able to diagnose me, either, but he might be able to lessen the pain.

"I want you to have an MRI immediately," the chiropractor said. "And make an appointment with a neurosurgeon."

The chiropractor sent me home with sit-down traction. I slipped my head into a harness that looped under my chin and then went up around my ears and attached to a bar dangling from a rope that threaded through a pulley fastened to the door. On the other end of the rope, a plastic bag filled with water served as a weight. I called the neurosurgeon and then sat down in the traction to wait out the three months before I could get in for an appointment. One half hour four times a day I stretched from the door frame. The first week was unbearable. The muscles in my neck went into spasm, hard knots the size of my fists. I backed off, iced my neck, let some of the water out of the bag, and tried again. Slowly, after another couple of weeks, the pain began to diminish.

But my boredom grew. While in traction I could do nothing but stare at the wall and listen to music or books on tape. Finally, I asked a carpenter friend to design a traction rig that could be placed over my desk where I might continue to do my writing. David banged together a wooden contraption that framed my desk and looked eerily like a gallows, the harness hanging down from the rope like a noose. I climbed back in my desk chair and tried to throw myself into a creative mode. I was productive, but my illness had again forced a baseline shift from solitude to loneliness. The traction sessions had to be spread out throughout the day and didn't allow for much free time. I was on sabbatical that fall semester, so I wasn't going to the university. I didn't go out of my house much and saw few people. My health care worker still came twice a week, cleaned my house and fixed my meals. Another friend did a once-a-week grocery shopping.

At last, in early October, my soup-making friend Marie arrived to drive me the fifteen miles to the neurosurgeon. Inside the clinic I saw the hazy white lines on the MRI that the doctor held to the light.

"Your disk ruptured at C6 in the car accident and punched a hole in the spinal cord," the neurosurgeon said. "Then the flu virus went into the cord and infected it. You have central cord syndrome and transverse myelitis, the same thing as polio but a different virus."

"What did he say I have?" I asked Marie, who was taking notes.

"Myelitis," she said.

I'd never heard of it.

"It's like poliomyelitis," the doctor said. "It means an infection of the spinal cord. Central cord syndrome paralyzes your arms, and myelitis paralyzes your legs."

"When will I be better?" I asked. My gait was unsteady, halting, but I still clung to the idea that I would eventually get off the cane.

"You're one lucky woman that you ever got out of that wheelchair, that you aren't on a respirator. At best, you should have been in heavy leg braces the rest of your life," the doctor said.

"Is there anything I can do for the pain?" I asked.

The doctor shook his head. "We could go in there and repair the disk," the doctor said, "but it wouldn't help the pain. We'd take out part of your hip and fuse it into your neck with a plate and screws."

"But the surgery wouldn't help the pain?"

"No, it would just be an attempt to stabilize your neck."

"What are the risks?"

"Well, once we do one fusion, often the next disk ruptures because it can't hold up the weight of the plate. Then we'd have to fuse the next disk. And to get at the disk, we have to cut through your throat, and there's a chance we'd nick your vocal cords and you wouldn't be able to talk again."

The third risk was chemical sensitivity. I had had a history of severe and dramatic drug reactions. Anesthetics were especially dangerous. The doctor ended up leaving me in traction and writing a referral to a world-famous pain clinic. The physicians there discovered a lesion on my spinal cord, stretching from C4 to C7— permanent nerve damage from the central cord syndrome and myelitis.

I returned to my neurosurgeon. I'd been offered a visiting professorship at the University of New Mexico and didn't know if in my condition I should take the appointment.

"Yes, by all means go," my neurosurgeon said. "That's absolutely perfect. The climate there will be really good for you. If you can possibly manage teaching, do it. We can't do anything more for you here. Take your traction and go to New Mexico."

I drove home that afternoon, searched for my road atlas, and flipped through the dog-eared pages: New Hampshire, New Jersey, New Mexico. New Mexico seemed like just another state, another residency, another visiting teaching gig. The thought of packing up and driving all the way across the country felt overwhelming. I still had a hard time driving the fifteen miles to the doctor. Yet the neurosurgeon thought there was some hope for me in New Mexico. A better climate. But just about any climate was better than Iowa in the winter. I flipped through the pages of the atlas: New York, North Carolina, North Dakota. No, North Dakota was definitely worse than Iowa in January. New Mexico it was.

I fingered a St. Christopher's medal I'd pinned to the cover of the atlas. Years ago an old neighbor had given me the medal during the last weeks of his life. He had kept it pinned to the dash of his car and in his eighty years had never had a major accident. I remembered the St. Christopher story from my childhood, how the giant had carried a small child across a turbulent river, the weight on his shoulder getting heavier and heavier with each step. When St. Christopher reached the opposite shore, he discovered that he had been carrying the Christ child and all the burdens of the world on his back.

"This medal is yours now," my neighbor had told me, squeezing the small tarnished object into the palm of my hand, "to keep you safe down all the roads you travel."

Travel away from all of this, I told myself. Carry yourself away. I was going away, literally going away, to New Mexico, although I didn't much want to take that road. I wanted just to stay put, but no one could do anything for me in Iowa. The doctors couldn't do anything, that was certain. I knew that New Mexico had a long, ancient healing tradition. Perhaps I could connect with healers there. I could try faith healing.

Okay, I said to myself, knowing that there was only one problem with this plan. In order to be healed by a faith healer, didn't you have to have faith? Wasn't that the glitch? The Catholic belief system of my childhood seemed silly to me now. Yet when all my religious trappings fell away, I still felt connected with some deeper current, a life force that couldn't be anthropomorphized. I could still muster a Hail Mary. I could still latch onto the lives of the mystics and feel that there was something sacred there to be honored.

But was this enough to be healed? I didn't know. I didn't know anything. I didn't even know how to pray anymore. "Mary, Mary," the child inside me begged the way the Christ child had pleaded with St. Christopher. "Carry me across the water." Over and over those words echoed in my head until they were the only words I heard. Was my faith in this entity strong enough to guide me through the wide river that has no bridge? What was I doing?

As a child, I thought I understood faith. I had made the leap. I believed in a being who was greater than any earthly construct. But as a child, it was easy to believe in whatever authority told you was true. Santa Claus. The Easter bunny. Paul Bunyon. Adam and Eve.

The Virgin birth. God. You believed. It all added up. Then little by little, as you experienced more of life, matured, and became more educated, you learned to question, to doubt, to understand that in many ways you'd been duped. You experienced the disappointment of learning that fantasy is not reality, and you weren't willing to go through that lesson again.

Where does this leave you? If you decide that a higher being is a fantasy, ironically, you put your trust back in those very people who told you those tall tales in the first place. You put your trust in the glorification of art, sports, achievement, or human institutions. And what happens when you become disillusioned with human order? What's to keep you from falling into despair? And once there, what's to pull you out?

They say there's no atheist in a foxhole. When confronted with a life-threatening crisis, humans opt for a belief in God either out of fear or out of a deep intuitive knowledge. In the cold, sweat, and blood of the muddy foxhole, all pretense of religion—the organized system with its prescribed rules and regulations—is dropped. Instead, panic and desperation, a sense of confrontation with death, put you squarely in the realm of the spiritual.

Deciding to go to New Mexico was one step toward that spiritual realm. I had to carry myself across the water. I had to fight the thought of drowning with the current, a heavy burden on my back. I made the decision to enter the river with the hope of one day reaching safety on the other side. I rubbed my St. Christopher's medal and knew that I was on my way.

4

With one big gust, the subzero January wind blew my Isuzu Trooper off the interstate toward the median. Sean, my neighbors' son and hired driver, righted the car, and we continued on in silence, the windshield wipers swiping away the snow. We were headed down I-35 through southern Iowa into Missouri. Our first night's destination: Topeka, Kansas. The second: Amarillo, Texas. The third and final stop: Albuquerque, New Mexico.

I sat upright next to Sean, the seatback vertical. I knew that I would have a very difficult time getting up from a reclining position. It was better to sit up and keep a small pillow tucked at the base of my spine. I wore my neck brace to support my head. If I dozed off, my head might flop down toward my shoulder, creating more spasms in my neck. The cold intensified the pain riddling my limbs, weighing them down with fatigue. My arms felt like lead pipes, my feet like anvils.

Sean and I were wrapped in layers of clothes—long underwear, wool pants, a pair of sweats on top of that, and down jackets and vests, wool stocking caps, and gloves. Even with the heater on full blast, our toes went numb with the cold. I had a bag of salt, a cell phone, blanket, an emergency fold-up shovel, flashlight, and flares tucked in a box in the back of the Trooper in case of emergency. I had my St. Christopher's medal in my pocket.

The state highway patrol had issued a warning: no travel unless absolutely necessary. For three days the wind had blown the snow smack into the rows of corn stubble in the fields outside the window of my home. The wind, with the whirling, twirling force of a prairie Poseidon, lifted the flakes up into the air and pitched them against the house. The walls creaked. The blizzard leaked a small, steady stream of its icy crystals through a crack in the windowsill. The snow swirled across my pasture, sticking to my garden fence, covering the roof of my goat's shed, covering my dog Bear as he lay curled up in a drift, only his nose poking out. The first morning I had watched an Amish buggy, a whole family snuggled together under a blanket for warmth, struggle up the hill. The horse's hooves pressed down on the gravel road, glassy and slick. No car dared make the trek. The ditches paralleling nearby Highway 1 were littered with semitrailer trucks jackknifed and flipped on their sides, the great white monsters of the midwestern deep, lying dying by the road. I fingered my St. Christopher's medal in my pocket. Patron of travelers, I thought, carry me through this storm. And he did.

By the time Sean and I reached western Oklahoma, the strength of the storm had passed. The wind and snow had stopped. The sun teased us with its presence from behind a cloud. For the first time since our departure, the road was clear. Yes, the wind had stopped, but when I looked out the window, the trees along the road were still bent over, their juniper branches like long manes of hair let down from an old woman's bun, nearly sweeping the ground. It felt as if we were still in the wind, but we were not. The trees whizzing by in their arthritic statures, their backs dowagers' humps, were bowing down to the forces of nature.

When we crossed the Texas border into New Mexico, we were in a different region, the landscape shifting from rolling hills to mountains, the light and land taking on a pinkish red hue, the canyons opening up around us like deep wounds. We had left the flat, steady drumming straight roads of the prairies and were caught up in the rat-a-rat-tat of the liftings and swelling of the American Southwest.

In Texas the soil was a large tablecloth draped over the ground for a picnic, its edges smoothed and unwrinkled. In New Mexico the cloth had been picked up and then tossed down again, covering the debris from the meal. A balled-up napkin became a gentle rise in the landscape, an orange, a more rounded, formed hill. The picnic basket itself poked up like a mountain peak.

We passed Santa Rosa and headed west toward Moriarty. I tried to make conversation, asking Sean about his classes during the spring semester, and for a few minutes we spoke of art, life drawing, and geology. Then silence gripped us again, the geology out the window growing increasingly dramatic, the geology inside me shifting back and forth from excitement to fear.

Gone was the wild white blizzard of the Midwest. Just a few lazy snowflakes tumbled onto the windshield. Gone was the dull brown bleakness of the Panhandle. Gone was the flatness. Instead, even in the dead of winter, there was a hint of pink color to the soil as if it were the face of someone racing across the land, the blood rising to her cheeks. I remembered a story told by a friend who had grown up on the Navaho reservation in New Mexico. When a Navaho girl reaches puberty, she is initiated into the tribe. She rises at dawn and runs as far and as fast as she can into the rising sun. When she returns, all the women in her tribe gather together and greet her. I could picture her dark hair flying away from her face, her feet sinking down into the desert sand then angling up into the air, her arms pumping back and forth, her whole body dashing toward the horizon.

We were just a little over an hour from Albuquerque, and I began to feel that same sense of accomplishment. I felt the anticipation of arrival, the satisfaction of finally reaching our destination, coupled with the anxiety of not really knowing what that end point would mean. I also felt as if my back would crack in two, that I couldn't possibly sit another moment, that I couldn't wait to lie down, stretch out, and take the weight off my hips.

Sean leaned back in the car seat, his elbows straightening. I could sense his relief, too. I could imagine how tired he was from three days of driving and his desire to sit down and relax and eat a real meal. Sean and I had both tucked our sleeping bags in the back of the Trooper. We planned to find my sparsely furnished one-room apartment, crash on the floor the first night, and then rise early and get him on the plane the next morning. Hey, we were going to make this in plenty of time after all. Our scenario was actually working out. We were even slightly ahead of schedule. We'd get into Albuquerque in early afternoon. No problem. A little bit of dry snow was coming down, but basically the drive from here on would be a cinch.

"We're coasting now," I said.

Sean nodded.

MORIARTY 10, the sign read. We sped on. Even though we were heading into more mountainous territory, I felt myself let go. Everything was going to be all right.

Albuquerque sprawled out in front of us, a flat, dusty city, its crevices filled with a thin dusting of snow. Against a backdrop of the Sandia

Mountains that rose up into the sky with a jagged dignity, the city at first glance looked dull and dirty. On the freeway we had passed whole suburbs of fake adobe houses with fake Spanish tile roofs, one looking exactly like another on winding streets with names like Saguaro Boulevard and Roadrunner Circle. Strip malls and major shopping malls linked one suburb to the next with their familiar low-slung storefronts and wide parking lots, the stores interchangeable with any in the United States. This looks just like West Des Moines, I thought.

When we turned off the freeway and headed into the central city, things got even tackier. The convenience stores and chain motels gave way to the pancake houses and doughnut huts. Litter clogged the gutters of the streets. Hamburger wrappers and paper cups snagged on the curbs. In the older part of the inner city, warehouses circled with high fences topped with razor wire squatted down next to graceful churches with brass bells stationed in their towers. A tiny bungalow shared an entire city block with a grocery store, an open field separating the two buildings. A palomino horse grazed on a clump of sagebrush, its head down and its tail swishing back and forth.

We stopped at a light, and a rooster ran across the street.

This is getting better, I thought. This is definitely getting better.

We tried to find my apartment building on the map, and after a couple of wrong turns found ourselves driving down a tiny, narrow street—not even a street, an old irrigation ditch, two slabs of concrete slanting toward each other at a forty-five-degree angle. The small bungalows on either side of the irrigation ditch sported rose trellises and brightly colored murals of Our Lady of Guadalupe. This cluster of houses butted up against a large cemetery, its rows of white markers trailing up the side of a hill where three ten-foot-tall white crosses, their tops disappearing into the spool of white clouds in the sky, stood guard over the city: The hodgepodge of businesses and pawn shops clumped together below selling piñatas, braided wreaths of cayenne peppers, guitars, and *guns*.

Not exactly enchanting, but funky, I thought. And I like funky. We pulled into my apartment complex, encircled by yet another high wall, a guard at the gate. I hobbled to the main office on my cane to sign my lease, my legs cramping and spasming from the long ride. Sean unloaded my boxes, piling them in one small corner of the tiny two- hundred-square-foot apartment. I peeked my head in the door. This is not what I had hoped for—just a square room with no charm—but it was clean and on the ground floor, which was all I cared about at that point. I realized they could've given me a three-story walk-up. My legs would never have made it up three flights of stairs. I flopped down on the sofa, and a wave of gratitude enveloped me. Tonight, Sean and I would venture forth into the city and buy the wooden braces for my traction. Tomorrow, I would go through the painful lifting and unpacking of boxes, my back aching, my feet scooting back and forth across the carpet, the chore taking twice as long as it would for a "normal" person. But for now I had arrived.

5

A thin layer of snow clung to the rooftops of the University of New Mexico's buildings, the brown adobe facades highlighted by decorative white lines—frosting on top of a square mocha-chocolate cake. The university is stunning in its uniformity, its attempt to create a congruent architecture. Many of the buildings are the real thing—old, low-slung, boxy adobe structures, their exposed ceiling beams made of hand-hewn logs. Other buildings are modern, nothing more than the standard 1970s six-story cement-block tombs, the windows sealed shut, the ventilation poor, the outside walls plastered over with brown stucco. Fake or not, at least the University of New Mexico has a master plan. Most campuses are a mixture of architectural designs, sleek gray high-rises wedged between gothic buildings with Roman pillars and squat English Tudor cottages.

The English Department is situated in the Humanities Building, one of the newer structures with an elevator and bulletin boards littered with posters for poetry readings, apartment subleases, and used couches. The Humanities Building faces the Zimmerman Library, one of the older buildings with wooden staircases, comfortable reading nooks, and busy computer terminals. A plaza stretches between the two buildings, its pinkish pavement stones reflecting the light back up into the faces of those who fill the space with constant motion: jewelry makers selling turquoise necklaces, weavers displaying rugs fresh from their looms, political speakers rallying a couple of dozen students, and roller-bladers playing a perpetual game of hockey, their ball flying across the courtyard.

My office was bright and warm. A bank of windows and a glass door opened onto a balcony that hung out over the plaza. At noon, the faculty gravitated to the balcony where they ate their lunches around patio tables and chairs. My office walls were lined with books on American literature, their owner off on a sabbatical. I set up my laptop and printer on the desk, deciding that this would be a pleasant place to work. Instead of lugging my computer back and forth to my apartment, I would leave it here, staying late or coming in on weekends to do my own writing once the school day was completed.

I hired a graduate student to carry the two-by-four boards up to the English Department and help me assemble my traction. I steadied the lumber, the student standing on top of a chair, power drill in hand. *Rrrr-rrrr-rrrr.* The wood screws joined the metal braces. *Rrrr-rrrr-rrrr.* The student made the rounds, hopping on and off the chair, securing one joint to the next on the three-legged contraption.

"Can I ask what you're doing?" My colleague across the hall appeared in my doorway.

I explained about the car accident and the spinal cord injury.

Her brow wrinkled. "Oh," she said, and returned to her office to grade papers.

Good, I thought. People are going to take my disability in stride. I'd only been in New Mexico a couple of days, but already I'd identified it as a tolerant place with many ethnic groups and cultures blending together. People came to live here from different parts of the United States, people longing for the adventure of the West, or people who had found themselves outside the mainstream in their former lives. I'll fit right in, I told myself, and reworded the state slogan: New Mexico, the Land of Eccentrics.

During the first week of classes, students and colleagues began drifting into my office. Some perched on the chair opposite me and began their discussions without a blink, stammer, or stare. We carried on our business as if there weren't an elephant standing in the middle of the room. One morning Karl, the chair of the English Department, strolled down the hallway, rounded the corner, and stepped into my office. He stopped dead still in my doorway and screamed, a high-pitched, screeching cry.

I unsnapped my harness and stood up, pressing my hands against my desk for leverage.

"What on earth?" Karl said.

I heard the footsteps of the secretary and administrative assistant running down the hall toward him.

I tried to explain the use for the apparatus. I didn't think I was getting through to Karl. Then, still standing in the doorway, Karl's face softened and took on a warmer hue. He told me that he'd had bad back problems for years, that he'd made the rounds for various treatments, that he understood the pain and frustration. He thought that maybe he might benefit from some traction like mine.

"Thank you," I said, acknowledging his support and returning to my work.

Waves of delight washed over me that afternoon when I began reading my students' essays. The weather had begun to warm up, the temperature rising to fifty-five degrees. The sky deepened from a robin's-egg to a sapphire blue. I sat at my desk in traction with the door open to the balcony. Warm, dry air blew in and rustled the papers in front of me. The sounds of the roller-bladers scraping their way through their hockey game in the plaza below provided an improvisational, jazzy beat.

The students' writing was sharp and focused. In class, we'd just had a lively, stimulating session, with students jumping into the discussion to offer their opinions and suggest further reading. We laughed. We had arguments. One man cried while he read his piece. The essays were about everything from their travels through Africa to do service work to travels through anorexia and eating disorders. We read about one man's job tending the ski slopes near Santa Fe and another woman's job tending a café near the uranium mines.

After class, Robert, a retired scientist, appeared in my office. He had immediately noticed my unsteady gait, the cane, and the fact that I couldn't stand up in class and had to ask a student to write on the board for me.

"I can tell you're having a tough time," Robert said. He opened his briefcase and pulled out the heavy Albuquerque phone book. I was perplexed.

Robert rested the book on my desk, flipping the thin yellow pages back and forth. Finally, he settled on the section marked "Physicians" and then "Physical Therapists."

"Look," Robert said. "I want to show you that we have facilities here in Albuquerque that can help you."

"Yes." I nodded.

Robert ran his finger down the page. "Right here at St. Joseph's Hospital physical therapy unit—just up the street—they advertise that they treat all sort of injuries. See, it includes 'spinal cord injuries.'"

Robert kept his finger on the spot and lifted the book up in front of my face.

"Thank you. I appreciate your concern," I said, and Robert slipped from the room.

I was grateful for this kind, sweet man's help. I hadn't had much luck with the standard forms of physical therapy, but perhaps he was correct. Maybe there was more I could do for myself. I didn't know that much about my injury. Perhaps there was some new treatment that might be helpful. I booted up the computer, clicked onto the Web, and typed in transverse myelitis.

A support group for the condition popped up, and I clicked on the names and photographs of the first fifty members on the roster. All were in wheelchairs. At least half were on respirators. One after another their pale, wan faces greeted me on the computer, their eyes staring out of a common pool of pain. All the patients had written the stories of their illnesses. I opened the first file and read the profile of a man in Ireland who had awoken one morning unable to move, pain spreading through all four limbs. I began to shake. Sweat broke out on my forehead. I clicked the file shut, tears beginning to well in my eyes.

I heard a knock on the door. I didn't want to deal with anyone.

"Professor Swander, it's Ernesto. Do you have a moment?" Ernesto, one of my students and a journalist for the Albuquerque newspaper, was from one of the oldest Hispanic families in the state.

Slowly, I pulled myself up from my desk and opened the door.

Ernesto entered my office, and for a few minutes we tossed around ideas for a book that he wanted to write about the people and landscape of New Mexico, running through the issues—from border patrols to bad health care for the poor.

Finally, Ernesto turned to me and asked, "And what are you working on while you're here?"

"I'm working on healing," I said.

"Sí," he said, his eyes scanning my traction rig.

"I'm looking for healers," I said.

"I can help you with that."

"Great. I'm looking for the real thing. Not some New Age person who's going to wave his hands over my body and tell me my energy is off."

"Sí," he said, taking out a small reporter's notebook from his shirt pocket. He scrawled an address in pencil and shoved it across my desk. "Here. If you want healers, you go down to the South Valley."

I took the slip of paper, folded it over, and placed it in my purse. "Thank you," I said.

"But if you follow up on this," Ernesto said, rising and edging toward the door, "don't go down to that neighborhood alone. And don't go there at night."

6

I shuffled through Albuquerque's barrio, my St. Christopher's medal still in my pocket, and rested on my cane in the middle of the sidewalk. I didn't know if I had the strength to go any farther. Contrary to all expectations, during my first few weeks in Albuquerque I actually felt worse. My feet became concrete blocks. I had to scoot into the driver's seat of the Trooper fanny-first, then reach down with my hands and lift my feet to the pedals. There, my feet could do their jobs, bending at the ankles, but I knew this wasn't exactly within the bounds of safety I'd been taught in high school driver's ed.

"Oh, it's too bad you arrived in such cold weather," the secretary at the university said. "You'll do better when it warms up."

But it felt luxuriously warm to me, the air dry against my skin, the sun wrapping my whole body in a relaxing fifty-five-degree heat.

"It's altitude adjustment," a colleague offered. "Everyone feels really rotten when they first land here."

Whatever it was, it made me nervous that my health seemed to be going downhill. So I found myself in the South Valley, in my hand the tiny piece of paper with an address scrawled in pencil by Ernesto.

Instead of healers I found homeless men lined up in front of the soup kitchen, dressed in tattered jeans and old jackets, hats shading their faces. One man lay in front of me on the sidewalk, his body curled in the fetal position, eyes closed, sound asleep. A mongrel dog, part chow, with intense brown eyes, sniffed the man's hands and face, then stepped over him. In the gutter, an empty beer can tumbled down the street, Route 66, the artery that still cut through the central city of Albuquerque.

A few miles away, closer to the university, the remnants of old motor courts, diners, and souvenir stands blended together with Wendy's and McDonald's fast-food stands. Tattoo parlors butted up against fashionable coffee shops. College students toted their backpacks full of books past street musicians with their guitar cases flopped open for tips. During my first week in the city, briefcase in hand, I was waiting for a light to change on Central Avenue when a woman dressed in a tight black skirt and high heels strode up to me and said, "This my territory, sister."

And what was mine?

The South Valley began where the university and downtown left off, Route 66 taking a turn, leaving behind the backpacks and guitar cases for the bundles and shopping carts of the homeless. The midday sun beat down on my blond head, the only blond head in sight. The sun was so intense that I knew in the future I'd have to wear a hat, lest my scalp become sunburned. The light bounced off the concrete sidewalk and back up into my face, my sunglasses shading my eyes. It was shortly after one in the afternoon.

The storefronts that were still operable needed paint and new roofs. Most had bars on their windows. I walked by the Catholic church with an icon of Our Lady of Guadalupe painted on its side, the Virgin's outer robes a brilliant turquoise against the pink adobe. Mary's inner garment was painted a darker rose, her brown skin accented by a dab of white at her throat and another near her hands that were folded in prayer. She stood on the horns of the devil, and

43

beneath them, an angel, his wings unfurled, showered roses down the side of the building.

Across the street on the front facade of a drugstore, a golden halo circled an icon of St. Francis of Assisi. A Russian inscription wound around Francis's toes, droplets of blood dripping from the nail holes in his feet. Near the drugstore door, a three-foot head-shot portrait of Christ—beard dark and scraggly, eyes brown and intense—stared out into the street.

On the opposite corner, an adobe wall held more icons in bright yellows, reds, and blues: St. Michael, Moses, and Mary Magdalene. His wings folded in, St. Michael stood eight feet tall, his outstretched hand beckoning toward the doorway of the building. Next to the door frame, Moses, the patriarch, presided over the street corner, his gray hair flowing down to his shoulders—shoulders strong and wide enough to hold up the Ten Commandments etched into stone tablets. Mary Magdalene created a softer, more haunting image, her face thin, wise with suffering, and nearly sunken behind her veil. Mary Magdalene's body was painted in profile, her visible brown eye meeting my own, her invisible eye seemingly veering off into another dimension.

"Do you want to know who painted these icons?" a man asked, suddenly popping up in front of me, his face close to mine and bearing a striking resemblance to that of Christ on the drugstore wall across the street.

"Yes," I said, taking a few steps back.

The man was dressed in a black pullover jacket and black stretch shorts. A heavy silver cross hung around his neck but did not weigh down his step. His body was trim. His legs were strong and muscular, and his feet moved agilely in his brown sandals. His mouth lifted into a huge grin. He seemed both inviting and scary, a man full of self-confidence and, at the same time, a man with a very large personality. He stood close to me, his face just a few inches from mine. I didn't know if I wanted to engage with him or turn around and run.

"I painted those icons," he said, hopping up on the curb and gesturing toward his work with an expansive exuberance. He introduced himself as Father Sergei, a Russian Orthodox monk who ran this inner-city monastery composed of two small bungalows and a garage transformed into a chapel. At sixty-seven years old, Father Sergei seemed more like a man of forty, his arms moving in quick bursts of energy. We stood on the sidewalk together, Father Sergei continuing to hop up and down, on and off the curb, excited to have an audience for his artwork. His eyes were alive, his face welcoming. Again, I vacillated between fear that I might be overtaken by this man's energy and a desire to embrace his untamed enthusiasm.

"I use the people in the neighborhood as my models," he said. "I sketch them inside on paper, then come out and just start painting. And I've been known to draw quite a crowd. When I painted those,"—he pointed to a portrait of the Madonna and child on the wall of the St. Vincent de Paul Center next door—"people came and sat in their lawn chairs watching me."

I imagined the audience gathered around this artist, the crack dealers setting up their chairs next to the homeless next to the Catholic priest next to the owner of the café down the street. I could see their heads tilted upward following Father Sergei's brushstrokes against the adobe wall, his feet firmly planted on the rungs of a ladder. The bright cans of paint sparkled in the sun, the azure blue color on the lid blending in with the New Mexico sky.

"See, in this icon"—the monk pointed to Mary Magdalene—"I used a fourteen-year-old neighbor as my model. Her family had kicked her out of her house because she was pregnant. I had my sisters take her in to live in the monastery. I made her Mary Magdalene.

"And look at this one." Father Sergei nodded at the portrait of the Archangel complete with wings and armor. "You see, we have a lot of crime and trouble in this neighborhood. The meter reader is a big, brawny guy, and he goes around from house to house and keeps the peace. I made him St. Michael.

"This man was a homosexual." The monk pointed to a painting near the sidewalk of a wounded man lying on the ground. "He had been severely beaten on the street, so he became the model for St. Stephen, the first martyr."

The homeless man who had been sleeping on the sidewalk woke up, pulled himself to his feet, gathered up his bundle—a blanket knotted together that held a few items of clothing—and wandered down the street in front of us. Father Sergei nodded to him and smiled. Otherwise, the long, wide street that stretched the five or six blocks down to the old tortilla factory was empty. In the middle of a weekday afternoon, the neighborhood took on an eerie feeling, as if some tragedy had just happened and everyone had rushed back into the safety of his or her house to watch the event on TV. No children played in the fenced yards. No cars stirred. No one entered the café down the block. No one came out of the hardware store with a newly purchased pair of pliers. No one went into the St. Vincent de

Paul Center to root through the piles of used jeans. No doors opened to the church.

"I myself have been beaten," the monk told me. Gang members had broken his bones and cracked his skull. He still suffered liver damage from the incidents. "The Fundamentalists have attacked me because I wear a crucifix, the Catholics because I don't believe in the Pope. But I always behave the same way, no matter what the denomination. I don't resist but simply hold up my crucifix and say, 'I absolve you for attempting to murder a priest of the Lord.'"

I stared at the monk, astounded by his attitude. Father Sergei leaned back into the wall, his face lost among those in his murals.

"You see, my people were conquistadors," he said. "They came over shortly after Columbus. If I've learned anything in life, it's what goes around comes around. And comes around again and again. You can see this most clearly when you study history. You must know your own history and the stories that shape your own life. You must read and reread and listen to the history of the lives of those around you."

Father Sergei led me to the bench at the bus stop. We sat together, the street still quiet, too quiet. But it felt good to sit, to get off my legs, to rest my feet. The bus stop bench and shelter made of adobe were decorated with hand-painted tiles in bright oranges, reds, and blues. Father Sergei explained that they had been made by the schoolchildren, part of a project designed to clean up, beautify, and instill pride in the barrio. In a few months' time, all the bus stops and shelters up and down the street would be adorned with the children's tiles.

"Yes, it's all a journey," Father Sergei said.

I stared at the priest blankly, having lost the thread of the conversation. "A journey for the children?"

"*Sí*. It's *all* a journey—down the street, through the desert, or across the water."

The priest seemed to be talking in riddles. Who was this man?

"And where one journey stops, another one begins," Father Sergei said. "That's the lesson to learn. We always want to stop the trip, get off the road, but the road continues on."

I leaned forward on the bench, the priest's voice assuming urgency. On the one hand, he seemed to be attempting to impart important information to me. On the other hand, he spoke as if I weren't there, as if he were repeating a mantra to himself, an old story he'd told over and over again.

"As a young boy, Christopher Columbus had heard the story of his patron saint, St. Christopher, and imagined his own journey across the water, the wide water that has no bridge," Father Sergei said. "And in adulthood, Columbus devised for himself his own test of faith. Oh, his crew thought he was crazy and tried to mutiny, to throw their admiral overboard. They clung to the idea that the world was flat and that they would sail right off the edge of the earth. As they voyaged into the unknown, Columbus tricked his men into thinking they were closer to Spain than they were, giving them false reckonings. He imagined the world differently and was willing to risk his life for his view. That's the important part of the story."

I was already beginning to imagine my world differently. I was imagining that this man sitting beside me at the bus stop might be a healer. I didn't quite know why he was rambling on about Christopher Columbus, but for the moment I was willing to tolerate his reckonings. Perhaps they would prove to be true. Perhaps false. I decided to let the journey find its own navigation. If this was a man I was supposed to meet, fine. If this was merely a crackpot on a bus stop bench, fine. I would know soon enough. But I would keep my cards close to my vest, my St. Christopher's medal in my pocket. I wouldn't blurt out my mission. Father Sergei's eye contact was intense, his deep brown eyes almost piercing mine. My midwestern sensibility couldn't distinguish intensity from threat.

"And when Columbus reached the New World," Father Sergei continued, "he knelt on the ground, kissing it and giving thanks to the Lord for safe passage." The monk dropped to his knees there on the sidewalk. A bus pulled up to our bench and stopped. The driver raised his eyebrows, as if to say, "Are you two lunatics getting on my bus or not?"

I shook my head and waved the driver on.

Father Sergei rose to his feet, the exhaust fumes from the bus clouding his face. "And there was another story behind the Columbus story, another event going on at the same time. You see, it's always the scene behind the scene that's even more important to the tale."

Oh, no, part of me thought. Now we're going to go off on another tangent. Yet another part of me thought, why not? This could be interesting. You've always loved a good story, even if you've heard it a hundred times. Father Sergei rocked back on his heels and sat down once again on the bench. I simply let his voice wash over me.

"When Columbus was getting his ships and crew ready to sail, Ferdinand and Isabella sent out a decree to rid Spain of all its Jews. Either the Jews had to leave the country, convert to Catholicism, or die. 'Hear ye, hear ye,' a herald shouted, unrolling the royal proclamation. Trumpets sounded a call throughout the cities and towns of the country. The unexpecting Jews, rich and poor alike, stood together in the square."

"And that was it? Nothing could be done?" I asked Father Sergei.

"Oh, a couple of brave men tried to buy the Jews' freedom. And it almost worked."

Father Sergei explained that Isaac Abravanel and Abraham Seneor, both high officials and advisors to the king and queen, tried to bargain with the monarchs to revoke the edict.

"Abravanel and Seneor reminded Ferdinand and Isabella of all that the Jews had done for Spain. Abravanel pledged his whole fortune—thirty thousand ducats. There was a moment when the monarchs wavered, an instant that could have sent history swerving in another direction. Ferdinand, always on the outlook for increased revenue, was attracted to the idea of ransom.

"But the context wasn't right," the monk said. "Look at the larger context of a situation. Momentous events often hinge on an individual choice, but those choices can be the work of the forces surrounding us."

At that moment, the forces that were surrounding us were young boys, a group of teenagers hanging out at the bus stop. They didn't seem intent on getting on the bus. Dressed in tight jeans and sneakers, their caps shading their faces, the boys crossed their arms and stared at the two of us, shifting their weight from one foot to another. Father Sergei met their eyes for a brief moment, a moment that held recognition and a brief flicker of fear. Then he turned back to me and continued with his story.

"You see, the Inquisition was in full swing. Anti-semitism was rampant across the land. Suddenly, a small side door swung open into the monarch's chamber. Tomás de Torquemada, the inquisitor general, burst into the magnificent hall, shaking. He held up a crucifix in front of the monarchs' faces and shouted, 'Behold the crucified Christ whom Judas Iscariot sold for thirty pieces of silver. You shall have to answer to God!'

"Isabella was intimidated and persuaded. She turned to Abravanel and Seneor. 'It appears that God, and not man, has decided the fate of the Spanish Jews. There is nothing more to say.'

"And so when Columbus traveled toward the small port of Palos where his ships were anchored, he must have passed thousands of Jewish refugees heading toward the larger nearby port of Cadiz. The Jews came on foot, women carrying babies on their backs, men toting bundles, and children tugging at the halters of donkeys that pulled carts loaded high with household furniture. The monarchs had decreed that the Jews could take their property with them, except for gold, silver, and gold coins. Since most of what the Jews owned was either on paper or in precious gems, the majority faced personal ruination. Some swallowed their jewels. Men, women, and children were assassinated en route and cut open by bandits."

The boys at the bus stop encircled our bench. They chewed gum loudly to try to gain our attention.

The monk merely lifted his head and nodded at them.

The boys nudged closer.

Uh-oh, I thought to myself. This isn't a group of friendly schoolboys. You've really done it this time. Who did I think I was? A *gringa* healer-hunter waltzing down to the barrio.

The boys stuffed their hands down into their pockets and found their cigarette lighters. Smoke curled toward us. From the corner of my eye I caught the expression on the boys' faces, one of disdain for the monk and the woman he was counseling. Father Sergei sighed and leaned back into the bench, crossing his arms, his eyes never straying from mine. Once again he acknowledged the boys' presence with a slight smile, his lips curling upward. The boys flicked their ashes on the sidewalk, the tips of their cigarettes glowing bright red.

Father Sergei held me in his gaze. I wasn't certain what our relationship would be. Would we be friends? Would his stories about Columbus take on any meaning in my life? In his? Perhaps I'd leave the barrio and never see this character again, leaving his persona and his tales to evaporate in the thin, dry air. Perhaps not. I was clearly intrigued by the man and hoped he was one of the people Ernesto had in mind when he sent me to the South Valley.

A bus pulled up to the curb. The boys stomped out their cigarettes with their sneakers and, without saying a word, stepped up into the bus, its black fumes engulfing us like incense.

7

After I had returned from the barrio to my apartment, pain surged through my system like a bolt of electricity, knocking me right out of my physical body. I felt as if I were floating somewhere above Albuquerque, floating and drifting without reckonings, floating and never finding a resting place, viewing everything from afar: the Sandia Mountains, splashed with snow on their peaks, cradling the metropolitan area on the north; the freeways, spewing diesel fumes and cutting the city into quadrants; the desert, dotted with sagebrush and opening onto flat, extended plains on the south. I circled over the five extinct volcanoes on the west, their tops round and flat. The petroglyphs carved into the rock—shapes of horses, birds, and stick figures, their legs bent in flight—spelled out a mysterious message that I could not discern, a code that no one had been able to completely crack.

I wanted to return to a familiar language, a grounded sense of reality. In retrospect, my encounter with Father Sergei and my quest for healers in the South Valley seemed unsettling. What was I doing sitting at a bus stop listening to a Russian Orthodox monk drone on about Christopher Columbus and the expulsion of the Jews? How did I suppose moments like these were going to heal me? I wanted to be more "normal," to blend into my own culture and find relief in the sanctioned medical methods of American mainstream society. I wanted to go to an M.D., take a pill, have surgery or whatever was recommended, and be well. I wanted to believe that the medical model could cure me.

I called Dr. Fox, a physician whom my neurosurgeon in Iowa had recommended, and made an appointment to see him.

"If you get in trouble in New Mexico, go see Dr. Fox," my neurosurgeon had told me.

I called the Employees Assistance Program at the university and made an appointment to see a therapist.

"In New Mexico, you can always contact the EAP and make an appointment to see a counselor," a friend at the University of Iowa had told me.

I was putting my faith back in the establishment and in the medical model, a model that no longer instilled confidence in me. It felt like a step backward, and I doubted the medical model could help me, yet I wasn't ready to continue my quest in the South Valley. I wasn't ready to embrace faith healing.

I'd lost my religion to the shifting, changing, questioning culture of the 1960s. Raised a strict Catholic, I had grown accustomed to being told what was right and what was wrong. As a child, indoctrinated in my mother's Irish culture, I thought the Church had a grip on "rightness." Then the Vietnam War heated up, the Civil Rights riots exploded, and the feminist movement targeted real problems in the basic ways in which we conducted our most intimate lives. Suddenly, the whole world, including every belief system I'd ever had, seemed wrong.

I went to Georgetown University in Washington, D.C., marched in the protests, raising my single lighted candle in front of the White House and chanting, "Peace now. Peace now." From the Jesuits I took theology courses like War and Peace, which blasted apart the "just war" theory, and Science, Myth, and Religion, which traced all great religions back to their mythological sources.

I returned home to Iowa for the summer after my freshman year and sat in a sweltering church one August Sunday morning, sweat pouring down my back, listening to the most uninspired, chastising sermon on sex from the most uninspired priest. He stood at the altar in front of the congregation, his pudgy little fingers wrapped around the cover of a *Playboy* magazine. He waved the publication in the air, admonishing all who turned its pages. At nineteen I thought the priest hopelessly boring. At nineteen I walked out, reasoning that religion was all myth anyway, and organized religion did nothing more than sanction a history full of horrible wars. Like most in my generation, I'd had it with the establishment telling us a bunch of lies so that they could simply make more money. That hot, muggy summer day, I officially became one of the multitudes of a generation of fallen away Catholics.

But my sense of spirituality was still intact. Even though my religion seemed ludicrous to me at that point, I still found myself wandering back into church for Christmas midnight Mass. I would still drop a quarter through the slot and light a candle for my grandmother on her death day, and whenever I was asked about my religious preference on any medical form, I would still circle "C" for Catholic. If I were near death, I couldn't imagine going out without the blessing of a priest, even if the very next morning he preached boring sermons on sex.

It was at this time that I became fascinated with the mystics. As I fulfilled my remaining theology requirements, I read everything I could about these odd holy people, these souls who holed themselves away from the world to find a deeper union with God. They seemed to be in a different realm. Yes, they were part of the Church, but they lived lives very removed from the outward trappings of the rest of Catholicism.

While the Church was growing fat and rich, these people gave up all their worldly goods and reached a consciousness far greater than those surrounding them. Most readily identified the corruption of the Church and initiated protests against it. The mystics seemed like hippies. They had visions. They levitated. They received the stigmata, the very wounds of Christ. Healings and miracles were achieved in their names. As fascinated as I was by these paranormal phenomena, even in my late teens I knew that these signs were just the outermost manifestations of a much more profound inner state.

Unlike the Spanish Jews, the Irish were converted to Catholicism voluntarily. Monks were sent to Ireland to establish monasteries and carry on the work of copying manuscripts in order to preserve sacred texts. Ireland, a remote rocky island, was not a strategic land for the Holy Roman Empire. Instead, the monks' presence was a kind of tokenism, a message from Rome declaring its authority, but at the same time a message making it clear that the Church wasn't putting a lot of effort into bringing the Celtic pagans into the fold.

The Irish became fascinated with the monastic scribes. They went to the abbeys to observe and slowly learned a written language. "Say, whatcha doing there?" I can imagine them asking. Previously, the Celts' legends and storytelling, their rituals and ceremonies, had all been in the oral tradition. The Irish desired the ability to record their words and communicate in a more connected way. The monks began to teach the people Latin, and with the language came Catholicism. "Oh, okay," the Celts collectively seemed to say, and slowly gave up their old mythologies or found analogies in Christianity. The Druids, fairies, and elves of their folklore merged with *The Lives of the Saints*.

Perhaps this historical heritage from my mother's side of the family, this nontraumatic conversion that I held in my genetic code, never allowed me to abandon my childhood religion completely. Perhaps the study of the mystics provided role models for me. Perhaps, at the core, I always felt more like a "crypto-Celt" and could juggle different belief systems at one time, knowing that there had to be a more inclusive, less culture-bound unifying picture. Or perhaps I intuitively knew the difference between religion and spirituality, and it was the latter that formed the walls of my soul.

Belief in science was the official creed in my family. Though we drifted through the sacraments, from baptism to extreme unction, we never found a safe harbor in these rituals. Though we fulfilled all of our formal duties and obligations toward Church rule, and though we never spoke openly of our doubts, I sensed that my family thought that Catholicism wasn't much more rational than the belief in druids, fairies, and elves. My maternal grandfather had been a horse-and-buggy doctor in rural Iowa. He had grown up poor on the west coast of Ireland, but through the patronage of a wealthy uncle was educated at Edinburgh—the most prestigious medical school of its era. Even though my grandfather had died just a few years before I was born, and even though he had not actively practiced medicine since the late 1930s when the Depression and his alcoholism conspired to put him out of business, his legacy still filled our house.

His medical texts lined the walls of my grandmother's dining room, their black leather covers, with bold red lettering, molding and cracking with age. Inside the books, the information was antiquated and obsolete. "When a woman is having her menses," I remember reading when I was twelve, the heavy dusty book in my lap, "she should go to bed and stay there for the duration of her sickness. She should have complete rest and not exert herself in any way." Good grief, I thought. Sickness? Go to bed five days a month? Loll around and do nothing? I understood that my grandfather had had to make adjustments for the discrepancies between his schooling in the British Isles and the reality of his practice in Iowa, but I couldn't imagine this advice being taken seriously by either the high society ladies of London or the pioneer women of the prairie.

"Why do you keep these books?" I asked my grandmother, knowing nothing then about poverty and grief.

"Because maybe someday one of your brothers will become a doctor and be able to use them," she replied.

Somehow I accepted the logic of this illogical answer. Until my grandmother died, the books remained on the shelves, honored and almost revered in their center-stage position, growing more valuable with time—at least in the collective household heart—like vintage wine.

"Those books represent your grandfather's education," my mother told me. "And he always said that education was the most precious thing you could have. It's the only thing that they can't take away from you."

The "they," of course, referred to the British who had taken away Irish lives, lands, and even their native tongue. As a child I knew nothing of this history, and so I only internalized "them" as an omnipresent oppressor who might at any time snatch up whatever you didn't carry inside your own head.

On the shelves next to the medical texts, my grandmother kept a set of the Harvard Classics.

"If you read the whole collection, it will be the equivalent of a college education," my grandmother had encouraged me. She had been the first female in her family and her new prairie town to finish high school.

And so, at twelve years old, I flipped through the brittle pages of the books and began the *Confessions* of St. Augustine. I was on my way to being an overachieving shanty Irish soul.

My lessons at school dovetailed with the heritage of my grandfather's scientific method at home. Life was rational. Life ran along the principle of cause and effect. If examined closely, phenomena could be explained. Nothing happened by magic or by chance. Superstition was a hangover from the illiteracy and ignorance of the Old World. This was America, after all. The land of opportunity. This was post–World War II society where our faith was in nuclear energy, in DDT, in better living through chemistry.

And when it came to medicine, complete trust was placed in the medical model. After all, the practice of medicine was the very thing that propelled my grandfather out of poverty, that launched his sea voyage to North America. We'd read his textbooks and could easily grasp the flaws in the system, but, yes, we firmly believed in the medical model. And despite the fact that my mother always hesitated to call a doctor, we kept on believing in the system. Cost was a factor for my mother. But having grown up driving her father on his rounds from house to house, my mother knew what crude knowledge the medical establishment actually possessed. "There's nothing much a doctor's going to be able to do," she would often say when my brothers or I begged her for medicine for a vast array of childhood ailments from chicken pox to flu to acne.

Of course, she was right. But no alternative was approved of, either. We scoffed at herbalists, at health food nuts, at osteopaths, at the chiropractor found on every corner of the state. Quacks. These people prescribed ridiculous things. They were dangerous and could maim you for life. Don't let them lay a hand on you. But the lowest of the low were those who did the actual laying on of hands, who believed in faith healing: the Christian Scientists. (They'd let their children die of appendicitis while they gathered around the bedside praying.) The evangelicals were even worse. (Put your hand on the radio, put your hand on the TV, my brothers and sisters, and you shall be healed!)

Bunk. Pure bunk.

So I believed in modern medicine throughout my youth. I believed more and more in the "rational" scientific approach to human suffering and less and less in answers that might come down from on high. I believed through my early twenties when my mother was treated for breast cancer at the University of Iowa Hospitals and Clinics, one of the largest teaching hospitals in the world. I believed bigger was better. I believed in experimentation, surgery, radiation, and chemotherapy. If these doctors said it would kill cancer, I believed it would. I believed over the course of the three years of her dying, watching the treatment strip her of her hair, her vitality, and her dignity. I believed all the way through the last months when the cancer had spread to her lungs and doctors injected her with mustard gas as a form of chemotherapy. I believed even when the war was finally lost.

And then I stopped believing.

8

The waiting room of the neurosurgery clinic at the University of New Mexico Hospital and Clinics was filled with patients. In wheelchairs, on walkers or canes, fifteen of us sat around an orange plastic coffee table full of outdated magazines, the covers ripped, the coupons inside torn out from their pages. We held on our laps large manila envelopes filled with X rays. I fingered the corner of my envelope and played with its string. Due to a cancellation, I'd been lucky enough to find an immediate slot in Dr. Fox's busy schedule.

The clinic seemed familiar, similar to most of the waiting rooms I'd experienced. There was comfort in the efficient bustle of the nurses and the clickety clack of the receptionist's hands on the computer keys. There was camaraderie in the gathering of patients with conditions similar to mine. I thumbed through an old *Newsweek* magazine, then tossed it back on the orange table. Just then a teenage boy in a neck brace and thick glasses picked up the magazine and turned to the sport section. No matter how tenuous, there was a sense of connection in the room.

My pain was so bad now that I would do anything, even return to the medical model or reluctantly consider surgery. I needed some immediate relief from the discomfort, but most of all I wanted to review my options—what I could do to improve my gait in the future. I wanted to discuss the kinds of physical therapy my student Robert had suggested. I wanted to ask about exercises and massage.

I remembered the children of my youth who had been stricken with polio in my small Iowa town. Those without resources dragged their damaged limbs in heavy leg braces, scrape-thunk, across the sidewalk on their way to elementary school. Those with more family support found their way to the rare swimming pools of rural Iowa where water exercises improved their mobility. I jotted down a note to myself to ask Dr. Fox about rehab programs.

"I'm sorry for the delay, folks," the charge nurse said, bursting through the heavy double doors. "The computers are down. There will be a wait."

"Yeah," an old man said. "Can't do anything without computers." Wrinkled and bent, he sat in his chair with his cane at his side, a large white cowboy hat on his head, and black cowboy boots on his feet. His hair trailed down the back of his neck in a thick braid. He moistened his lips and smiled, shaking his head slowly.

"Whatcha here for?" asked a thin, wiry man sitting next to him, his scraggly beard bobbing.

"Oh, just have to come back so they'll give me more medicine."

"Sí. They always have you come back," said a middle-aged woman in a flowered dress in the corner. She sat in a wheelchair next to her daughter, a solid woman in her early twenties with bright red lipstick and fingernails to match.

"And back and back and back," the daughter said, thumbing through a magazine.

"I come back every year," the mother said, "have more X rays, then get the same medicine."

"When I was a boy, my mother gave me a certain kind of tea," the old man said, "and that was our medicine."

The charge nurse rushed through the doors again. "I'm sorry, folks, but we're just not having a good day. Now the telephones are down. I ask for your patience."

"I didn't know I was going to talk to the doctor on the phone," the old man cracked.

The thin man shifted in his seat. "Have you ever tried homeopathy?"

"Home-ee-what?" the old man asked.

"It's a kind of herbal medicine. It's really intense. It isn't even the herb itself but the energy field from the substance."

"The energy field?" the old man said.

"There's a new way to make corn bread," the young woman said, looking up from her magazine at her mother. "See, it says here that you add applesauce instead of oil."

"Ah, no." The mother scrunched up her eyebrows.

"It makes it real sweet and cuts down on the fat," the daughter said.

"I'm not using applesauce," the mother said.

Suddenly, all the lights went out. Over the intercom, security called for any available doctor to stand by in the emergency room.

"No. See, when we'd get sick"—the old man's voice rose through the darkness—"when we'd come down with the flu or whatever it was, my mama made us drink this tea."

"And that probably kept you as healthy as any medicine," the thin man said.

The daughter closed her magazine. "But, Ma, we need to cut down on fat."

"No, now I don't make corn bread that often anymore, but when I'm going to make corn bread, I'm going to make corn bread," the mother said.

And then the phone rang, the computers bleeped, and the lights came back on. The charge nurse called my name and squired me down the hall to an examining room. I rested my cane against the wall, changed into a gown, perched on top of the table, and waited for the resident. Soon, she stood beside me, her rubber mallet protruding from the pocket of her short white jacket. Hurriedly, she jotted down my history, condensing the effects from five car accidents into an equal number of sentences in my chart.

Then the safety pin appeared from the resident's pocket and the familiar neurological exam began. The doctor pricked me with a pin up and down my arms and legs. "Can you feel that?" she asked. "Here? Here?" The rubber mallet surfaced, and the resident tapped her way from my ankles to my knees. My leg swung out in an arc, then fell back toward the table. She moved up my body toward my elbows, poised to strike them.

"Don't touch my elbows," I said. They had become hypersensitive to touch. Just brushing my elbows against a hard surface caused nerve pain, as if I'd hit my funny bone.

The resident let the mallet fall toward my elbow, and I pulled it away.

"Don't touch my elbows," I repeated. "They really hurt."

The resident tried to hit my elbow again, and I dodged her blow.

The resident grabbed my arm. "Ms. Swander, in order to do a full exam, we must strike your elbows."

"Then let's not do a full exam," I said, pulling my arm away from her hand, my elbows tucked close to my torso.

The young doctor stopped, jammed her mallet back into her pocket, spun around on her heel, and without a word exited the room.

Oh, dear, I thought. This is not going well. I was trying to be a cooperative patient, but my symptoms were not fitting into the examination protocol.

I watched the old man outside the door, shuffling from his examining room into the hallway. His white gown reached below his knees, meeting the pointed tops of his cowboy boots. He clutched a small urine bottle in his hand. The mother and daughter were getting settled in the room across the hall. The daughter wheeled the mother into place, then plopped down in the single chair and spread her magazine in front of her face. The mother stared straight ahead, into space.

Dr. Fox, a trim, athletic man in his late fifties, bounded into my room in running shoes. He smiled and stood in front of me in a sports shirt and khaki pants, cocking his head. "So I hear you wouldn't let my resident do a full exam."

I tried to explain the pain in my elbows, but while I spoke, he sat in the chair and read the notes in my chart, head down, eyes cast on the page. After less than a minute he slammed my chart shut, grinned up at me, and said, "This isn't so bad." He scrawled a prescription on his pad and handed it to me. "Come back in three months," he said, twirled around, and headed out the door.

I picked up the prescription for a muscle relaxer that I had tried years before without success. "This doesn't work on me," I called to Dr. Fox.

He turned around in the door. "It will."

I looked at him skeptically.

"Trust me," he said and walked out the door.

I pulled on my sweater and slacks, picked up the prescription in one hand and the cane in the other, and hobbled back down the hallway past the mother and daughter who were now deep in conversation about angel food cake. I passed the next examining room. The door was partially open, and the old man was stretched out on the table, his eyes closed, mouth open, a snore vibrating from his lips. I headed back to the waiting room, stopping at the desk to gather up my X rays and MRI reports. I walked toward the door and dropped the prescription in a large trash can, its hood swinging open, swinging shut.

Even though I had experienced similar medical visits in the past, I was stunned by Dr. Fox's dismissal and abruptness. Perhaps, though, I had come to the wrong place for a discussion of my injury. I knew that these kinds of visits were limited to about seven minutes per patient. This was a busy university hospital clinic with little time to sit down and talk, with little time to do anything but the quick and dirty. Perhaps the best I could wish for was a prescription and a date for another visit. If I wanted talk, I rationalized, I'd already set up an appointment with a counselor. Perhaps she could give me some references for rehab programs or at least help me set off on a path of my own research and discovery.

A couple of days later I sat in another waiting room at the University Employees Assistance Office. As a new faculty member, I understood that I was allowed three free counseling sessions here. I figured that would be enough for me to sort out my situation and find firmer emotional grounding. I had an appointment to see a therapist named Nancy.

"Oh, you're Mary Swander," the receptionist said. "I've read your books. So happy to meet you."

I've come to the right place, I thought. I've actually met a fan.

The secretary spun around in her desk chair, glanced up at me, then lowered her voice. "Nancy refused to see you," she said. "But I begged her. I told her, 'You have to see this woman. I feel like I know her.'"

Nancy refused to see me? She must be overscheduled, I thought. A busy time of the year.

"Please come in," Nancy said, appearing in the doorway. She was a tall, smartly dressed woman wearing a long hand-knit sweater that draped below her knees. She crossed her legs at the ankles and leaned back into a cushy black office chair that supported her head.

"My secretary has filled me in on part of your story," Nancy said.

Good, I thought. I won't have to waste time giving a lot of background.

"I'm afraid I won't be able to help you."

"No, I understand. I have to help myself," I said. I thought Nancy was giving me the "you're the only one who can figure this out" routine. I agreed with that. I didn't expect anyone to rescue me or come up with solutions that I needed to initiate.

"Then why are you here?" she asked.

"I need to sort out my feelings about my injury," I said.

"That's exactly why I can't help you," she said.

I was puzzled. Wasn't that the point of going to a counselor? Did I come to the wrong office?

"You'll have to see someone else," she said.

"Another counselor?" I asked. Perhaps this wasn't her specialty, I thought. Maybe she only dealt with marriage counseling or people trying to break addictions.

"That's right." She dashed off some names on a sheet of paper, names of therapists who were not connected to the university and who would charge a significant amount of money.

"Isn't there anyone in this office who can see me for a couple of sessions?" I asked.

"No," she said. "I'm the only counselor here." Then her eyes welled with tears. She blurted out her own story, how she had had three ruptured disks in her lower back, how the pain had been relentless, how she had undergone surgery, and how she'd endured the agony of the recovery period with multiple complications.

"I'm so sorry," I said.

"I can't have you come in here and talk about your injury," she said. "I can't handle it. It's too traumatic for me. It brings up too many issues that I can't face."

"Thank you for your honesty," I said, picking up the slip of paper with the referrals.

I stepped out of the office into the New Mexico sunshine on Central Avenue. The old man in the neurosurgery clinic probably had it right all along. His mother's tea may have been just as effective as our modern medicines. His mother's voice and presence probably did as much to cure her son as any counselor. Yet folk cures still scared me. I wanted a more scientific treatment, but I clearly wasn't making progress on that front. Trash blew up and down the street in the gutters. Cars, motorcycles, and trucks sped by. I let go of the slip of paper and watched as it was lifted up over the flow of traffic and carried away by the blowing wind.

9

In the South Valley again, I stood next to Father Sergei's monastery and stared across the street at the drugstore.

"There's a *curandera* there that you'll love," Ernesto had told me.

A *curandera*, I thought. My feet barely able to work the pedals, I had driven back down to the barrio, the neighborhood where I could be killed by a stray bullet, to search out a *curandera*—a *curandera* who was now going to have to deal with this *gringa*. But what options remained? I'd tried the standard medical routes, and they hadn't panned out.

But was I ready to entrust my life to a folk healer? Someone who believed equally in the power of herbs and prayer? I had less trouble with the herb part of the equation. I believed the old man in the neurosurgery clinic. In the past I'd used an herb here or there with success—willow bark and feverfew for mild headaches. But the idea of saying chants and incantations over dried-up twigs to enhance their power was a little out of my realm.

The traffic whizzed by me, my feet seemingly merging with the concrete sidewalk. I braced myself against the bench at the bus stop, the sun shining in my eyes and down on my head, covered with a beret. I couldn't bring myself to cross the street. I steadied myself with my cane. I felt like one of the juniper trees I'd seen en route to New Mexico. The trees spaced apart—a half dozen or so to a ridge—were the elders of the highway. They had been blown so hard and so long by the wind that they remained permanently bent, locked into their version of reality.

How true those trees were, I thought. Once you become accustomed to one mode of existence, one mind-set, you forget what it would be like to right yourself, to entertain another kind of thought. Once you live with a strong force, you forget what it's like to be without it. You have braced yourself and been blown that way for such a long time that you simply stay that way, even when the wind is gone, even when you know better than to repeat the pattern again.

I let go of my grip on the bus stop bench. I forced myself to enter the drugstore.

The walls were lined with pictures of the saints, their robes sweeping their feet, their halos circling their heads painted with bold yellow strokes: St. Michael and Gabriel, St. Joseph and Our Lady of Guadalupe, the Sacred Heart of Jesus, and St. Christopher. Each saint carried a name tag in both English and Spanish, as did the plastic boxes of herbs and Mason jars filled with twigs, flowers, and leaves that lined the shelves: *diente de león* (dandelion), *hinojo* (fennel), *moscada* (nutmeg), *cola de caballo* (horsetail). On the top shelves were still more religious, primitive wood carvings: St. Francis in his sandals, a bird perched on his shoulder, St. Teresa of Avila in her ecstasy, Christ nailed to the cross.

A woman with short graying hair, who appeared to be in her early sixties, stood behind the counter. Her frame was solid, her back straight, her head and arms moving in steady, self-assured motions. She was dressed in a white button-down western shirt and jeans, and on her left wrist she wore a silver bracelet with a large turquoise stone in the center. She did not appear magical or mystical. Rather, she seemed like someone who might be clerking in an old-fashioned department store, a twenty-year veteran who knew where every item was located in each aisle. She peered up at me from behind her glasses with her large, round brown eyes and introduced herself as "Luisa" or "Lu."

"Oh, you're from Iowa?" Lu said. "I have another friend from Iowa. She's a social worker."

"How did you know I'm from Iowa?" I asked. I hadn't given her any information—not even my name.

"I recognized you right away because you wear a little hat. My friend wore a little hat, too, from Iowa. I met my friend when she had just been transferred here. She needed a toothbrush and was walking down the street and saw the sign, so she stopped in."

When my fellow Iowan entered Lu's drugstore, she probably didn't find a toothbrush. If you rooted around hard enough, you might find a can of deodorant or a jar of linament in the store, and you can still get a prescription filled in the tiny pharmacy tucked away in the back, but ever since Lu became part owner, the place took on a different character.

On one long, sweeping counter near the cash register were jars of bubble gum, Mounds bars, and Dickie's Pecan Rolls. A rack held a pile of Spanish newspapers: *El Hispano News*. Tootsie Roll pops and pickled peppers were wedged in next to glow-in-the-dark Jesus nightlights. Small packages of individually wrapped herbs hung on pegs along the wall closest to the door. Baskets filled with tiny aloe vera plants perched on metal shelves in front of the window.

To reach the rack with the hot water bottles and the hair nets, you had to maneuver around Lu's easel and paints, her watercolor of the New Mexico landscape just beginning to fill in with pinkish brown earth tones. Next, you passed the glass case jammed full of Lu's handmade rosaries, the prayer beads made with everything from the smoothest, most polished turquoise to tiny, fragrant rose beads fashioned from crushed petals. Then you slipped past a baby's playpen filled with blankets, rattles, and a pacifier tied to a white shoestring anchored to the frame. Next to the playpen, a whole row of mortar and pestles—ten inches in diameter and made of rough gray limestone—stood guard over a display of Acoma pottery, the Native American water jars as delicate and finely designed as the receptacles were heavy.

The tiny gold bell attached to the front door jingled. In shuffled an older man, a blue knit stocking cap pulled down over his head. He stood near the cash register, speechless, lost in his jacket and trousers, his clothes much too big for his body. A few sparse whiskers were sprinkled across his sunken cheeks.

"*Buenos días*, Lu," the man said at last in a soft, whispery voice.

"Oh, Pepe," Lu said. "You need a sandwich. I'll fix you one." Lu opened an old white refrigerator filled with bottles of Coke and pulled out a loaf of bread and a package of bologna. She spread two slices of the bread with mayonnaise and mustard, added a leaf of lettuce, cut the sandwich in half, and placing it on a piece of waxed paper, handed it to Pepe.

"*Gracias, gracias, muchas gracias.*" The old man smiled and disappeared out the door.

"Poor Pepe," Lu said. "The gangs keep stealing his Social Security checks, so he has nothing to live on. His water and electricity have been turned off in his apartment. If I didn't make him a sandwich once a day, he would starve to death."

The bell rang again, and two little boys, one with a backpack slung over his shoulder, walked into the store. They fingered the licorice and candy bars on the counter, then stacked up a little pile of pennies to buy bubble gum.

"*Uno, dos, tres, cuatro, cinco …*"

"*Bueno,*" Lu said, and the boys scampered back out to the street where they'd locked their bicycles to the lamppost. Two teenage boys—the same two who had appeared at the bus stop bench several days before—waited for the smaller boys. The teenagers bent over them, one holding out his hand for gum and the other flicking his lighter, bringing the flame close to the young boys' faces.

Lu sat on her little swivel desk chair at her card table, her recipe box in hand. She took out an empty white card and picked up a pen. "You want herbs, no?"

"Yes," I said, taking a couple of steps back from her table. I was a juniper tree bent by the wind.

Lu tolerated no hesitancy. "Now, *Señorita Iowa,* what's your real name?" she asked.

I said my first name and spelled my last. In neat, clear, bold letters she wrote at the top of the card: MARY SWANDER. Then she took a medical interview, asking me about my symptoms, the car accident, the pain, and how it had affected my whole system.

"Ah, we need something to boost your immune system, something to boost your whole body."

She thumbed through her herbal manuals that lined the top of her desk, books that included everything from Chinese remedies to medicinal plants of the desert Southwest. She wrote notes on her index card, then came up with a suggestion of three herbs: yerba del manzo, damiana, and echinacea.

She scurried through her store and located each of the herbs on the drugstore shelves. Unscrewing the lids of the jars, she reached her hand deep into the glass containers and withdrew the dried herbs, testing their freshness between her fingers, holding them up to her nose to absorb their bitter smell. She placed the herbs in separate plastic bags and handed them to me.

"You combine all these herbs, then boil them together for about ten minutes. Strain and sip throughout the day, and each time you sip, you say a little prayer. Put the herbs in a water bottle, and it will be convenient to carry around with you," Lu said.

"And you've had good success with these herbs?"

"*Sí*! Of course, everyone's different. I don't give the same thing to *todo el mundo*. Look, people come in here sick with everything from dry mouth to hemorrhaging, and I recommend a potion, and a few days later they call and say, 'Hey, I feel better!'"

Lu's whole face lifted in delight, her high, rounded cheekbones pressing against her oval glasses. She twirled around on her stool, her movements quick and spirited, her hands pressing and straightening the cloth that covered her card table.

I tried to pay Lu for the consultation, but she insisted it was free.

"No, I don't charge," she said. "My talent as an herbalist is a gift from God. And when you have a gift, you have to give something back."

The telephone rang, and Lu leaped up to run behind the counter. "*Sí*, that's right," she said. "I told you to take inmortal. Same thing. *Sí...* inmortal. Everlasting. *Bueno*." Lu hung up and returned to her desk. "You see, I have people call from all over the United States."

She spun around on her stool and directed her attention back to me as if I were the only person in her life at the moment. She looked at me and smiled, her whole face consumed with hope, as if to say, "This will work. Don't worry. I'm good at what I do, and these herbs are potent healing agents. You must place your faith in their power."

"You take those herbs and come see me in a week," Lu said at last. "We'll get along. You're from Iowa. You'll be fine. As long as you don't need a toothbrush."

10

Fortunately, I'd brought my toothbrush with me from Iowa and had placed it in its holder in my apartment in Albuquerque—everything in its own place. The studio was so small that it dictated orderliness. The main piece of furniture—a sofa bed whose mattress sagged nearly to the floor—took up most of the space. I spent one night on that bed, and it felt like sleeping in an ice-cream scoop, my back a bar of chocolate snapping in two. So I pulled off the blankets and camped on my exercise mat on the floor. Mornings, the light poured through my one window, cheery and bright, but I moved slowly, the pain in my limbs riveting me to the floor.

One morning I awoke and bent my knee, the pain shooting down my leg into my foot. I bent my other knee, the pain shooting up into my hip. I reached over to turn off the alarm, and my biceps and triceps throbbed. I lay back, and pain nailed me to the carpet. Any move, any attempt to right myself, blasted pain down my neck and spine. I lay back and drifted into sleep, my body carried out into a vast ocean to some unknown destination.

I opened my eyes and tried again. I reached over and turned on the radio, hoping that the strains of the news would rouse me to get up and make it through another day. That was the mission. That was my test of faith at the moment. To get up and hold firm in the belief that I could make it through another day, that things would actually get better, that the pain would lessen, and I would reach land before the whole ship went down.

To get up meant getting up on my knees. That was the first position. I would roll over on my side, then slowly bring my knees to my chest. When the pain subsided, I'd rock myself onto my knees, bracing my hands against the floor. That was the first step, the easy part.

I can do that, I thought. Then I thought of the second step, actually trying to stand up, my legs straightening. The events of the last few days trilled in the background of my mind. I had launched myself into the world of faith healing. I believed that I had found genuine healers. At least Lu seemed like a genuine healer. But should I take her herbs? They might work. Think of that. They just might work. But they might not. They might be contaminated with something. After all, where did they come from? They might make me even worse.

At least Lu had a steady flow of customers going in and out of her shop. If she wasn't any good, she'd go out of business. What about Father Sergei? For all I knew, he could be a cult leader. He hadn't even mentioned anything about healing. But had he done anything to harm me? No. And he was interesting, seemingly totally committed to living his faith. I can respect that. I lay back and let myself drift into sleep.

In that fuzzy state between drowsing and dreaming, I encountered a pair of eyes, eyes in the middle of storms in the Atlantic Ocean, eyes in the middle of storms encountered by Christopher Columbus. I encountered deep-set brown eyes staring through me. They were the eyes in the icon of Christ on Lu's drugstore door. They peered out of a face dotted with blood, framed in long brown hair and a long scraggly beard. They were Father Sergei's eyes. The pupils grew large and round, riding the waves of a barren desert, once an ocean.

The pupils grew to the size of the moon, the dark side of the moon, with only a sliver of light shining through. The light shone down on a man, a man dressed in a loincloth, brightly colored feathers in his hair, the same dark eyes in his head. The man lay under a tree in the forest, ill, alone. Birds sang and then stopped. Birds circled overhead. The man's fever rose. He shivered and tossed back and forth in his bed of leaves. Days passed into a week, two weeks. The man had no food. His fever rose. Finally, sweat poured from his body, cascading down his chest and back. Birds sang. The man pulled himself up and walked back to his village full of people.

After that, whenever someone in the village fell ill, relatives approached the man, this shaman. One day, they carried a woman on a stretcher to the shaman and begged him to help the lame woman walk. The man chanted and danced and chanted and danced his way into a trance. He spun around and around the lame woman's pallet. He spoke to the birds, to the trees, to the spirits in heaven. He crossed the waters, traveled to the underworld, and brought back news from the woman's dead ancestors, and when he returned, he chanted and danced until the evil spirits departed, and the woman slowly rose up on her feet and walked. The villagers cheered. The man followed her with his eyes. Years passed.

The eyes were the eyes of storms. The eyes of the shaman were Father Sergei's eyes. They were Christ's eyes during the time of his healing ministry. In that era, in that culture, the ill and the lame were despised. The lepers were shunned, living outside the cities, wearing bells around their necks to warn others against coming near. Illness was an expression of God's will, something that had to be endured. Or, worse, illness was the fault of a sinful soul.

But Christ embraced the sinners and lived among the shunned. "Out, unclean spirit, come out," Christ commanded, and the ill were healed. Lepers were cured. Christ stretched his hands on top of a lame man's head. "Pick up your bed and walk." A hemorrhaging woman touched the tassel of Christ's robe, saying to herself, "If I touch his clothes, I shall be cured." Immediately, her problem disappeared. Christ said, "My daughter, your faith has healed you. Go in peace, free forever from this trouble." The woman walked down the road. Birds sang, their eyes open wide.

Their eyes were Christ's eyes. They were the eyes of his disciples, men with tongues of flame over their heads. The flames fanned up into the air. The disciples fanned out all over the world, through the deserts, over the mountains, across the oceans, to obey Christ's command to "Heal the sick, cleanse the lepers, raise the dead, and cast out devils." The disciples laid on hands and cured the lame. They exorcised demons and healed snakebite, blindness, and dysentery. They spread their nets and welcomed the ill, the sick, the misfits and outcasts into their boats.

My eyes opened. The FM station chimed the tone at the top of the hour. The day's news beamed through my brain. I have to get up, I told myself. It's a quarter past the hour. It's half-past the hour. I have to get up. What if disease and illness were just to be endured? Never to be alleviated? What if I stayed in this kind of pain for the rest of my life? Okay, what if? I still have to get up. I have to get up and go to work, I thought. I can't just lie here all day even if I'm stuck with this disability. I felt like a member of Christopher Columbus's crew, hoping to stop the force of the water carrying my ship away from Spain. But even if you try to stop movement, I told myself, even if you lay here all day, even if you tried to will the currents to stop, they scurry on, pushing you forward, carrying you along with them.

I had been easing myself back into the Christian world, the Catholic world. I had done this on purpose, hoping against hope to come into contact with that ancient thread of shamanism, of finding some remnant of that old healing tradition. The Catholic world encompassed truly holy people with healing abilities, but it also included dull priests holding up *Playboy* magazines. The Catholic world included domination and oppression—all the things I had rebelled against, all the things I had grown conscious of as I matured. Was I going backward with this search for faith healing? Falling back into the grip of the patriarchy? My search for faith healing seemed to be the only way out of my pain, but it cast me into swirling waters.

My eyes closed.

The eyes were Lu's eyes. The eyes were the eyes of the Virgin Mary. They were Mary Magdalene's eyes, the eyes of a prostitute, the woman Christ chose to be his mate. They were the eyes of Christ ignoring the stares of the Pharisees for his association with women. They were the welcoming eyes of Martha and Mary who fed and lodged him on his travels.

The eyes were the eyes of the Virgin Mary and Mary Magdalene at the base of the cross. They were the eyes of Veronica wiping Christ's face with a rag. They were the eyes on the visage left on the cloth. Judas, the man with the kiss and the bag of coins, had run away. Peter, the sleepy man with the rock, had run away. The cock, with its beak open wide, had crowed one, two, three times.

The pupils of the eyes grew to the size of the moon, the dark side of the moon, without a sliver of light shining through. The guards cast lots for Christ's robes. They offered him vinegar to drink and ran him through with a sword. It was three o'clock in the afternoon. The ground shook. "Father, forgive them, for they know not what they do."

Mother-Father, forgive them for what they do. The early Christians prayed to Mother-Father God, a god of male might, a goddess of compassion, courage, and wisdom. Male and female eyes alike opened to the world, caring for and healing others.

The Lives of the Saints opened with female healers stepping out of the pages. Healers such as St. Fabiola who opened her heart, gave up her wealth, opened her home to the sick, and founded a hospital in Rome in 394 A.D. St. Fabiola gathered up people from the street— the poor, the blind, those reeking of disease. She waited on the patients herself, making her rounds from bed to bed. She tended to all, never shying away from the most repulsive wounds and sores. She was a physician, a healer. She was never referred to as a nurse. She built a large hospice for pilgrims coming to Rome. Her friend Paula founded a hospital for the Jews, bathing and caring for her patients while she wore sackcloth.

I pulled the sheet up over my face. The FM station chimed the tone at the top of the next hour. I needed to get up and take a shower. I needed to find some clean clothes. I needed the will to voyage through my world of pain and get up and function through another day, acting as if nothing was happening, coursing through the waters, tricking my own crew into thinking we were closer to land than we were, keeping my own private reckonings.

I had to get up and get on with my mission, my discovery, or the surprise discoveries I would make along the way. I needed to kiss the land and pray for healing, for healers, for something, someone who could help me get up on my knees in the morning. For someone who would help me balance the male and female sides of healing. For someone in contact with the ancient rituals who could integrate the positive power of shamanism with the Christian tradition. For someone who could call my spirit back from the grip of demons. For someone who could help me find a story that would explain my life.

I rolled up on my knees and bowed my head, stretching my arms out in front of me as far as I could reach. My back muscles released. Then, with one hand braced against the seat of the kitchen chair and the other against the coffee table, I accomplished the most excruciating move, rising up, straightening my whole body, my crippled arms trying to do some of the work for my crippled legs. Once up, I used my cane to steady my shifting gait. My weak legs wobbled, casting me this way and that as if with the waves.

11

The classic condemnation of the Midwest is the dismissal: It's flat and has no ocean. But I've lived in that so-called flatness long enough to have a feel for the contours, the slight rises in the land, the dips and dives of a place capable of supporting so many living things. Viewed this way, it's not all flatness, it's all subtlety. It's all in the way you attune yourself to your surroundings, appreciating what others might chalk off as unimportant, what others might never stop to see.

In New Mexico, I had begun a similar process of tuning in to the slight changes in the landscape. The state's high dramas stunned me: the Sangre de Cristo Mountains in the north that turned blood red at sunset, the subalpine forests near Cloudcraft that sheltered you from the wind in the folds of their conifers, the White Sands National Monument that blinded you with the stark glare of its dunes, and the Carlsbad Caverns that dwarfed you with stalagmites and stalactites. What I valued more were the little surprises: the tiny hand-lettered sign in the high desert with its warning to stay on the path lest you tangle with a rattlesnake; the roadrunner scurrying across the adobe wall outside my apartment door each morning; the color of the sand becoming pinker the closer I walked to the Rio Grande; the voices of the children playing in the park, carrying far over the sagebrush in the dry air.

My trips to the barrio were beginning to take on this same sense of subtlety. In some strange way I was slowly beginning to feel at home there and began drifting down to the neighborhood a couple of times a week. While I had seen posters tacked up on bulletin boards along Central Avenue advertising New Age healers who had national reputations for their psychic abilities, I preferred to connect with the little-known people I had discovered in the area of town that most ignored or didn't dare approach. Even though the barrio stood in direct contrast to my Iowa landscape and culture, something about the place seemed comfortable and familiar.

Quickly, I discovered that the people of the barrio did not run on standard American timetables. They did not answer to message machines and e-mail. A couple of times I tried to call and set up an appointment with Father Sergei, but one of his monks answered the phone and told me he had no idea how to locate the priest. "You want to see him?" the monk asked. "Just come to the monastery." When I called the drugstore looking for Lu, I got her brother-in-law, the pharmacist, who had a similar response: "Lu's not here now, but she will be later."

Having lived for years around the Amish in Iowa, I understood how to function in a culture without dependence on technology. The "visit" was a key part of the Amish way of life. The Amish prized these face-to-face meetings with others, which they thought fostered honest communication and community. So I set off to visit the barrio. I knocked on Father Sergei's door, and when he wasn't there, I chatted with one of his nuns or another monk who might be out tending the garden. I watched them turn the compost heap and prune the apricot tree. I helped them spoon food into the bowls for their dogs.

On the sidewalk, I bumped into Father Corazón, the Catholic priest, and introduced myself. He was a dashingly handsome extroverted man with a sweep of jet-black hair and an all-encompassing intellect. Sometimes I found myself slipping into the back pew of the church at his daily Mass to hear his homilies. He was interested in my job at the university, in the worlds of history, politics, and theology, but when I confessed that I was in search of healers, he simply nodded his head and said, "You're in the right place."

When Lu wasn't in the drugstore, I visited with her sister, her husband, or her granddaughter—whoever was minding the store. I watched Lu's husband spread some yerba del manzo, or swamp root, on a newspaper to dry. He'd just returned from a trip to the Rio Grande to dig the herb. I helped Lu's sister plant pansies along the boulevard in front of the store. She leaned into a spade and told me of her struggles with breast cancer.

"I have trouble in my life," she said, kneeling down around the holes she'd dug in the ground, patting the dirt next to the flowers, "but I have no fear." Then she looked up from her work and stared me in the face. "Fear gets you nowhere. Fear is merely a lack of faith in God."

I stepped into Lu's drugstore one day in February after I'd just begun taking her herbal concoction. I'd finally gotten up the courage to boil the brew on top of the stove. A woody, moldy smell had filled my apartment. I'd sieved off the herbs and poured the liquid into a coffee mug. I held my nose and chugged it down like horrible-tasting cough medicine.

So that February day I returned to Lu to check in, to give her my report that I'd seen some slight improvement. At least the altitude adjustment had receded. My feet were working better, and I had returned to my more "normal" state of pain. I didn't know the causative agent for my improvement—the herbs or the simple passage of time—but I was hopeful to see change.

I sat beside Lu at her card table, but my eyes kept landing on the pairs of eyes that were staring down at us: St. Francis, St. Teresa, and Christ nailed to the cross.

"Would you like to see one of those?" Lu asked, pointing to the hand-carved wooden statues on the very top shelf of her drugstore.

I nodded.

"I'll get them down," Lu said, wheeling out a tall ladder from the back room. She scampered up to the top rung to reach for the statues, past the jars of alfalfa, ginger, fennel, and juniper berries. Her hands grasping a piece of soft cloth, she lovingly dusted off the statues and placed them on the counter, whispering to each one as if to a real presence.

The statues were made from a soft wood, poplar, the fibers still white and unstained. The cuts in the wood were precise, careful, but bold. The saints' bodies were at the same time very realistic yet out of proportion, their fingers and toes too boxy and too large and undefined compared to their more delicate facial features.

"*Bueno*," Lu said. "A man was selling these out in front of the church one Sunday after Mass. He was so thin. He was starving. I swept up the statues and bought them all."

Lu told me the wood-carver had grown up in Albuquerque and had journeyed down Route 66 to Hollywood where he claimed to have carved parts of movie sets—the banister for *Gone with the Wind* among his more famous pieces. In his old age, he returned to Albuquerque penniless and took up his old, more traditional subject matter.

I held the crucifix in my hands, the massive, bulky body of Christ assuming a weight that was different from the trim Jesus renditions of my youth. There was at once something very childish and yet serious about this representation of suffering, something that at once repelled and drew me to the cross.

I thought of my childhood convent school days and the crucifixes that had been stationed at the front of every classroom. The crucifixes had been dark, stamped out of pitch black wood, with a skinny Jesus—his body made of cold, twisted, steely metal, with his ribs sticking out—nailed to the cross. Over the altar in the chapel, a life-size version of the same crucifix hung above the tabernacle. On top of each filing cabinet in each classroom, a statue of the Virgin Mary held reign over the room. In the hallways, in the stairwells, and in the chapel, more statues crowded in together, their affiliations well known to all of us. St. Joseph was the Virgin Mary's reluctant husband. An angel had to talk him into the marriage. St. Francis de Sales and St. Jeanne de Chantal were the founders of the Visitation order. In France, they had designed the nuns' habits that were mysteriously held together by straight pins.

We crossed ourselves, chanted, and recited our prayers and "ejaculations" in front of these statues. In May, we processed through the hallways, into the chapel, and outside to the shrine, carrying the statue of the Virgin Mary on our shoulders, forming a "living rosary"—ten girls for each decade rattling off the Hail Marys, the president of each class taking up the recitation of the Our Father. We stepped along, medals around our necks, round, tarnished impressions of our patron saints wedging into our developing bosoms. I loved the reliability of the crucifixes—one in every room.

I loved the stories and images of the saints represented by their statues—St. Joseph's staff that was said to have burst into blossom when he agreed to take Mary as his bride, and St. Francis's plume that became the symbol for all writers.

We had our crucifixes, statues, and medals blessed. We carried them around with us in special cases or boxes. The church forbade the destruction of any blessed article, so we never threw them away but passed the crucifixes, rosaries, and medals down the line to other relatives. What we had lost was the history behind our actions. I never questioned these images until early adulthood when a Quaker friend asked why Catholics filled their churches with "bad art." In contrast, her meetinghouse was stripped bare.

About this time I discovered that when the number of healers in the early Church declined, the healing powers of the imagination flourished. People put their faith in the powers of relics, shrines, and statues. Pilgrims reported cures at shrines such as St. Ursula's in Cologne that retained its popularity even after the skeletons of the eleven thousand virgins proved to be those of males. At the shrine of the blessed St. Rosalia in Palermo, the saint's miraculous bones, which were credited with many healings, were later discovered to be those of a goat. The substance of the relic didn't seem to matter as much as the degree of faith it engendered.

At my convent school, Sister Mary Ignatius carried with her at all times a relic of the French mystic St. Jeanne de Chantal, concealed in a little silver case and hidden deep in the pocket of her habit. Sometimes the nun took the relic out and showed it to the girls in her classroom. It was a very precious item, she assured us—a piece of hair from the saint's head. I was told that the nuns had to crop their hair very short, that they had crew cuts under those wimples.

So I reasoned that this hair from the head of St. Jeanne was very precious indeed. Never mind the fact that the hair had not deteriorated after 350 years, the hair was a first-class relic.

During the Crusades, these kinds of relics had become the spoils of war, and through their sale they brought the Church considerable wealth. Later, Martin Luther and others objected to this commerce. But until that time, the masses venerated the body parts of biblical heroes and saints. Gallons of Christ's blood, buckets of milk from Mary's breasts, splinters from the cross, leg bones, arm bones, skulls, shriveled hearts, and whole skeletons were enshrined.

Sister Ignatius had claimed that all relics were capable of producing healings. The Virgin Mary, of course, was the first line of defense. Her intercession with Christ could cure all ailments. Then, in the tradition of the idols of ancient Rome and Greece, the Church tagged some relics with specializations. St. Lucy's relics were supposed to cure eye disease. St. Teresa of Avila became the healer of cardiac patients. St. Jeanne de Chantal herself served as the therapist saint, the healer of dysfunctional families. There were saints who healed leprosy and others who dealt with infertility or the plague. Rather than taking herbs like the "pagans," the medieval Christians scraped the gravestones of saints and ground them into potions or wore them as amulets.

Yet all the statues and all the relics hidden deep down in the pockets of nuns' habits did not completely override the existence of women healer herbalists. In *Tristan and Isolde*, Isolde knows how to use the drugs in her chest of herbs. In *The Canterbury Tales*, Chaucer describes women who use herbs to heal and cure the sick, lovely ladies saving wounded knights with bandages and potions, baths and lotions. In the Scandinavian epic *Edda*, women receive knowledge from spirits on how to care for wounds and where to dig for roots and herbs.

"I'll take this one," I said, pointing to the wooden crucifix, not really knowing why I was making this purchase. I rationalized that this herbalist, this *curandera*, was helping me, and I needed to pay her back. I needed to buy something in her store—more than a couple of $2 bags of roots and herbs. Heaven knows, I didn't need another crucifix. I had a box in storage filled with fifteen to twenty crucifixes, all having been removed from the coffins of my dead relatives, all having been carefully wrapped in newspaper and deposited in the same box, then passed from one generation to the next.

"I love this crucifix," I told Lu. Then for some inexplicable reason I blurted out my story about my box. Not even my best friends knew about that box, and here I was telling this near stranger. Most of my friends, like me, had drifted away from their childhood churches, the old Catholics among them, the most rebellious and rejecting of their former paths. The thought of the box was brutally painful. It was also slightly embarrassing to admit that I still clung to its contents.

"I've never known what to do with all those crucifixes," I told Lu. "They're blessed," I added. "I can't throw them away."

"No, no, no. You must get them out and hang them all on the wall, all together, with this new one, too. This will be yours, you see."

"Oh."

"You must be proud of your past. You must celebrate and honor your dead, not hide them in a box in the attic. Understand?"

"*Sí,*" I said and felt lighter. In this completely foreign place, I was connecting with a deep strain of my existence that I hadn't been able to access before.

I thought of Isaac Abravanel and Abraham Seneor, of all who had been terrorized by the symbol of the cross, all who had been forced to accept its weight or reject its tyranny. I remembered all the horrors of all the wars the crucifix had engendered. I had preferred to journey away from the politics of this emblem, its institutionalized power. Yet here was a woman who in some small way was echoing the roles of Fabiola and Paula. Here were the faint strains of *Tristan and Isolde*, *The Canterbury Tales*, and *Edda*, a woman who was helping to restore the role of women healers, of women's place in the original scheme of spirituality. At this moment I felt it was all right to set down some of my reservations and doubts, and begin cautiously to approach my religious belief system again—at least with one small step. I could return to my faith as an adult and relearn what I could learn. "Whatcha doing there?" I thought to myself, looking down at Lu's desk as if peering over a monk's ancient manuscript.

Lu was showing me that it was okay to embrace the cross again—not necessarily the oppressive structure it had historically symbolized, but the sense of family ties and tradition it could represent. She was giving me permission to descend to the underworld and contact my spirit guides. I still wasn't sure what it meant to have true faith, but I could accept this link with my heritage. Lu's herbs seemed to be helping me, and perhaps the letting go of this old religious antagonism would help me just as much.

With every bag of herbs Lu gave me, she instructed me to say a prayer, a favorite invocation of my own design. She seemed so firm, so sure about her instructions that I couldn't help but feel her sense of reverence and power. I still had doubts about this, but as I stood there in the drugstore with the refrigerator constantly humming behind me, I decided that at this moment I would weave my doubts into my very being, as if they were Druids, fairies, and elves. I would trust Lu. I took a breath and quietly and ever so calmly decided I would take this step down a very crooked path.

"There are different ways to heal," Lu said, climbing back up the ladder to replace the statues on their shelf. She turned her head around and beamed down at me. "There's physical healing and spiritual healing. We need both. You need both. You're on a pilgrimage, no? The important thing is not the destination but the discoveries you make along the journey."

12

I journeyed north from Albuquerque, past Santa Fe through the Jemez River canyon, discovering a rugged landscape of piñon- and juniper-studded steppes that gave way to the dramatic red sandstone and volcanic outcroppings of the mountains. I downshifted to gain some momentum up the steep highway, the Trooper chugging with the change of altitude. After my last visit with Lu, my legs began to feel even better, and I set out in the Trooper one Sunday morning with a map of sacred sites that Ernesto had given me. I passed through the tiny town of Jemez Springs, a village Ernesto had marked on the map, the site of ancient healing waters. A handful of spas, restaurants, and small inns hugged the roadside. A Zen center hung out its sign near a Catholic retreat house. A few cars nosed into the small parking lot in front of the Laughing Lizard Motel, its facade painted bright pink. The mountain walls above Jemez, formed by thickened layers of ash spewed from a massive volcanic eruption more than a million years ago, dwarfed the tiny town. Spruce and fir trees spread across the mountain crests.

I was tempted to check into the Laughing Lizard and soak in the mineral springs. The motel reminded me of all the mom-and-pop motels of my youth, one-night stops my family had made on our vacations across country. "She'll be coming around the mountain when she comes," I could hear my mother singing in the front seat of our 1955 Ford station wagon. She kept a thermos of hot coffee at her feet. She had spread peanut butter on sandwiches and passed a half to each of us, the car putting along through northern New Mexico. My two brothers and I were stretched out on the air mattress that lined the cavity of the car. We curled up and abandoned ourselves to the swerves and curves of the highway, our T-shirts and khaki shorts dissolved into a mass of wrinkles clumped around our bodies. I lay on my right side, then rolled over and shifted to my left. In my pocket was a small statue of the Virgin Mary that Sister Mary Ignatius had given me. It was made of translucent, glow-in-the-dark plastic. "Let the Virgin be your guide through all your journeys in life," the nun had said to me. "And expect miracles."

I was tempted to stop at the Laughing Lizard, but I decided to press on, taking the narrow road that wound past Redondo Peak, its elevation rising to more than eleven thousand feet. A secondary volcanic cone, Redondo Peak had grown from the crater floor and now seemed to preside over all below: the Valle Grande, a circular fifteen-mile-diameter depression in the heart of the largest system of volcanic craters or caldera in the world. I cut east on Highway 502, the road twisting past dry gulches and eroded blocks of sandstone, the "badlands" of the Espanola Valley.

Then I veered northwest toward the Chimayó Valley, famous for its apples, chili peppers, and fine handwoven rugs. The valley is wedged between the Rio Grande on the west, which brings irrigation and fertility to its fields, and the Sangre de Cristo Mountains on the east, which shelter it from harsh winds and weather. The town of Chimayó, a two-mile string of houses, shops, and a Catholic church along the highway, had a more earthy quality than Jemez Springs. No pink B and Bs grabbed my eye. Rather, the adobe houses faded back into the natural brown tones of the surrounding hills.

A couple of miles to the north, I rounded a curve, pulled into a driveway, and found El Santuario de Chimayó, a site that Ernesto had starred on his map. New Mexicans pilgrimaged here every year on Good Friday, some walking miles on their knees to dip their hands into the hole in the floor with its healing dirt. I had expected a quiet, out-of-the way church, but instead I found the parking lot jammed with cars and pickup trucks. I was just in time for Sunday Mass.

Three generations of families—grandparents, parents, and children—poured into the shrine, prayer books in hand and rosaries wound around their wrists. Fathers carried ill babies in their arms. Mothers pushed their mothers in wheelchairs. A blind man was led by a seeing-eye dog. Some worshipers walked on crutches. Some scooted along the dirt path with walkers. Others, like me, used canes to steady themselves. We all ducked through two hand-carved wooden doors under the arch of the adobe wall in front of the small church. The melting snow stained the top of the wall a darker shade of brown. Two steeples on either side of the entrance rose up into the clear sky, their bells swaying back and forth, *bong-bong, bong-bong.*

Thigh pressed to thigh, we squeezed together in the pinewood pews, the ninety-by-thirty-foot church filling instantly with a couple of hundred people, the overflow standing in the aisles. The smell of damp earth permeated the air, but as the church quickly warmed, the heat held in by the three-foot-thick adobe walls, the space became dry and crisp. The walls were adorned with *santos*, brightly colored statues of saints mounted behind glass frames. *Reredos*, a series of sacred symbolic paintings done in equally bright colors, decorated the main altar and framed a large six-foot-high hard-carved crucifix, Christ's arms outspread, his head hanging down in agony, blood trickling down his cheek.

The priest stood on the altar and fiddled with the microphone, flicking the switch on and off, checking all the connections. Finally, he threw up his arms and said, "I'm sorry, but we don't have a sound system today. Yesterday the mike was working, but not today. It's a mystery. But it's all a mystery—this church, the dirt, the miraculous healings that take place here."

The mystery of Chimayó can be traced back to the creation myths of the Tewa Indians. Legend has it that the Twin War Brothers, who were already credited with creating mountains and saving people from monsters, slew an evil giant in this secluded valley, sending fire, smoke, and boiling water spewing out of the earth. The geysers became New Mexico's fabled curative hot springs, but eventually the Chimayó pool dried up, leaving only miraculous mud and then dirt. Oral history suggests that the Tewa once had a pueblo site where the Spanish shrine now stands. There is evidence that the Indians used the dirt and mud from their old sacred pool for healing.

When the Spanish arrived in the valley in 1700, the sick were drawn to the miraculous soil of Chimayó. Then, in 1813, Bernardo Abeyta, a pious man of the Brotherhood of the Penitentes, found a bright light shining over the pool of dirt in the ground. Abeyta dug down in the soil and uncovered a miraculous crucifix that he brought to the church at Santa Cruz. Not once, not twice, but three times the cross disappeared from the church and reappeared in the dirt at Chimayó. Soon a chapel was built over the holy place. A short time later, Christ appeared to Abeyta on the spot and cured him of a ravaging illness.

I slipped out of the last pew and entered the small room near the altar with the healing dirt. The walls were filled with crutches, braces, and canes, all testimonials to the miracles that had taken place there. A small hole in the floor held a pile of loose reddish soil from this fertile valley. Bracing myself with my cane, I knelt down beside the hole. What, oh, what are you doing? I asked myself. Putting your trust in dirt? I'd put my trust in Lu and her statues, and now I was going to believe that dirt in a hole in the ground could cure me? Then I thought of my garden in the spring, kneeling like this on the ground, struggling so hard to plant those seedlings and encourage them to take root. Dirt. Why not dirt? I didn't need to believe anything more. Dirt was magical. After all, dirt nurtured all growing things.

I bent down and fingered the dirt, allowing it to fall through my hands. I pinched a few specks and held it between my thumb and index finger. I held it up to my nose and took a breath in. I held it up to the light streaming in the one small window. Then I pushed up my sleeve and rubbed it on my right arm. I rubbed it on my left arm. I picked up more dirt and rubbed it down my right leg, tracing the painful, damaged nerves all the way from my thigh to my ankle. I swooped the dirt down the same path on my left leg. Next, I bent my head over the hole, my spine curling, and placed a whole handful of dirt on my neck. I closed my eyes and pressed the dirt, cool and powdery, against my skin.

Suddenly, I was back in the 1955 Ford again, my neck pressed against the air mattress, my glow-in-the-dark Virgin Mary statue in my pocket. The car was parked at a roadside café. I waited until the whole family had disappeared into the restaurant, then I climbed into the front seat. On the dashboard was a compass, a glass bulb with the large letters N S E W that spun around and around when you changed directions, and around and around again, always coming full circle. My Virgin statue had a suction cup on her feet—just like the compass on the dash.

I brought the Virgin's feet to my lips and spit into the cup. My saliva pooled into the plastic. I placed the statue on the dash right next to the compass, pushing down hard on the suction cup. The Virgin stuck! Her hands were folded in prayer, and her serene translucent face gazed out over the dusty interior of the Ford. The Virgin and the compass would guide our way. The Virgin would preserve our little family, keep us together, bless our trip.

"You crawl in the back now." My mother stood at the window with the thermos of coffee in hand.

I heaved myself over the front seat. My brothers hopped in the back tailgate. My father started the car, my mother unfolding the map of New Mexico on her lap. My father craned his neck toward my mother, glancing down at the map, then his eyes fell on the Virgin. "Jesus Christ, what's this?" he yelled.

He grabbed the statue, his thumb and index finger circling the Virgin's neck, and yanked it off the dash. The Virgin's feet gave way with a *pop*. My father rolled down the window, and threw the statue out on the highway. The Virgin's head broke away at her neck.

We sped back down the mountain road.

WHETHER YOU HAVE A HANDICAP,
WHETHER YOU HAVE A BROKEN HEART,
FOLLOW THE LONG MOUNTAIN ROAD,
FIND A HOME IN CHIMAYÓ.

I raised my head and read the poem on the shrine wall, the dirt trickling down to my shoulders. Years ago in New Mexico, my father had literally thrown my statue of the Virgin Mary out the window. In my twenties, I had symbolically done the same. Now in my forties, I was inviting her and all that she represented—all the associations, all the resonances, all the superstitions, and all the true powers that she possessed—back into my life. The Virgin statue, the healing dirt, the miraculous crucifix, all became part of the larger scope of possibilities.

"Let us proclaim the mystery of faith." The priest launched into the Mass in the next room, his voice booming, carrying through the crowded church over the heads of the crying babies, up into the choir loft.

I reached down and scooped up some dirt to fill a little leather pouch. I pressed the pouch to my neck. I pressed the pouch to my heart. Then I walked out onto the path, expecting guidance, expecting blessing, expecting miracles.

13

"I hate traveling down straight paths," Father Sergei said a few days later when I visited him at his Russian Orthodox monastery.

When I'd arrived, I stopped at the white picket fence running around the two bungalows that house the monks and nuns. I unlatched the gate. A trellis of climbing roses, their blooms bright red and fragrant, arched over my head. The roses created such a contrast to the earth tones of Albuquerque, where splotches of natural color are rare and, due to the dryness of the region, gardens are scarce. I stood there under the trellis, taking in the roundness of the rose petals, the gracefulness of their stems winding up and around the wooden laths. A little hand-painted sign tacked to the trellis read: YOU KNOW THAT IN MONASTICISM THERE ARE MANY THORNS—BUT WHAT ROSES!

I stepped onto the path that cut through the front yard, and suddenly, a pack of Chihuahua dogs charged my ankles, ten or twelve pure breeds and mixed mutts, not one of them more than six inches tall, jumping up to my knees, pawing at my jeans, barking with high-pitched *yip-yip-yips*. The door to the monastery flew open, and Father Sergei bounded down the steps.

"Hello, my daughter," he said. "I've been expecting you." The monk led me around to the backyard, the pack of little dogs trailing after us. "Let's talk in the garden," he said.

I didn't know how the monk knew I had planned to visit him that day. We strolled along his paths that wandered this way and that through an intensely landscaped plot. Blue plastic whirligigs spun around and around in the late afternoon breeze among densely packed vegetable patches filled with broccoli and cabbage, Swiss chard and zucchini. Pink flamingos clustered under fig and pomegranate trees laden with fruit, the branches bending toward us.

"People say, 'You can't grow those trees here!'" Father explained. "But I say to them, 'Where is your faith? What was the story of the Garden of Eden all about but to go out and face the challenges of the world?' Gardening is what keeps me alive. See, I can die, but these trees will live on." The monk paused. Tibetan prayer bells and sets of chimes hanging from the trees tinkled, some with high pitches, others with low, creating a harmonious sound in the background, a chant of their own.

We sat on a bench, another red rose–covered trellis above our heads, holding us as if in an embrace. A pink rosebush framed a birdbath next to us.

"See, this garden symbolizes the Resurrection itself. Life begins and begins again, and everything here has its own significance. The red roses there represent the Virgin Mary, and the pink petals on that bush stand for the shedding of Christ's blood."

The perfume of the perfectly formed flowers drifted toward us. The music of the chimes carried out toward the street on the other side of the adobe walls, the street filled with dust and barrenness, poverty, drugs, and crime.

"And when I do die," Father Sergei said, "I want to be buried right there under those rosebushes. Just tell everyone that I've gone back to Jerusalem."

I nodded and we sat in silence for a moment, a couple of sparrows swooping down from the sky and landing on the fig tree. They wound their claws around one of the twigs and swayed back and forth to the rhythm of the chimes. A blue swallowtail butterfly glided past our vision, its wings outstretched, catching the light, then folding in on itself on the trellis. *Just tell everyone that I've gone back to Jerusalem.* The words twirled around in my head like the wings of the whirligigs. This man understands the meaning of pilgrimage. What a beautiful metaphor. *Just tell everyone that I've gone back to Jerusalem.*

"And I don't mean that as a metaphor," Father Sergei said. "My people originally came from there."

"Israel?"

"Yes. I'm Jewish. That's the scene behind the scene for me. Now you must discover your own subtext."

"I thought you were a Russian Orthodox monk—well, an Hispanic Russian Orthodox monk."

"That's right," Father Sergei said.

This monk's original path had begun in Israel. Then because of persecution his family fled across Europe to settle in Spain, where they lived for hundreds of years. Sometime around 1492, in order to save their own lives, Father Sergei's family converted to Catholicism, secretly practicing Judaism in their homes, becoming crypto-Jews. They survived the Inquisition. Whether crypto-Jews or *conversos* struggling to assimilate into the Christian culture, Torquemada, the inquisitor general, suspected anyone who had any Jewish blood in his veins. Soon after the Expulsion, many crypto-Jews left with the conquistadors for the Americas and remained there with their secret for the next five hundred years.

"So that's how my family left for the New World. Many of the Spanish Jews who refused to convert to Christianity left Spain for unknown destinies during the Expulsion from Cadiz on or before August 2, 1492," Father Sergei said. "Out they went. Nobles of the court, shoemakers, tanners, artisans, butchers, the old and infirm, the young, the pregnant, all made their way over the rough roads through the stifling heat to exile. Some stumbled, some fainted, some died, and others came into the world en route. The rabbis urged the young people and women to sing and play the pipes and tabors to keep their spirits up.

"Some rabbis promised that once they reached the water, God would lead them to safety as he had Moses in the book of Exodus. Many bands of Jews walked right up to the water's edge and stood there, waiting for the sea to part. When the waves didn't budge and the Jews stared instead at the gangplanks of the ships that were to carry them away into the unknown, many panicked and converted on the spot. Priests were handy to raise a crucifix before their eyes and pour water over their heads in baptism. The women proved more courageous and faithful to their religion than the men. Husbands turned back at the last moment and let their families float out to sea. About fifty thousand converts remained behind."

"And your family stayed in Spain?" I asked, trying to piece together the monk's story. Now I understood why Christopher Columbus was so important to him, why "a test of faith" had particular resonance for him, and why he could go into vast detail about the Expulsion. Father Sergei was offering his background in little bits and pieces. I was beginning to understand him as a teacher and spiritual guide. I didn't tell him my problems, and he didn't give advice. Rather, he instructed, drawing on history, theological ideas, politics. My job was to listen and pull the threads together, apply his thoughts to my own life and the world around me.

"Oh, yes, as I said, my family stayed in Spain for a while," the monk replied. "My family and many of the nobility chose to convert. Even Rabbi Abraham Seneor. *Sí*, that was bitter news for many exiles."

Father Sergei shook his head and clicked his tongue, leaning back, his hands locked under the bench for support. The Chihuahua dogs began their yipping, dancing around my shoes, pulling on my laces. They backed up, rushed forward, pawed at my shoe, and then barked, a shrill, high, squeaky yap. They charged my shoe and chewed on the end of my toe. The Tibetan bells jingled in the wind, and on the other side of the fence, a hot rod car zoomed down the street.

I waved the dogs away.

"But you see, the monarchs were very foolish," Father Sergei continued. "They miscalculated the Jews. They thought that once Seneor converted, the rest of the Jews would follow. They hoped to gain more souls for the Church and prevent a brain drain from the country. Ferdinand and Isabella also pressured Isaac Abravanel to convert. They even went so far as to attempt to kidnap and baptize his one-year-old grandson."

The plot didn't work. Father Sergei explained that on July 31, 1492, Isaac Abravanel, the man who had pleaded to save Spain's Jews, departed from the port of Valencia. Sea travel was dangerous, and there were reports of overloaded ships that sank and others that caught fire. Passengers were thrown overboard and their possessions stolen. Captains sold boatloads of Jews into slavery, claiming they were prisoners of war. One captain reportedly stole the Jews' clothes and left them on an isolated island where they were attacked and killed by wild animals. Another boat came by, and the survivors were picked up and wrapped in old sails and taken to Genoa. Plague broke out on another boat, and the captain left the Jews on an island without food or water.

At the same time, thousands sailed for Italy because Pope Alexander had asked all the Italian states to receive the Jews. Others left for North Africa, Flanders, the Low Countries, and the south of France. Thousands more sailed toward the Ottoman Empire where Sultan Bayezid II welcomed the refugees. Some Jews thought he was the messiah who would eventually lead them back to the Promised Land. When asked about Ferdinand's expulsion edict, the Sultan replied, "Can such a king be called wise and intelligent—one who impoverishes his country and enriches my kingdom?"

"New Mexico was enriched by the immigration of hidden Jews," Father Sergei said, smiling. "Some scholars say we crypto-Jews don't exist in New Mexico, but I'm here to tell you we do. In northern New Mexico, there's a whole town full of us who have been there for centuries."

"Where's that?" I asked.

"Can't tell you. It's hidden," Father said, throwing back his head in laughter, his gray beard jutting away from his chest. The Chihuahuas yapped and skittered about my feet, mouths open wide, tongues out.

What wasn't hidden was the monk's immediate past. Having grown up Catholic and knowing he was Jewish, Father Sergei set out on a religious quest in early adulthood to find his path. He studied comparative religions and in the process picked up fourteen languages, finally choosing his own faith.

"I like what Buddhism has to say about our particular garden paths," Father Sergei said. "If you want to know about the present, look to the past. If you want to know about the future, look to the present."

The monk's beliefs tilted toward Christianity, and he knew that he wanted to be a priest. Russian Orthodoxy seemed as close as he could get to Hasidic Judaism, so there he found a fit.

"I wanted to remain Christian because we need a model for suffering," Father Sergei said, holding up his crucifix. "But, oh, yes, there are many of us hidden Jews here."

He remembered a day when one of his parishioners came to him with an object that had been in her family for generations. The woman had perched on the bench next to the monk under the fig tree, gazing down into her lap until she pulled a small crucifix from her dress pocket. Father Sergei asked if he could take the crucifix apart.

"But what if you wreck it?" the woman asked.

"If I wreck it, I will pay you for it," Father Sergei said, then pried open the crucifix with his nail file. Inside was a tiny piece of ancient paper, crumbling and yellow, with writing in Hebrew.

"You see," the monk said. "This means that you, like me, are really Jewish. This is part of the Torah from Granada that the Jews smuggled out with them when they left Spain, hoping to keep their faith alive. Other little pieces of that Torah have been found all over Mexico and New Mexico."

"That can't be right." The woman shook her head.

"But it is."

"I can't be Jewish."

"Why?" the monk asked.

"Because I'm so anti-Semitic," the woman said.

"God has ways of humbling us, my child," the monk said. "Sometimes he leads us down strange paths."

14

My path led me back to my pallet on the floor in my apartment. Ill with the flu, I lay in the twilight watching the light from the window play across the contours of the hand-carved wooden crucifix I had placed on my bookshelf. The rays from the setting sun speckled the figure of Christ with shadow. The dark descended, and my fever rose, a pink tint spreading across the terrain of my cheeks and chest. I'll feel better in the morning, I told myself, and tried to sleep. By ten o'clock my skin was burning, pain ricocheting up and down my limbs. In a couple of days I'll be fine, I told myself. I need to get up and drink some fluids to flush this bug out of my system. When I tried to rise, one hand on the cane, the other bracing against a kitchen chair, my legs buckled beneath me.

I called a colleague from the university, who insisted on taking me to an all-night clinic. Slowly, one hand on the cane, the other on my friend's arm, I shuffled out to her car, still in my pajamas, now fearful that this flu virus might be heading in the same direction as the last—down the hole in my spinal cord. I arrived back in my apartment around one in the morning with a diagnosis of bronchitis, a prescription for antibiotics, and an exhaustion so profound that it sent me into a fitful sleep filled with Technicolor nightmares of the Twin War Brothers slaying monsters and erupting volcanoes spewing ash down on my head.

In the morning, my fever was lower but still near 101 degrees. I tried to get up and fix myself some breakfast, but in just a few minutes I collapsed back onto the floor in a heap. I called the Visiting Nurses Association, and within a few hours a nurse pulled up in front of my apartment—on a motorcycle. There was pounding on the door. I pulled myself up, teetered across the room, and peered through the peephole. A man stood in front of me holding a helmet under one arm and a medic's kit under the other. He looked like Cookie in one of the old Western TV shows with close-cropped graying hair and a five-day beard. He was short, five feet six at the most, his legs slightly bowed. His feet were stuck in cowboy boots, his belly spilling over his jeans, a pair of black suspenders holding up his pants.

I pulled open the door. Cookie quickly assessed the scene, then ran cool water in the tub and helped me into the bathroom. I slipped into the water, hoping to quell my fever. I soaked in the tub, letting the cool water lap at my arms and legs. I leaned my head back on the porcelain and thought that maybe it was time to go back home. Maybe my body was telling me that this faith healing quest had reached its natural end, that it was time to pull back and evaluate my progress. In the past few weeks, I had been feeling better, but now I'd landed back in bed, unable to function. I thought about calling Sean to hire him to fly down to Albuquerque and drive me back to Iowa. But we hadn't even reached midterm time at the university. I couldn't stop teaching and leave my classes in the air, my students disoriented.

I had to keep going, push through. I had to believe that I could make it through the semester, that there was something yet undiscovered or unexplored on my quest. If faith meant trusting an all-connecting force, it also meant trusting myself. It meant opening myself to my own strengths and intuitions—my hunches, my guesses, and my gut reactions that I had worked hard to repress. Faith meant accepting my intuition and not dismissing it as superstition. It meant accepting the nonscientific part of myself, the nonrational fairies, elves, and Druids there in the back of my mind, insisting on their own voices.

I called for Cookie. He stood discreetly on the other side of the bathroom door, listening for any mishap, while I dragged myself out of the tub. I dried off with the towel and slipped back into a pair of pajamas. With Cookie's help, I returned to my pallet.

"You can't sleep on the floor," Cookie said, but when I explained the situation, he helped me to the daybed and went to work wedging pillows around my body to create firmer support. The ice-cream scoop still sagged, but I could lie flat on my back without my neck craning up at a right angle.

Suddenly, Cookie picked up his helmet and was out the door. *Zoom. Zoom.* He revved his motorcycle and rumbled down the street. In a half-hour, he returned with a bag filled with fresh vegetables, stew meat, a bottle of garlic pills, and a copy of *The New York Times*.

"News of the day?" Cookie asked, placing the paper on the coffee table. He busied himself in the kitchen, chopping and slicing onions and carrots and potatoes, and browning a package of stew meat. He searched around in the cupboards for spices, and when his concoction was simmering in its own juices, he dipped a spoon into the liquid and made pronouncements. "More pepper" or "Needs a dash of sage." He shook spices into the pot and stirred the stew with a wooden spoon. My head ached so much that I could barely tolerate the clanging of the cast-iron lid or the sound of the spoon hitting the counter.

But then, just as if we were sitting around a campfire, the wagons drawn in a circle, Cookie sat down beside me on the chair and told me stories of other culinary delights. Cookie had been a medic in the Marine Corps. During survival training, he had been driven out into the desert and left for a week without food or water. "I split open cactus for liquid. I gathered up any piece of dry crud I could find to make a fire. I did what I had to to survive. And then I had myself a feast."

Cookie's voice reverberated through my skull. I didn't know if I could handle anyone's life history at this point. I could barely concentrate. My fever drove me back into myself, and I longed for complete silence. Yet I also longed for a survival story—any morsel of truth that might propel me through this setback. I rolled over on my side. "What did you eat out there in the desert?" I finally asked, trying to be polite.

"Rattlesnakes," Cookie said.

Cookie described catching rattlers in more exquisite detail than any Alabama evangelical snake handler. He explained how you had to tease the rattlers out into the open and how, contrary to popular opinion, the snakes were not just sitting there at all times, ready to strike. "Once you've found one, you sneak up real slow so they don't get on to you, and you grab them around the neck with your fist and squeeze," Cookie said, "so they can't attack." He held his left hand in the air, an imaginary snake winding around his arm. "Then you cut off their heads with your knife." Cookie brought his right hand down to make the fantasy kill stroke. "And, boy, do they make some of the finest stew meat you've ever tasted."

My stew pot bubbled over, and Cookie dashed into the kitchen area to mop up the spill. Then I began to laugh, a coughing, wheezing laugh, a giggling laugh that seemed to shake the virus right out of my body, a chortling laugh that made Cookie grin and hop from one foot to another in a little dance, the wooden spoon in his hand, the steam from the stew pot clouding the window.

My pot of stew dwindled over the next week and my illness slowly, ever so slowly improved. Cookie arrived every afternoon to replenish my dish, madly chopping more root vegetables, helping me into the bath, and bringing me the newspaper. While the news of the day changed, my fever rose at sunset and lowered at dawn. At night my dreams became a kaleidoscope of dirt, ash, broken necks, and snakebites, a glow-in-the-dark Virgin Mary hovering high in the sky over all, shaking a rattle, fairies and elves dancing in a ring around the moon. At week's end, my fever finally broke, sweat cascading down my body, the exhaust fumes from Cookie's bike trailing down the street for the last time, my Druid gone.

I had survived another bout of flu. I was left weak and wan, but the worst hadn't happened. The virus hadn't gone down through the hole in my spinal cord and infected my central nervous system again. I was going to be okay. I could return to teach my classes for the rest of the semester at the university. Is faith just a means of survival then? I asked myself. A way to get through a tough time? A dish of rattlesnake stew in the middle of the desert?

"After all, what is faith?" I remembered Sister Mary Ignatius asking my fifth-grade religion class. She sat at her desk, the blackboard dark and blank behind her. The large Virgin Mary statue was perched on the filing cabinet beside her, and the metal crucifix hung over her head. A small crèche—the Christ child in the manger, the three kings kneeling in adoration, with lambs and camels looking on—was set up on a card table in the corner of the room. A sprig of mistletoe was tacked to the coatroom door.

"It's believing," one of my classmates said.

"That's right," the nun said. "Believing in mystery. Believing without having scientific data but still knowing a truth."

We wiggled in our seats, the itchy wool of our school uniforms clinging to our legs. We gazed out the window, the long bank of glass that rose to the ceiling and looked out onto the playground, with its swings and teeter-totters and merry-go-rounds, its softball diamond and tennis courts—all places buried under a layer of snow but all places that held more interest for us than the cardinal virtues. The nun rose from her desk and, taking the pole in her hands, hooked it into the handle of one of the windows and opened it outward. On these late December afternoons, the boiler often overheated, the radiators steaming and clanging. Jarred loose by the window pole, a fly awoke from hibernation, buzzed the room in confused circles, then landed on the nun's veil near her ear. With her peripheral vision cut off by her wimple, the nun failed to notice the pest.

"Now, for example," the nun continued, "I've been standing up here teaching you for this whole year, and how do you know that I'm not making up a bunch of lies? How do you know that what I'm saying is true?"

No one raised her hand.

The nun would not relent. "Mary," she said, "how do you know what I'm saying is true?" The fly flew up and landed on the top of her head.

"I don't," I said.

The nun swatted at the insect.

"But I can always check up on you. I can always go home and ask my mother."

I guess I didn't have faith in nuns.

I did have faith in my mother and the stories she told me. Ours was a storytelling family from the Irish tradition with a layer of midwestern taciturnity superimposed on top. When someone wanted to make a point, we didn't sit around the dining room table and debate the idea or dissect the thought. We didn't argue our opinions. Rather, one person would assume the floor and sit back and tell a tale that illustrated his or her point. All other eyes focused on the storyteller. All other mouths remained shut. At the story's end, we were left to figure out the point and apply it to the situation at hand. There was no further discussion. When someone wanted to entertain, we engaged in a similar process. One person assumed the floor and told mostly humorous, self-deprecating stories on him- or herself.

While my mother enjoyed the limelight and could spin a yarn as well as the next person, her stories tended to be shorter and quieter, and often slipped into the routine of everyday life. Her family was dark-haired, the "black Irish," a group that had intermarried with the Spanish during the great period of trading around 1492. Her stories were family tales of survival, of a people who had gone through unimaginable traumas such as the potato famine. As we hung the clothes on the line, she told me that for years during the Depression she had only one dress, a hand-me-down from her mother that had been cut down to size. When we took a ferryboat ride across the Mississippi River, she told the story of my great-grandmother Anna coming to America alone on the boat at age sixteen. The trip was so rough that Anna never wanted to get on a moving vehicle again, and when the Homesteading Act opened up land in Iowa, she walked almost the whole distance of the state to stake her claim. When we visited the cemetery, she told how my grandmother had nursed her favorite brother to his end from tuberculosis and had lived with him in a tent at the foot of Pike's Peak.

These stories, like *The Lives of the Saints*, provided models of strength and courage, of empathy and fortitude. They wove their way into the fabric of my being, and when much of my family had died, their stories lingered after them. The ability of these family members to face the unknown, to, as Father Sergei said, leave the Garden of Eden and go out and confront the challenges of this world, was an example to me. And what pulled these family members through tough times? I'll never know the depth of their spiritual connection, but if these family members didn't have faith in the Divine, they certainly had faith in themselves and their own ability to cope.

I gazed up at the bookshelf in my Albuquerque apartment, my eyes fixed again on the wooden crucifix. Christ was a model for suffering. The Bible stories of his passion flooded my memory. I'd always wondered at his acceptance of his torture and death. The Way of the Cross was bloody and horrifying, but Christ's calmness in the face of the worst kind of imaginable adversity was inspiring. Throughout the years I had flipped back and forth, embracing the mysteries of his existence as the literal truth when I was young, then doubting their veracity as I grew older. But whatever my state of belief, I always loved the triumphant recounting of his Resurrection. On a much larger scale, he, like my family members, was a survivor. No matter how his followers eventually used his image to oppress and stifle others, his basic story still gave me courage and strength.

The lives of the mystics imparted that same sense of strength. Once again, I vowed to delve more deeply into their biographies. And I vowed to do what Lu had urged me to do: delve more deeply into my own box of crucifixes, the symbols of death and resurrection that had graced the coffins of my family members. As I lay there on my daybed recovering from bronchitis, I understood that survival meant connection to other survivors. Would I have survived my bronchitis without Cookie and his rattlesnake tales? Probably. But I'm certain I wouldn't have healed as quickly. How would my life be different if I'd had a different family history? Father Sergei had discovered his family's past. I pushed myself to pick up my pallet like the lame man in the Gospels and stroll down my garden path to uncover strength in my own.

15

It was a day of survival stories in the barrio, a day I would learn about the interconnectiveness of the neighborhood. It was a Saturday morning, the sun unimpeded by a single cloud beaming down on the concrete city sidewalk. One car, then another pulled into the parking lot behind Lu's drugstore. Whole families tumbled out of the vehicles: parents with two or three children of varying ages—four, eight, and ten years old. A boy of about ten pushed himself along the sidewalk in a wheelchair. More children, both girls and boys, rode in on bicycles, careening into the lot with wide grins on their faces and heavy bike chains dangling from their necks. They padlocked their bicycles to the lamppost and squinted at the sign on the back room of the drugstore that read: DANCE STUDIO. Life-size figures of Mexican folk dancers, their skirts and pants black, their blouses and shirts bright red, were painted on the building's facade. The swirling, twirling forms danced all the way to the edge of the wall where they were met by Father Sergei's icon of St. Francis of Assisi.

Lu's granddaughter, Carmen, and her husband, Rafael, had cleaned out the back storage room of Lu's drugstore and converted it into a studio to teach authentic Mexican folk dancing to the children of the barrio. Both Carmen and Rafael had taken a course of study in Mexico that not only taught the traditional dances, but also provided instruction in set making and design, lighting, costumes, and puppetry. The dance troupe drew students from throughout the South Valley, but Carmen and her husband especially tried to recruit "at-risk" children who might otherwise end up in gangs. They also reached out to children who had been injured by crime and drive-by shootings in the area, incorporating wheelchairs and crutches into their choreography.

Carmen and Rafael did not charge for their dance lessons, nor did they receive grants from city, state, or national arts agencies. Instead, once a year they put on a fund-raising dinner, with Lu rolling out tortillas and making up hundreds of enchilada dinners. People from the barrio poured into a rented hall to sit at long folding tables, eat together, and stuff enough money into a glass jar to keep the dancers afloat for another year. Businesses donated yard goods for costumes or scrap lumber for the sets. If the dance troupe ran out of money anytime during the year, Lu bought more sacks of flour, rolled out more tortillas, and the whole process began again.

Inside the drugstore, I sat at Lu's card table and tapped my foot to the strains of the muffled mariachi music played on a boom box in the back room.

"Uno, dos, tres," Carmen called, and then a small herd of thundering feet fell into a rhythm that punctuated the music.

The screen door to the drugstore creaked open, and a thirteen-year-old boy entered, a boy I recognized from my first visit with Father Sergei, one of the group of young men who had surrounded me at the bus stop.

"Hurry, Antonio," Lu said to the boy. "They've already started the lesson in the studio. Go on, now."

Antonio scurried down the aisle past a statue of his namesake, St. Anthony, and a rack holding thermometers and heating pads. He disappeared behind the pharmacy counter, heading into the converted storage room.

"Antonio was on the streets, homeless," Lu explained. "Oh, his family had illnesses, and his father had lost his job. It was sad. So Antonio stopped going to school and hung out with a bad crowd. He didn't have enough to eat. He didn't have a place to sleep. He didn't want to go back home for fear he'd get beaten. So Carmen and Rafael took him in. They fed him and found him some new clothes. They've made him the star of the dance troupe. He does so well! He's back in school, and he's out of that gang. His life has begun to turn around."

When I turned around, I found Pepe staring up at me, his eyes wide. He fidgeted with his hands, the sleeves of an old suit coat falling down almost to the ends of his fingertips. His face was thinner than the first time I'd seen him, his cheeks hollow. His pants hung down over his shoes, a pair of work boots, the heels worn thin. The soles were stuffed with newspaper, a dash of bright red color from a cartoon in a comic section sticking out of his toe.

"Oh, Pepe, is it time for your sandwich?" Lu asked, heading for the refrigerator with its stash of bread and bologna.

"*Sí. Gracias, muchas gracias,*" Pepe said, holding out his cupped hands as if to receive a communion wafer.

Lu patted the meat and bread together, wound the piece of waxed paper around the sandwich, and handed it to Pepe. He accepted it and, closing his eyes, bowed his head, as if to once again acknowledge his gratitude.

"Pepe, you remember that tomorrow is the day. *Correcto?* I'll come for you at nine o'clock in the morning. *A las nueve en punto.*"

"*Sí,*" Pepe said. He slipped the sandwich into the pocket of his suit coat and smiled, his mouth opening around his few remaining teeth. With one foot and then the other sliding across the wooden floor, the newspaper rustling in his shoes, Pepe shuffled out of the store. The bell rang behind him, and the trumpet from the mariachi band sounded a long, sustained call.

"He's survived all winter without heat—goodness—and no water. I couldn't let him go on living like that. I've made arrangements to take him to a home. I wrote the Social Security agency, and they're going to deposit his checks directly into an account at the home for him. No more theft. He'll be so much better cared for at the home. *Bueno. Mañana*," Lu said, bending back down over some receipts that she was filing at her table.

"*Mañana, mañana*," a woman said, suddenly appearing at the counter with a small infant in her arms. "I think it's going to be better tomorrow, and it isn't. It's no better."

Lu rose slowly from her chair and made her way to the counter. "Can I help you?"

"I hope so," the woman said. "I called earlier."

"Oh, yes, you're the woman with the colicky baby." Lu smiled across the counter at the baby whose eyes were closed, his head resting against his mother's shoulder.

"This is the first wink of sleep he's had for days. I can get up and walk him, walk, walk, walk, and he quiets a little, but then he starts in again. I've had no sleep, either. I'm exhausted."

"I can see that," Lu said, quickly making her way through the store to a jar of herbs marked *Peppermint*. When she returned to the counter, the baby was awake, his head thrown back, his eyes intensely fixed on his mother, a loud, lurching howl emanating from his mouth.

"Heat up some milk …" Lu began, but the baby's cries were drowning out her words. The woman jiggled the baby on her hip and walked around and around in a circle in front of the counter, the baby's cries dimming to a lower pitch.

"Okay, heat up some milk ..." the woman said, repeating the directions.

"And stir in a couple of peppermint leaves. Let them steep in the milk for a few minutes, and then remove the herb. Then feed the milk to your baby."

"*Gracias,*" the woman said, pulling a few quarters out of her pocket and plunking them down on the counter. She passed Father Sergei in the doorway on her way out of the store.

"Look what I have! Look what I have!" Father Sergei called to Lu. He held a large blanket in his arms. Spilling out of one pocket of his cassock were long stems of dill, their feathery leaves dark green and wiggling with each of his steps. Oregano, its leaves oval and tightly woven together, poked out of the opposite pocket of the monk's cassock.

"Fresh dill and oregano! Bless you, Father, bless you," Lu said, then turned to me. "He grows herbs for me."

"You can use them?" Father Sergei asked.

"Of course," Lu said, pulling the herbs out of his pockets and placing them on the counter.

"But look what I have. Just look!" The monk motioned to me with a flick of his head and set down the blanket on the counter, unfolding its edges. Inside were a mother Chihuahua and six tiny puppies the size of plums. The tiny creatures snuggled up to their mother, their eyes closed, their smooth, thinly furred bodies exposed to the air. The mother lay on her side, and the pups nosed toward her, rooting out her teats.

"They're beautiful," I said. "How old?"

"Just six weeks today. This is their first outing," Father Sergei said. He patted the mother's head, and she panted into his hand, mouth open and tongue out, surveying the scene, her eyes taking in her surroundings.

Lu picked up a pup and held it to her cheek. I held one of the puppies in the palm of my hand, stroking it with my index finger. The puppy licked my hand and looked up at me with its dark eyes. All puppies are cute and vulnerable, but these were some of the smallest and most defenseless domesticated animals I'd ever seen. Their legs were thin, wiry, and quick, their bodies without weight, well adapted to the desert environment.

"Show the children," Lu said.

"Of course," Father Sergei said, sweeping the litter up into his arms in the blanket. In the studio, the music stopped, and the young dancers circled around the monk. The blanket fell open on the floor. The room teemed with energy and spirit, from the dogs to the children to the brightly painted papier-mâché masks that hung on the wall depicting dragons, tigers, and eagles.

"Can we pet the dogs? Can we hold them?" the children begged.

"Sí," Father Sergei said, placing one of the pups in the lap of the boy in the wheelchair. The boy stroked it and held it to his chest.

The children reached for the pups, their small hands matching the small contours of the animals' bodies. Carefully, gently, the children held the Chihuahuas, lifting them in the air. They pressed them to their faces, the puppies' tiny pointed ears pressing back into their noses.

"He likes me," Antonio said. The puppy in his hand licked his finger. "He likes me!"

Lu appeared with a pitcherful of mint tea and twenty small cups on a tray. "I had that jar of peppermint open, so I thought it was time for a break," she said, pouring the tea and passing it around the room.

"Thank you," Carmen said, lifting her cup to her lips and wiping away a bead of sweat from her brow, the mother Chihuahua scampering around her ankles. "Thank you, Grandma."

16

I had two very different grandmothers representing the two branches of the family, the two different cultures, the two sides of myself—the survivor and the relinquisher, the "good" witch and the "bad" witch. We called my maternal grandmother "Boo-boo." Silently, I called my paternal grandmother "Doo-doo."

When my oldest brother was a toddler, Grandmother Lynch played peek-a-boo with him for hours on a long train ride. Ever after that, he simply referred to her by the suffix of that game. When my other brother and I were born, we took up the habit, and then as nicknames spread, my mother's mother was called "Boo" by all the neighborhood children and even many adults in town for the last twenty years of her life.

Boo was only five feet six inches tall, but because she was two inches taller than my mother and had a fuller, sturdier frame, I thought of her as a large woman with a large presence. In retrospect, I can see that she had a shy nature and continually had to push herself to be assertive. Once she crossed over that line, though, there was no return. Boo was the youngest of nine children, the only girl. Her father had doted on her, and her mother had made her the servant to all her older brothers. But once her Irish mother died in the 1920s, Boo became the matriarch of the family, and once she made up her mind, she made up her mind.

I remember one winter day when we went to Carroll, the county seat, for some Christmas shopping. The whole family packed into the car. We braced ourselves against the chill December wind and scurried up and down Main Street, buying stocking stuffers and fingering yo-yos and paddleballs in the dime store display cases. At the end of a long afternoon, we slumped back toward the car. My mother, visibly exhausted and wanting a break before she tackled the twenty-mile drive home to our small town where we all lived together in a large white house, turned to Boo and asked, "Mother, do you want to stop in the café and have a cup of coffee?"

Boo never hesitated. "No, we'll go home now," she said. And home we went.

Home was a place of growing things, of chickens that lived under the porch, of a garden in the backyard filled with cucumbers and tomatoes, of canning jars steaming in the pressure cooker, of a clump of irises planted around the back door, of a patch of wild strawberries growing on the top of the cave where the potatoes were stored for the winter. Home was Boo making her own soap from lye and a slab of fat she'd saved from her butchered sow, the sharp smell lingering in the basement for days. Home was home remedies, poultices she made for her aching knees, and a shot of whiskey at bedtime to induce sleep. Home was a pitcher of Kool-Aid poured into jelly jars for all the neighborhood gang. Home was a gold crucifix placed on top of her bureau, a dog-eared volume of Thomas à Kempis's *My Imitation of Christ*, and an amethyst rosary that she carried to church every Sunday.

Boo drove an old 1940 Ford until the day she died in 1964. The windshield wipers had to be manually operated, a job that usually fell to me. You pulled the knob out and the wipers spread across the windshield. You pushed the knob in, the wipers returned. The trunk was held shut with baling wire, and under the seat, Boo kept the multipurpose corn knife that she used for chopping the cockleburs out of her bean rows and slaughtering a fresh chicken for Sunday dinner.

While there was nothing chicken about Boo's domineering qualities, they were tempered by her generosity. With her teeth in the cup on the kitchen counter, her lips pressed together in a mischievous smile, and her wiry white hair brushed back from her face in a short bob (she hated the feel of hair trailing down her neck), Boo often had the look of a giant banshee. She owned two small farms, and on her daily visits to them, she might tell the tenant very directly that it was time to walk the beans, then turn around and pull lollipops out of her purse for his children.

On Christmas morning, she put her foot in the ashes of the fireplace, then banged a spoon on the radiator pipes. My brothers and I flew downstairs and into the dining room, where the sprig of mistletoe was tacked to the door frame and the stockings hanging from the mantel overflowed with apples and oranges and little trinkets and goodies that we'd coveted for a whole year. Happy, the dog, jumped off the chair where she slept and wagged her tail at her treasure, an old sock filled with a fresh new bone.

"Look!" Boo said. "Santa's just left! His footprint's there in the ashes."

Doo-doo had made the Christmas stockings, knitting them with her fine long needles flashing in the Florida sun where she and my grandfather had moved in retirement. Doo had an arthritic condition. She had to keep her hands moving, or they would seize up and stiffen into claws. So she quilted and knitted, our Christmas stockings beautifully made in white, red, and green, with a portrait of Santa and our names in large letters woven right into the design.

Grandfather Swander and Doo were never with us for Christmas. They remained in their comfortable retirement home, a new ranch-style house with sleek, modern lines, filled with the newest conveniences, such as a dishwasher, a disposal, and a clothes dryer. They even had air-conditioning. The Swander grandparents celebrated Christmas there by themselves and sent us presents that appeared under the white pine that we had chopped down and pulled home through the snow on a sled. After we dumped the contents of our stockings all over the dining room floor, we hurried into the front room where the tree stood, decorated with lights, ornaments, and tinsel that we had thrown down on its branches from the top of the stairway.

Doo had wrapped our presents in bright paper, the tied bows still retaining their spunk after their long train trip up from the South. For a week before Christmas we picked up the gifts, turning them over and over in our hands, shaking them to try to discover the contents.

"It must be a new baseball glove," my brother said. "The box is just the right size."

"It has to be an Etch-A-Sketch," I said. "When I knock on the box, it sounds hollow."

But on Christmas morning when the wrapping paper began flying off and the tissue paper was strewn across the floor, the boxes held a man's belt—the leather old, cracked, and smelly and five times too big for either of my brothers—and a mismatched pair of dirty mittens.

Out of politeness I tried to feign excitement. "Look what I got," I said. "Mittens."

"And I got a stinky old belt," my brother Jim said.

My father sat in his chair, completely silent.

We stared at my mother for some explanation.

"Your grandmother buys your presents at the Goodwill," my mother said matter-of-factly, trying to divert us by passing out other boxes that had been clearly labeled FROM SANTA.

One year, long after Santa had left, Doo and my grandfather arrived. It was their first and only visit to our home where we lived with Boo in our small Iowa town. Doo and Grandfather pulled into the driveway in their sleek new Buick to be greeted by a headless chicken flapping wildly through the yard, blood flying in all directions.

"How do you do?" Boo introduced herself to her daughter's in-laws. She stuck a friendly hand, one covered with blood and feathers, through the open window of the Buick.

"It's a pleasure," Grandfather said.

Doo refused to answer.

"Come in. Come in." Boo pried open the screen door with her bloody corn knife.

Inside, five more decapitated chickens lay in a bucket on the floor. Another, scalded and plucked, sat on the table, its entrails mounded in a pile beside it.

"I'm cooking for my threshers," Boo explained.

"I see," Doo replied, and hurried through the house to find my father. When she did, she began to lobby. Night and day, day and night, she told him that she wanted him to buy her a mink stole. It was fashionable then for women in high society to go out in their best attire wrapped in mink pelts—the stoles draped loosely over their shoulders, the fur brushing their chins. The women grasped the corners of the garments to keep them from falling off into the snow.

So despite the fact that Doo lived in a tropical climate, she had to have a mink. Finally, one night my father came home from his job in Omaha with a large box. Like a child on Christmas morning, Doo ripped open the tissue paper and held the stole up to the light. She fingered the pelts and enveloped herself in the mink. She ran to the landing in the hallway, the platform that faced a long, full-length mirror on the opposite wall. Doo, a tiny woman, a bantam with dyed frizzy auburn hair, twirled around in front of her reflection.

"Don't I look pretty?" she asked the rest of us gathered around her. "Don't I look pretty?"

Her skin, shriveled and wrinkled like a chicken's wattle, clung to her bones. Her eyes, brown and beady, sank into her skull, large black circles encasing them. In its darkness, her face seemed to drain away all the light of the day beaming through the picture window, all the light bouncing off the walls of the room. While she preened on the landing, her shadow enveloped the room. Once, I was told, Doo had been a big woman but put herself on a diet and lost a tremendous amount of weight. Then she became thin, very thin and brittle, her cheeks sallow, her neck lined and scrawny. She was a chain-smoker with a voice to match, scratchy and discordant.

"Don't I look pretty?" Doo clucked, dipping and diving in front of the mirror, her arms pressed to her side like tight little wings.

Boo turned and left for the kitchen where she had been washing the dishes, her house slippers scuffling along the linoleum floor. I followed and took up a towel to dry. Boo's lips pressed together in banshee mode. She ran more hot water and plunged her hands into the sink, furiously scraping at a burned spot on a pot.

"Yes," Boo said. "She'd be really pretty—if she weren't so damn ugly."

17

One night I stirred Lu's herbs around and around in boiling water in my one little pot in my one little room in Albuquerque. Their scents filled the air. I glanced over toward the bookshelf where I'd placed the carved crucifix. I hadn't yet hung it on the wall. I'll do it tomorrow, I told myself. I don't want to punch a hole in the plaster and lose some of my damage deposit.

What I really didn't want to do was confront this symbol again. I had accepted my crooked path, but I was taking only one step at a time. I had let go of some of my doubts and was learning to trust my intuition, to develop faith in my own strength to face the unknown. In the past, I'd lived a life of superimposed structure—of academic course schedules, of medical routines. Now the routines were more intense than ever: neck and back exercises, weight lifting, the stationary bicycle to build up the muscles around the injury, and traction four times a day. These regimentations tended to silence that internal voice with its hunches, with its guidance. Yet after my bout with the flu, things began to change. In the stillness of my Albuquerque apartment—the same stillness that had produced feelings of anxiety and loneliness—came a sense of trust in that inner voice. I could be secure enough in my own self-esteem to value my own hunches and feelings. But could I embrace this crucifix, actually hang it on the wall? I was back to the old game of pull and tug.

How did I lose faith in my inner voice? Was it just regimentation? The scientific method? It seemed like a larger force. The oppression of the patriarchy. Yes, but that force was too vague, too easy to blame for everything. Still, most women did seem cut off from their intuitions. That was a fact. I'm sure that women's loss of their own voices occurred over the centuries in progressive, subtle, and not-so-subtle ways. I'd wager that the severance could be traced back at least as far as the Middle Ages when the Church set forth the doctrine of original sin, the dogma that made all women ugly in the eyes of God.

The doctrine blames Eve, the first woman in the Judeo-Christian tradition, for original sin. You know the story: God created Adam and Eve and placed them in an idyllic garden living off the land under the shade of an apple tree, or the tree of life. They wandered around naked, free of pain and suffering, their needs provided for. They had only to obey one command: not to eat the fruit of the tree. The serpent tempted Eve who tempted Adam. Then all was lost. After that, humans were born with a blot on their souls—original sin. Adam and Eve were forced out of paradise, forced to clothe themselves, forever ashamed of their bodies and its functions, forever destined to experience misery and suffering. Any pain that woman suffered, from menstruation to childbirth, was her just punishment for conspiring with the devil.

For some, the doctrine justified beating and denigrating women. Women were inherently evil. Later, during the Spanish Inquisition, the dogma served as the basis for the mass persecution of women, condemning them as witches responsible for any misfortune. St. Thomas Aquinas wrote, for example, that a witch was likely to blame if a man's penis wilted. The feminine part of nature, of creation, then became not a joy but a curse. Many women absorbed this negativity and adopted the attitude that sex was for procreation only and not for pleasure, that menstruation, pregnancy, and childbirth were all shameful and should be hidden, that their own very beings were tainted and second-rate. Women became cut off from their own bodies. Is it any wonder that they became cut off from their minds and souls?

When I glanced down at the wooden crucifix on my bookshelf, once again I was haunted by the picture of the Spanish clergy holding up the cross in front of "witches," claiming that these women were evil. I saw members of the Inquisition holding up the cross in front of the Jews, trying to drive them out of the country, as if they were the very personification of the devil. One image engendered another. I saw the conquistadors holding up the crucifix in front of the Native Americans at Acoma, trying to eradicate their "pagan" ways. I saw all the oppressors of the world through time using this symbol to terrorize, to loot, and to kill. To hold power over a more disadvantaged group.

I knew the history. I knew what this cross had done. Yet Lu, a "wise woman," a woman who seemed to exude pure goodness, instructed me to put aside my view, embrace this crucifix again, embrace my ancestors, and say a prayer over these healing herbs. The prayer had to go with the concoction. Yes, I had been doing this every few days—brewing the herbs and gulping them down—and now I needed to heed her other directions. But could I do more than utter a Hail Mary? Could I put my heart in this ritual and believe that the prayer would work?

I realized that if Lu had been doling out these herbs five hundred years ago, as surely her ancestors had, she would have been killed. Rounded up by the Inquisition with their crucifixes. Scapegoated for the plagues and misfortunes of the day. Oh, the little ironies that weave back and forth throughout history, the connecting threads of the past that surprise and illuminate our present.

Just when Christopher Columbus was embarking on his trip to the New World and the Spanish Jews were sailing toward their unknown destinies, the Black Death was ravaging Europe. The disease returned again and again throughout the Middle Ages, and in 1478, the Black Death wiped out one-third of the remaining European population. Syphilis, leprosy, smallpox, measles, and St. Vitus' dance all took their toll. A fatal disease called sweating sickness, which often left its victims dead within hours, devastated England between 1486 and 1551, then crossed the Channel and ripped through the Continent.

Everyone who had enough money to leave fled their area in hopes of outrunning the plagues. The few physicians who were sanctioned by the Church and state seldom stayed behind. Who was left then to minister to the sick? Mostly women healers who used a combination of shaman-like techniques—chants, rituals, and prayers—in addition to their knowledge of herbal remedies. They cared for the ill at their own risk, the risk of contracting these dread diseases and of being labeled a "witch." In a complete turn of twisted logic, the women healers who carried a knowledge of remedies that often helped relieve misery were blamed for the great suffering of the era. But these "wise women" were not rounded up and sent to a holocaust at sea. The establishment placed their faith in an easier solution.

In my apartment, the smoke detector fired off its shrill, steady blare, sending me running to the stove to turn the pot of herbs down to a simmer. Steam fogged the windows, and an acrid, burnt smell filled the room. I opened the window, but the smoke detector kept up its wail. I opened the door, and the cry of the alarm carried out into the dry desert air, where I imagined the roadrunner ducking for cover and the rattlesnake burrowing back into its hole. I fanned the door, back and forth, back and forth. I saw the light go on in the neighbor's apartment beside me. I heard the door open in the apartment above me.

Finally, the alarm stopped.

I poured my herbal concoction into a Mason jar. I'd made enough of the mixture to last several days. I planned to put daily doses in my plastic water bottle and place the rest in the jar in the refrigerator. I stared at my daily dose and added a little more water to the bottle. The herbs, still smelling pungent and strong, took on an amber hue.

Well, I realized, being burned at the stake would probably cure you of using herbs or chants again, let alone using your intuition. With the power of the Inquisition and the rise of the guild system in the Middle Ages, medicine moved out of "wise women's" hands into the deep pockets of male physicians, who banned together to make more money. The physicians' guild practiced medicine based on astrology and alchemy, with the barbers joining the surgeons in 1493. The barber-surgeon guild then defined who could do what to whom. Executioners could set bones. Barbers could bleed, cup, and give enemas. These rising middle-class guilds also dictated "standard" cures, including the use of dragon's blood, mummy dust, and incantations while they condemned the lower-class "quacks" for using "nonstandard" medicine.

Women fared even more poorly than the quacks. Women could practice midwifery, but "wise women" healers could be executed if they assisted at the birth of a stillborn or deformed child. By this time the medical and law guilds were webbed together under the protection of the Church, so the women healers had nowhere to turn when faced with this kind of condemnation. Instead, the patriarchal elite accused the "wise women" of the "crimes" of "aiding the sick" and "caring for the dying."

A "wise woman" named Jacoba Felicie was brought before a French court in 1322 and charged with practicing medicine without proper credentials. Felicie was probably a Jew, banned by the Church from the medical field. Many Jews were such skillful healers, however, that nobles often hired them on the sly. One by one, young and old, male and female, witnesses swore that Jacoba Felicie had doctored them with herbs and other remedies. On cross-examination, the same witnesses also testified that Felicie had cured them when physicians failed. In the final arguments, the prosecution argued that "a man can always heal the sick better than a woman." The jury bought it. The judge fined Felicie but allowed her a limited practice and forbade her to take a fee for her services.

By 1518 the College of Physicians in England incorporated itself and issued a decree against quackery. The barber-surgeons had no intention of treating the ill-paying poor and didn't want anyone else aiding them, either. The guild harassed the "wise women" who treated the poor for free as charity cases, and it tried to get the women to stop helping the destitute. Fearing that the peasants might revolt, the King of England finally revoked part of the "Quack's Charter" to enable the poor to receive some medical care. The folk healers and "wise women" were once again grudgingly allowed to treat the poor with their knowledge of "plant rootes and waters" and to cure surface maladies with ointments, poultices, and plasters.

I held up my Mason jar to the light. My "plant rootes" swam in the water, the liquid turning a darker brown. Fascinated, I watched the coloration deepen and the twigs sink and settle down toward the bottom of the glass. The brewing of these herbs seemed like a high school science project—something to observe with attention. I was having some trouble thinking of it as anything more: as a healing ritual or a mystical process. Yet if the Spanish Inquisition had caught me holding these herbs up to the light, they would have charged me with possessing secrets of the occult or, worse, with killing babies or performing orgiastic and bloody rituals. By giving me these herbs, Lu was what the medieval Church would have called a "good witch" who practiced "white magic." The "bad witches" were accused of casting spells and curses. Still, the "good" witches met the same fate as the "bad."

These witches, good and bad, were often older women who had no networks and had to find some way to support themselves. They may have turned to midwifery or folk healing as an alternative to starvation. Still other witches had nothing to do with the healing arts at all. They were women who were simply deemed too independent, too "obnoxious" or "needy," a tiresome wife, a meddling mother-in-law. They were often spinsters, the physically and mentally handicapped, or anyone who just happened to be mistrusted or disliked or near a tragedy or accident.

The "good" witches, like Jacoba Felicie, were often mature wealthy women who had extensive medical knowledge. At the same time, witch-hunters rounded up thousands of beautiful, innocent young girls and accused them of devilish acts. William Perkins, a Scottish minister and leading witch-hunter, summed up the general opinion of the clergy toward "blessing witches" when he wrote, "The good witch is more a monster than the bad." English authorities admitted that "good witches" existed and that they should be consulted when a physician failed to cure a patient, yet at the same time any problem that eluded the physicians was readily attributed to witchcraft.

Gradually, over the course of that evening, I came to think of the brewing of these herbs as an act of solidarity. I came to think of the brewing of the herbs as a sacred act. I let go of the idea of a science project and replaced it with the thought of connecting myself to the threads of women's history, threads that had nearly been snipped off, threads that I might be gathering up again. I connected to the thought of my two grandmothers, the "good witch" and the "bad," both historical archetypes. I picked up my Book of Psalms, the steam from my pot of herbs still clouding the room. I trusted Lu, the "good witch," and myself to follow her instructions.

But could I let go of my critical eye and accept the cultural and gender contradictions of this act—praying over herbs, this "feminine" medicine, with "masculine" Judeo-Christian psalms? It felt incongruent. It felt crazy. Then again, I'd come to understand that the whole history of healing made little rational sense. I trusted this body of women's medicine that certainly had a longer, more successful, and more noble history than the male medical model. At the same time, I trusted the ancient power, familiarity, and meta-phors of the psalms. Hesitantly, I decided to give it a try. In a clear, strong voice, I chanted Psalm 141 over my concoction:

> O Lord, I call to you; come quickly to me.
> Hear my voice when I call to you.

May my prayer be set before you like incense;
may the lifting up of my hands be like the evening sacrifice.

Set a guard over my mouth, O Lord;
keep watch over the door of my lips.

Let not my heart be drawn to what is evil,
to take part in wicked deeds

with men who are evildoers;
let me not eat of their delicacies.

Let a righteous man strike me—it is a kindness;
let him rebuke me—it is oil on my head.

My head will not refuse it.
Yet my prayer is ever against the deeds of the evildoers;
their rulers will be thrown down from the cliffs,
and the wicked will learn that my words were well spoken.

They will say, "As one plows and breaks up the earth,
so our bones have been scattered at the mouth of the grave."

But my eyes are fixed on you, O Sovereign Lord;
in you I take refuge—do not give me over to death.

Keep me from the snares they have laid for me,
from the traps of the evildoers.

Let the wicked fall into their own nets,
while I pass by in safety.

18

I found safety in the barrio, the most dangerous part of the city. On my trips to the neighborhood, I gradually discovered which houses were filled with honest hardworking people trying to raise their families in a decent manner, and which houses were filled with crack dealers trying to exploit the poor and oppressed. I saw enough petty crime that I stopped carrying a purse and just stuck my driver's license and a couple of dollars in my pocket. I drove right up in front of my destination and parked adjacent to the drugstore, monastery, church, or café, keeping the Trooper in sight at all times. The streets were mostly deserted, so parking wasn't a problem. Car break-ins and thefts were common, and if someone attacked me on the street, I knew that my legs weren't healed enough to carry me on a long run.

I told few where I was going. Once when I mentioned my haunt to one of my colleagues at the university, she said, "You have to be kidding. You're not going down there." So before I set out on my journey, I scratched a little note on a pad on the kitchen counter: Gone to barrio. Expect to return by 4 P.M., Monday.

And I didn't find myself running down the street. Instead, I often found myself in step with the homeless shuffling along toward the soup kitchen. After a while, their faces became familiar. I nodded to them and smiled.

"*Buenos días,*" they said.

"*Buenos días,*" I replied.

I came to love sitting in the café in midafternoon, in the hustle and swirl, the click and clatter of the neighborhood's afternoon coffee break, waitresses running back and forth, balancing large metal trays filled with sloshing cups of coffee and tall glasses of Coke. Customers laughed and traded jokes. They told stories with warmth and flare. They spoke with each other in hushed tones about serious matters. The whole atmosphere reminded me of my family dining room table. In the middle of the throng, I slid into a small booth, its seats covered with red vinyl. On the other side of the counter, the grill sizzled.

Just six months before, the café had been a boarded-up storefront, its windows cracked and broken, the counter stripped bare of the cups and saucers, the plates and small boxes of cereal that once were an emblem of a more prosperous time. In hopes of rejuvenating the area and providing a safe gathering place, Lu had donated all the kitchen equipment for the restaurant, and the café had opened its doors once again to the public. I sat for hours grading papers and seemingly minding my own business. The waitresses clapped and applauded when I hesitantly managed the correct pronunciation of an item on the menu.

"Steak de lomito, por favor."

"Excelente!" they said.

"La comida es fantástica."

"Gracias."

I dropped a quarter in the jukebox, and the whole café rocked to the strains of Enrique Iglesias.

One afternoon after leaving the café, I headed for Father Sergei's monastery. I dipped my head under the trellis of bright red blooming roses in front of the house and knocked on the door. No answer. No dogs. No wind or tinkling of bells. I circled around to the backyard and found no one there, either. The day was warm, the garden inviting, so I sat down on one of the benches and tilted my head back, grateful for the sun on my face, the bright shining sun that was probably hidden behind a cloud in Iowa at that moment. I took some breaths in and out and allowed myself to feel good about my journey here, about the people I had met, about the changes that seemed to be happening in my life. I still had doubts about my whole exploration, but for now it felt fine to lean back on this bench in this Russian Orthodox monastery, in this refuge from the crime outside the gate, and value whatever might transpire.

I watched a sparrow flitter from the apricot to the pomegranate tree. The bird dove to the ground, picked up a weed, dead and dried, pitched by the side of the vegetable patch. In the apricot tree, the bird had begun to weave a nest in the crotch of a couple of branches. I followed the bird's movement, its flying away to return again and again with one weed, one long piece of string, a couple of feathers to blend into the nest. After an hour, the nest was still just a small ball of fluff. Okay, I told myself, have patience with yourself. Does anything worthwhile happen all at once? Isn't every exploration a process?

Suddenly, the door to a shed in the back of the lot opened wide, and the mother Chihuahua and all her pups charged out and raced to my feet. Over the weeks, the pups had grown to the size of baseballs, but they were still so small, I was afraid I might inadvertently crush one of them if I stood up and took a step.

"Hello, my daughter," Father Sergei called from the shed. "I'll be with you in a moment."

The door of the shed ajar, I saw the monk perched on a stool, jars of bright red, yellow, and green paint surrounding him, and a partially finished icon resting on an easel.

"Oh, please. I don't want to disturb you. I didn't even know you were there."

"No, no, it's all right. I've done as much work as I can for the day." The monk stood in the middle of the garden, cleaning his paintbrush, dipping it into an old tin can full of turpentine. "I began this icon a couple of days ago. I fasted and prayed. I asked for guidance in my creative energies."

"Please don't let me stop you."

"Don't worry. My inspiration had vanished for the day. They say that an icon is the meeting between heaven and earth. And that's what my visit will be with you: the meeting between heaven and earth."

"Whom are you painting?"

"St. Anthony—one of the original desert fathers."

"The patron of lost and stolen things."

"That's right. You see, last week, I'd lost my large ring of keys with keys to the monastery, keys to the chapel, keys to every part of our lives that we feel so compelled to lock up and keep safe from the outside world. Well, first I thought, so be it, maybe we shouldn't lock ourselves away from our own people, and then more things began to disappear—a candle here, a plate there. I searched everywhere, my monks and nuns tearing the whole place apart for days, and we could not find the keys. At last I said we must pray. We must pray to St. Anthony to help us locate those keys. Well, right in the middle of our prayer, we heard a loud noise—a rattle, a crashing thump, and a squeaking sound. What in the world? I wondered.

Then I walked into the hallway, and there was my ring of keys smack dab in the middle of the rocking chair seat, the rocker creaking back and forth and back and forth with the weight."

"And no one had been sitting there?"

"No. All the monks and nuns were in the other room praying."

"That's amazing," I said, but privately I registered my own disbelief. How could a set of keys just drop out of the sky?

"How could the son of God just drop out of the sky?" Father Sergei asked.

The man had an uncanny ability to read my thoughts.

"I know, I know what you're thinking. But you see, that's what an icon is all about. We paint icons to make the idea of God concrete. We paint the images of the saints to serve as pathways to God, to provide role models. Christ was not just a shadow or a concept. He was a living, breathing human being who is still active in our lives—if we let him in. We can close the door to the shed and keep all our puppies in one place, but this will only work for a short period of time. Eventually, the door will have to open, or the dogs will grow so big that they will chew a hole right through it to release themselves.

"'Thou, thyself, O Lord, art the fulfillment and completion of all good things. Fill my soul with joy and gladness, for thou alone art the Lover of all creatures.' You see, that's the beginning of the prayer we say when we finish an icon. It's joy that's emphasized. There is joy in the very act of iconography itself. It's a creative act. But there's even more joy than that to the process. There's the joy of spreading icons in the world. There's the joy of giving the saint the possibility to shine through his icon. There's the joy of being in union with the saint whose face you are painting. I am painting St. Anthony as a joyful act of thanksgiving for finding my keys for me.

"See, you are living with that shed door pulled shut. Open it, my daughter. Open it to the daylight. You must invite creativity and joy back in your life. Think of each day as if you are painting an icon. Before we paint, we make the sign of the cross and pray in silence to pardon our enemies. Then we work with care on every detail as if we are working in front of the Divine. During work, we pray to strengthen ourselves physically and spiritually. We avoid all unnecessary words, work in silence, and pray to the saint we're painting so that he or she might be close to us. When we choose a color, we stretch out our hands and ask for guidance and counsel. We are not jealous of our neighbors' work. If they succeed, we succeed. When we are finished with our paintings, we thank God for the grace that we received to accomplish our work. And then we give our work away. We light a candle, we say a prayer in front of the icon, we kiss the icon, then we give it up to others to enjoy."

I bent down, picked up one of the puppies, and edged my way through the pack of little dogs toward the shed. On the easel was a block of wood, the figure of an ancient monk outlined on the surface, his facial features just beginning to take form, a halo traced around his head with the feathery strokes of a brush dipped in gold paint. I could already sense the power behind this piece and that it was more than just a pretty religious picture.

"Yes, you see, it isn't me who is painting this icon," Father Sergei said.

"No?"

"No, it's a collaboration of me, St. Anthony, and the Holy Spirit— all three of us working together."

"And you feel this energy while you're working?"

"If I didn't, I would stop. If I didn't, I wouldn't be painting an icon. And you must understand that every part of an icon has symbolic meaning, from the colors to the items the saints hold in their hands, to the landscape in the background. We have to look at all of life symbolically. Only then will we truly be able to embrace it."

"*Los cuadros son maravillosos.*"

"*Gracias.*"

I let the pup down out of my arms to scamper under the apricot tree where the sparrow had added a few more strands to its nest.

"That's right," the monk said. "Open the door and let those puppies out. Let them out now before they grow into howling dogs and keep you up all night with their cries and moaning. You have your own icons, your own models. You must contact them, search them out, learn from them. You have your dead, your ancestors. Talk to them, embrace their examples, let them work their magic in your life. Then find your saints, those who will push you farther along your path. Search them out. You have connected with your intuition, with your feminine side of yourself, but you are afraid to act on it."

"No, I've acted on it some."

"Some? You are sitting inside the café while life goes on around you, but you are afraid to speak the language."

"I'm trying."

"Ah, but you must jump in and not be afraid to make mistakes."

"Okay."

"Look, my daughter," the monk said, drying the bristles of his brush on an old paint rag, "let these icons teach you and bring you joy. You are inside the shed with the door closed and locked. Open up, open up and throw away the key. Only then will you find safety."

19

Twenty-five years earlier, my mother had found safety in a motor court during her last days. When my parents divorced, my mother had gotten in the car and driven Route 66 to take a job in Arizona. She had only been there a year when she discovered a lump in her breast, and she wanted to return to the University of Iowa Hospital for treatment. I was twenty and my mother was fifty-five years old. I left Georgetown University in Washington, D.C., for the summer. We landed in Iowa City together and quartered ourselves temporarily at the Blue Top Motel, an old motor court on the edge of town that still had kitchenettes, swing sets on the grounds, and the flashing sign: VACANCY.

Like everyone else at the motor court, we thought we would be transients at the Blue Top. We thought we might be there a month. When the doctors performed my mother's mastectomy, they removed one breast and lymph nodes, then simply sewed her back up. The cancer was that widespread. They gave her little hope and thought that her life could be counted in months. But the months went on, and the radiation began. She got no better, only gradually, very gradually worse.

I returned to Georgetown for the fall semester of my junior year. By Thanksgiving, my mother seemed to be declining even more, the cancer spreading into her bones. Her eyes were ringed with deep, dark circles. In December I dropped out of Georgetown and went back to take care of my mother, hoping to finish my studies at the

University of Iowa. Soon after Christmas, my mother was in the shower washing her hair when she found a lump protruding from her skull. The cancer had spread to her brain. The chemotherapy began.

At this time, Iowa City was experiencing a dire housing shortage. With little money, little housing was available, so for the first year of our sojourn, we moved first from the Blue Top to house-sit one place or another until the proprietors returned. Finally, the yardman at the Blue Top moved out of the garage apartment, and the motel owner called and said we could rent the "penthouse." Back we went, up the long drive where the individual cabins clustered in a circle, their blue roof shingles shining, flower boxes under the windows filled with blossoming petunias.

The penthouse was situated at the northern end of the "ranch," as my mother called it, a shotgun-style, two-room apartment with no more than two hundred square feet. But what the place lacked in space, it made up in windows. Thirteen windows ringed the flat, opening out onto the expanse of maple trees that shaded the park benches below. The sun poured in on the south, brightening the walls, beaming down on the narrow little inside steps that led up from the drive. On the tree outside the kitchen window I hung a little suet feeder, and every morning while doing the dishes, I watched the blue jay swoop down and bite the downy woodpecker's derrière, driving it away from the food.

My mother and I ate our supper on our laps, the apartment too small to contain her bed, the couch I slept on, and a kitchen table. So we became as adept at juggling trays as we did our lives in such close quarters. With our "stuff" cut down to the minimum, we kept things tidy by returning everything to its exact place and wedging items down into the eaves. I kept my growing poetry collection on a shelf in the bathroom, and my mother organized her financial records in file folders that she slipped into a suitcase that fit neatly under her bed.

We settled into a home that was a home away from home for many. The epitome of the American pilgrimage. A culture with a lingo of its own.

"Did you hear about the couple that was headed out west, their car loaded down with furniture and possessions?" the laundry man asked.

"No."

"They stopped at motels and each night unloaded all their things and carried them inside. Then in the morning they packed everything up again. Well, one morning they met a Buddhist in the unit next to them. He traveled with nothing, not even a single bag.

" 'Why are you packing up all your possessions?' " the Buddhist asked, watching the couple squeeze things into their trunk.

" 'Because we're not staying,' the couple replied.

" 'No?' the Buddhist asked.

" 'We're driving all the way down Route 66 to California,' the couple said. 'We're just passing through.' Then they looked at the Buddhist and asked, 'Why do you carry nothing?'

" 'Because I have no possessions,' he said.

" 'Nothing at all?' they asked. 'Why?'

" 'Because I'm not staying,' he said. 'I'm just passing through.' "

After a month in the penthouse, we pulled up the carpet and replaced it with a brighter, more cheerful remnant. I painted over the hospital-green walls, transforming them into a soft yellow that made the one strip of flowered wallpaper with its garish roses look planned. We hung mirrors to make the space appear larger, installed old wicker furniture found at garage sales, and replaced the ratty old dark burlap curtains with white organdy. We decorated with Audubon prints of great blue herons and sandhill cranes, and the penthouse became a cozy tree house. In the winter, its two little radiators sputtered and clanked, and the steam from the kettle on the stove fogged the windows.

In the spring, the winds blew so hard that the windows bowed. When the tornado siren blasted its warning, we raced down the penthouse steps, scurrying up the drive to the owner's house, which had the only basement on the "ranch." These drills often found us huddled together with a few fertilizer salesmen, the motel managers and their three small children, and the owners and their eighty-something mother who was afflicted with Alzheimer's disease.

"Sinbad! Sinbad!" she called, the storm howling around us. "We're all going to be lost in the wreck."

One autumn, I was just about to fall asleep when the whole penthouse shook and my glasses fell off the nightstand. I didn't think much of it because the walls shook every time the owner opened the heavy garage door below and started up the tractor to mow the great expanse of land.

It's a funny time to be mowing, I thought, and turned over and went to sleep. In the morning, I stumbled down the steps to get the paper, and the headline read: RARE MIDWESTERN EARTHQUAKE SHAKES EASTERN IOWA.

That winter, I began working as a desk clerk at the motel for a little discount on our rent. I perched on a chair behind a long, high counter, the room keys dangling on hooks at my shoulder. The reservations were kept on index cards in a metal box and the registrations in a large red "Week at a Glance" daybook. I had explicit directions not to rent to anyone with a local license plate (this was the Blue Top, after all, not a brothel) unless it was the coach of the Iowa football team, who had been known to check in with his assistants and draw up their secret tactics for the next week's game. Those were the days when Iowa went to the Rose Bowl.

I learned the names of the traveling salesmen who stopped on a regular basis, of the other hospital "visitors" who came for treatments of one kind or another, of the football fans who, win or lose, returned year after year to cheer for the Hawks.

> *We're going to fight, fight, fight for Iowa. Let every loyal Hawkeye sing. We're going to fight, fight, fight for Iowa Until the walls and rafters ring.*

Mostly what rang was the phone, and I soon learned the rhythm of the switchboard, pulling the long black cord out of its hole and plugging it into its designated peg. The cabins, perhaps for some superstitious reason, were numbered one through twelve, then fourteen and fifteen, and finally seventeen and eighteen, and as easy as that may seem, you had to keep your wits about you when you were moving those long black cords around the switchboard. Mostly, I sang the tunes of the country and rock bands who played for the Black Stallion bar down the road. The musicians, who were often our only clients on January subzero days, pulled up in their vans, renting one cabin for slumber and another for rehearsal.

In the penthouse, my mother was engaged in rehearsals of her own. She made out her will, gathered her papers together in her suitcase, made arrangements for her burial plot, and kept her address book updated so that I would easily know whom to call.

She prayed her rosary and kept it in a little leather case by her bed. I never saw her cry, although sometimes she would lash out in anger when drugged with this toxic chemical or that, or lapse into an impenetrable silence. She read voraciously, *The New Yorker* and the *Chicago Tribune Book Review* her favorites, listened to all the Iowa football games on the radio—the announcer was an old family friend—and watched every second of the Watergate hearings. I drove her to the hospital twice a week for her chemo shots, and we learned that the later she was scheduled in the day, the later we would be up at night.

Around midnight the nausea usually set in, and from there on out, it was a night of fitful sleep at best for the two of us. Our lives became nocturnal. Often I would find myself rubbing her back, trying to soothe her to sleep. Sometimes I would read to her. I took an American novel course at the university, and we read *The Grapes of Wrath*. I took a class in classical and biblical literature, and we read the Bible.

"I don't think I want to hear anymore," my mother said one night as I made my way through Genesis. "All these people live nine hundred and ninety-nine years."

Often I just sat quietly by her bed in the yellow vinyl-covered chair, the two of us listening to "Jazz with Jim," the radio show that ran from midnight until 6 A.M. Duke Ellington, Count Basie, and Ella Fitzgerald became our companions, the strains of their melodies growing louder and louder as my mother gradually lost her hearing. At other times I found myself just listening. In the pitch dark of the tiny apartment, with the moon and the constellations of stars shining through the windows, my mother told stories of how she used to dance to the big bands in the ballroom at the Memorial

Union at the university, of how she'd met Tennessee Williams who had written *The Glass Menagerie* while he was here, and how Grant Wood had begun the regionalist movement while teaching at the university. She told stories of her college days, dropping in and out of classes during the Depression, teaching school to earn more money to return.

And then once when she was flattened by the chemo, she told me of a dream that she had had five years before when my grandmother had died of cancer. A stranger appeared to my mother on the road, dressed in a long cloak. It was nighttime, very dark. No moon in the sky. My mother couldn't make out the stranger's face. She approached slowly, getting closer and closer. My mother strained to get a look at the stranger. Finally, she stopped, and my mother recognized her own mother, who looked at her calmly and said, "Pick up your cross and follow me."

My mother kept her rosary with her at all times. When she removed it from its leather pouch, the beads fell into shifting landscapes on her bedside stand, the cross hanging over the edge of the table, dangling in the air. She kept the rosary with her even in her last illness when she stopped going to Mass, even when she waved away the priest who appeared unannounced in her hospital room and gave her the last rites at least three different times.

"I'm too old for that now," she told him, and he hustled back out into the hallway, only to reappear again and again. My mother grew up in the pre–Vatican II days when the last rites were called "extreme unction" and they meant what they said—a last-ditch effort to save your soul before you died. When a priest appeared, you knew you were done for. My mother told me stories of people who had serious illnesses who could have rallied but simply gave up when they saw the priest walk through the door.

Instead, when my mother was still ambulatory, she drove herself to St. Patrick's Church one morning and received the blessing for the sick. She came home, a little unsteady, sober, and a bit shaken, but told me she'd taken care of that end of things herself and didn't want me calling in any priests at the last minute.

My mother's rosary came with us when we made all of our little pilgrimages from the Blue Top to the surgery clinic at the hospital for chemo and radiation. She kept the blue leather case tucked inside her purse. I held her purse on my lap when she sat in the old classroom chair in the hospital hallway, her right arm resting on its rigid desktop, while one of the residents wiped her arm with alcohol and injected the butterfly needle. The chief of surgery and my mother's physician, a balding, rotund man dressed in a long white coat, often strolled by during this procedure, smoking a cigar, grumbling, barking orders, and yelling at the unit clerk for some minor problem.

Over a period of three years, I got to know the clerks who deflected this abuse, the nurses who seemed genuinely caring, and the parade of medical students and residents who were all trying to work their way up in the system. I got to know the other women who were coming to the clinic to be treated for breast cancer. Some came in with friends, some with their husbands. There was a continuum of the progression of the illness among the women. A few were better off than my mother, in earlier stages, but most were worse. Since this was a university hospital, this was a place of last resort, a clinic that saw the most severe cases throughout the state.

All were treated with experimental drugs, the newest chemotherapy in use.

We sat in the waiting room together, patients and caretakers. We passed back and forth, in and out. We learned each other's names. Pictures were circulated, photos of sons and daughters, of parents, of houses and pets. There was a strained pleasantness to the group. All were in this together, dealing with the same disease, but no one was getting better. No one was getting cured. All were dying, and at an early age. My mother, at fifty-five, was one of the oldest of the group. All were enduring the treatment that our society, our culture, told them they must.

And it was difficult for those in the earlier stages of the disease to face those in the later stages. They received a flash of things to come, a fast-forward view of themselves in the mirror. And it was difficult for those in the later stages to face those in the earlier stages. They received an idea of how far they had slipped. Cancer was never mentioned. Chemotherapy and its side effects were never discussed. The futility of what they were doing was never confronted. No one questioned the fact that they were subjecting themselves day after day, week after week to an expensive treatment that not only wasn't working but was causing horrible suffering.

In the early 1970s when everyone was questioning everything else—the Vietnam War, the military-industrial complex, religion and its prejudices, and attitudes toward minorities and women— few confronted the contradictions of the medical model. Or if they did, they seldom voiced their doubts. Most of the people in the waiting room just retreated into stoic midwestern silence, blanking out their minds. Perhaps facing the insanity of what they were doing was just too much to handle. Perhaps doubting the humanity of the medical model placed them too far out of the mainstream American culture. They didn't want to be labeled kooks. They had to cling to some kind of hope. They had to put their faith in something.

To cope, my mother and I usually entered into the gallows humor of the nurses and doctors. We laughed with the old Navy nurse who had been on duty in the Pacific in World War II and spoke about the clinic as if it were a submarine.

"Dive, dive," she'd call when she saw the chief of surgery approaching down the hall.

Over time, we got to know not only the nurses but their spouses and families on a first-name basis. We knew who liked to go to the Cubs games, who went fishing after work, who got a new car—the currencies of friendship. We were even invited into the staff lounge for birthdays and given a piece of cake. My mother was grateful to these people, and every time she was hospitalized in a crisis, she'd instruct me to go out and buy each of them a bottle of wine or flowers or some token of appreciation.

My mother especially liked Gertrude, the head nurse, who ran an orderly clinic with a Nurse Ratchet forthrightness, but also exuded a warm and nurturing presence. Once when my mother slumped to a hump in the hallway after hearing the news that the cancer had advanced again, Gertrude confessed that she, too, had had a double mastectomy. When my mother's hair was finally gone, nothing left but a few strands, Gertrude urged her to buy a wig. A few days later, my mother waltzed into the clinic with her new "do," turning and modeling the wig for the nurses. Gertrude applauded. Like a child who has been given a brand-new present, my mother beamed.

One day, though, the smile fell from my mother's face and the cheerfulness drained from her lips when we stepped into the lounge for Dr. D.'s birthday celebration. Dr. D. was a dashing young staff doctor, quick, efficient, his wavy blond hair combed back away from his face with flair. He flirted with the nurses, his blue eyes meeting theirs, and he exchanged a sexual energy with them every time he entered the clinic.

There on the table was a huge mound of a cake covered with pink frosting and shaped into a woman's breast, complete with a nipple on the top. Dr. D. picked up the knife and cut right down through the sugar-coated mammary gland while everyone laughed, licking frosting from their fingers, the icing sticking to their teeth.

My mother turned quietly and left the room. I trailed after her. She sat down at the chemo "desk," her arm out, readying herself for the treatment. Quietly, without expression, she said, "That didn't strike me as funny."

After the cancer had spread to my mother's lungs, after the doctors had given her mustard gas, she decided to stop. Dr. A., the chief of surgery, pulled us out of the hall and into the examining room to suggest further surgery, going in through her nose to remove her pituitary gland.

My mother looked at me, tears in her eyes, and said, "No."

I nodded my head in agreement.

Instead, Dr. A. admitted her to the surgery unit for another blood transfusion. There, she was rigged up with an IV, a catheter, and oxygen. For the next month the nights became days and the days night. She drifted in and out of a coma, her liver shutting down, her abdomen swelling. She called for her mother. She called for her father. She called for her childhood friends. She had seizures. She was given morphine even though she protested that she had no pain. She had hallucinations. She was given more blood, and she had allergic reactions to each transfusion, always administered in the middle of the night when the unit had one nurse for fifty patients. The IV infused and her arm swelled to twice its size. The resident was paged. He stumbled into the room, having been awake for thirty-six hours, a three-day growth of stubble sprouting from his face. He started an IV at three in the morning and shuffled out of the room, leaving the tourniquet still tightly bound around my mother's bicep.

The next day Dr. A. appeared on his rounds.

"You're dying," he pronounced to my mother. "You have to leave. We need the bed."

"Leave?" I said.

"Yes, she's *dying*," Dr. A. said. "Take her away."

"Where?"

"She'll have to be out in forty-eight hours," Dr. A. said, exiting.

My mother looked at me, perplexed. "This has to be a mistake. Call Gertrude. She'll straighten it out."

I rang the clinic downstairs, and in about a half-hour, Gertrude appeared. She stood in the hall, refusing to go in the room and meet my mother's gaze.

Her voice took on a cold affect. "This is a teaching hospital," she said. "It's no place for a dying person. We need the bed. She'll have to be out in two days."

I drove back to the Blue Top. I called the Visiting Nurses and asked to reserve a hospital bed, but found that it would not fit up the narrow steps to our apartment. I reserved a suctioning machine and asked to be trained in the management of a catheter. I rented an IV pole and an oxygen tank. These were the days before hospice care, before home health care, before grief support groups—any of it.

I ran back down the stairs and threw open the car door. There stood my landlady.

"How's your mother?" she asked.

I told her she had been "evicted" from the hospital, and I was making arrangements to bring her home.

"Oh, no," my landlady said. "I can't have her dying here."

I raced back to the hospital to find the nurse pulling out all of my mother's support lines.

"What's happening?" I asked.

"They can't manage these lines in the nursing home," the nurse said.

"What nursing home?"

Dr. A. entered the room. "I've made arrangements for her to go to the O.K. Nursing Home," he said. "The ambulance will take her there shortly."

"But who will be her doctor?" I said.

"I'll come visit her," Dr. A. said. With that, he turned and strolled out the door. Neither my mother nor I ever saw him again.

Instead, we saw the inside of the infirmary of the O.K. Nursing Home, a dark and dingy corridor in the basement of a squat brick building surrounded by a parking lot and not a single tree or dab of green space. The nursing assistants lifted my mother into a bed and pulled up the railings. I busied myself by hanging up my mother's nightgowns in her closet and placing her slippers on the floor at the foot of her bed. I slipped her rosary in the drawer of her bedside stand. Then we sat silently together, my hand searching for hers through the railings. The walls, completely blank and hospital-green, stared back at us. The one small window that looked out on parked cars was darkening with the setting sun.

My mother, who hadn't said anything all day, turned to me, a jumble of syllables spilling from her lips, words so garbled I couldn't understand. I nodded to her as if I did, playing along, but she knew I wasn't connecting with her and kept repeating the words again and again.

"What?" I said. "Try saying it again."

Finally, on the third or fourth try, the words, slowly, very slowly, formulated by my mother's lips and tongue, came into focus.

"This is my cross," she said.

20

So I crossed myself—the Father, Son, and Holy Spirit—and began chanting again, the act becoming a weekly ritual in my Albuquerque apartment. My face filled with the steam from the boiling herbs, the sun going down, the pink glow on the mountains fading to a soft silvery hue.

I chanted Psalm 91, the pilgrimage psalm, the same prayer that Christopher Columbus's crew had sung each night at sunset:

> He who dwells in the shelter of the Most High
>> will rest in the shadow of the Almighty.
> I will say of the Lord, "He is my refuge and my fortress,
>> my God in whom I trust."
> Surely he will save you from the fowler's snare
>> and from the deadly pestilence.
> He will cover you with his feathers,
>> and under his wings you will find refuge;
> his faithfulness will be your shield and rampart.
>
> You will not fear the terror of the night,
>> nor the arrow that flies by day,
> nor the pestilence that stalks in the darkness,
>> nor the plague that destroys at midday.
> A thousand may fall at your side,
>> ten thousand at your right hand,
>> but it will not come near you.

You will only observe with your eyes
    and see the punishment of the wicked.

If you make the Most High your dwelling—
    even the Lord, who is my refuge—
then no harm will befall you,
    no disaster will come near your tent.
For he will command his angels concerning you
    to guard you in all your ways;
they will lift you up in their hands,
    so that you will not strike your foot against a stone.
You will tread upon the lion and cobra;
    you will trample the great lion and serpent.

"Because he loves me," says the Lord,
    "I will rescue him;
    I will protect him, for he acknowledges my name.
He will call upon me, and I will answer him;
    I will be with him in trouble,
    I will deliver him and honor him.
With long life will I satisfy him and show him my
    salvation."

I chanted and boiled herbs and boiled herbs and chanted. Father Sergei had told me to look to my own ancestors for icons. I placed the image of my grandmother and mother in front of my mind as if their photographs had been painted on a block of wood. I drew strength from their courage, their humor, their sense of fun, their dignity in the face of adversity. I could imagine myself a spry eighty-year-old woman like my grandmother, walking the beans in an Iowa field, swinging a corn knife. I could imagine myself as my mother driving through the desert, red bandana tied around my head, thermos of coffee at my feet, singing at the top of my lungs, "Home, home on the range, where the deer and the antelope play."

I chanted and boiled herbs and boiled herbs and chanted, but I wanted more than the lives that my ancestors had lived. I wanted to open the door to my shed, let the dogs out, and paint my life on a different kind of wood. I began to place my faith in a way of being, a way of healing that was completely different from my mother's. I could pick up my cross, yes, but I no longer wanted to be part of the system that shunned her in the end. I wanted to find a different approach to medicine. I wanted to find a different worldview. I wanted to be part of a vision of existence that was more expansive, that allowed for more mystery, more caring and compassion. I wanted a permanent refuge, a spiritual garden with an apricot tree that would put an end to my nightmare terrors of broken necks and monsters. I wanted to find a firmer base for my beliefs, my sense of self. Now that I trusted my own intuition, I wanted to find role models, other icons, other women who had developed their spirituality from a deep connection with their own strengths and talents. I longed to find safety under their wings.

Since my bout with the flu, my physical strength had been rebuilding and my energy level increasing. I'd returned to my old level of functioning and even pushed beyond. Another thin layer of pain had lifted. Was this step in my recovery the result of the sun, the dirt, the herbs and chants, or the new friends that I was making and the stories they had to tell? Probably a combination of all those factors. All I knew was that my legs and arms seemed lighter, less burdensome, more connected to my body. At the same time, my spirit felt as if it was going off in another direction. I strolled along the plaza in front of my office building at the university in a seemingly normal fashion, one foot in front of the other, but my emotions felt as if they were wound up inside the little black ball in the student hockey game, controlled by one team, then the other, bouncing back and forth across the paving stones, sometimes flying uncontrollably out of bounds.

I chanted and boiled herbs and boiled herbs and chanted, thinking of all the women before me who had done this very thing, all the women in the "Age of Discovery" who had set sail but never found refuge, who never reached safety. I projected myself back in time, wondering if any of the women in my family would have survived the Inquisition. I decided to reencounter the mystics I'd remembered when I was first stricken with central cord syndrome and transverse myelitis. I trooped off to the Zimmerman library to study the lives of some of the clever women—the Lu's of this world—who had a larger, different vision and dared to express it, who outwitted the patriarchy, who healed themselves and others, who were carriers of a cultural wisdom that could have been easily forgotten.

I brought home a bundle of books and CDs from the library and knelt down on the floor, spreading the materials in front of me, hoping to find something in them—anything—that would center me and pull me out of my deep, dark sense of alienation. I focused on two of the mystics I'd discovered when I was younger: Hildegard and St. Teresa of Avila. Like me, both women had had severe health problems that had landed them in their own states of paralysis and fear. Both had pushed through their illnesses to go on to write great books, finding outlets for their creativity and clarity for their bold ideas.

I listened to a choir chanting Hildegard of Bingen's words, their fresh voices lifting up out of the speakers of my tiny boom box, filling the narrow walls of my apartment. The CD spun around and around, and around and around again, the herbs boiling, droplets of water running down the wall behind the stove, the sun completely hidden behind the Sandia Mountains in the distance. I sat in the darkness, not rushing to get up and turn on a light. The chants floated through the air, surrounding me. Who was this woman who created such haunting melodies?

I first heard of Hildegard in the early 1980s when I read a review of Judy Chicago's "Dinner Party" and found that the mystic was a featured guest in the exhibit. Hildegard's writings were published for the first time in English in 1982. Soon after that, I was going through another serious illness, battling insurance companies, doctors, and difficult work situations. A friend stopped by my house and said, "Here, you need Hildegard," and handed me her books of *Illuminations*. I thumbed through the pages and was engulfed by the mystic's series of mandalas, their subtle colors, the browns and grays whirling and swirling together, always in circular motion, the mouths of goats and dogs open, spewing out a visible stream of breath, propelling the images forward on the page. Immediately, I sensed a shift of energy inside myself. Just by looking at these reproductions, my mind seemed to expand, to leave its narrow, constricted view of the world behind and open up to a wider array of possibilities.

I picked up my library copy of the *Illuminations* and opened its cover. I imagined Hildegard of Bingen as a compact woman with quick movements, a fast walk, a quick, clipped way of speaking, short of stature but long on energy. Today, she would probably be medicated for her "mania," tranquilized to better fit into a society of passive women. A twelfth-century German Benedictine nun, Hildegard was a mystic, theologian, poet, composer, painter, and naturalist. She left herbal treatises that are still valid today, treatises that people like Lu would find both fascinating in their scope and effective in their application. No shy violet, Hildegard wrote more than three hundred opinionated letters to the Pope, the emperor, and other noblemen. She confronted problems and personalities head-on. She was direct and definite, and I can't picture her waffling or trying to appease anyone. She preached in the cathedrals of Cologne and Mainz. Almost one thousand years later, I've rarely heard a woman preach in any Catholic church.

Hildegard began her life in a conventional way for a young girl in Bickelheim on the Nahe River, a tributary of the Rhine. Her father was a German knight, and she was the youngest of ten children. She was tutored by a holy anchoress at the Benedictine monastery of Mount St. Disibode and schooled in the traditions of music, spinning, biblical history, prayer, and work. She was trained to become a "lady" in German society. But even as a child, she had visionary experiences. At about age eighteen, Hildegard took the Benedictine habit.

Yet it wasn't until she was forty-two that she began writing of her visions. First, she developed all of her other talents. She made architectural drawings for her convent, led a center for producing manuscripts, and created numerous sketches and paintings. She became a scientist, recording her findings about horticulture and pharmacology. She wrote of the medicinal properties of 485 plants and advocated small homeopathic-like doses. She recommended treating diabetes by omitting sweets and nuts from the diet. She wrote about what happens to people during sexual intercourse and menstruation. She wrote about preventative health, the human body and personality types, and how the paleness of a monk's face reflects his vegetarian diet and celibate state.

Then in middle age her visions overwhelmed her. "The heavens burst forth with a fiery light," she recalled. She was so dazzled by the phenomena that she didn't know how to put it into words. She lacked confidence in her abilities as a writer, caving in to learned feelings of feminine inferiority. Even though she was accomplished in so many other ways, she froze at the thought of putting pen to paper. She fell ill until she gathered up all her resources and wrote about her thirty-three visions. Her writing energized her, allowing her to throw off some of the remaining bonds of her patriarchal conditioning. Her writing literally got her out of bed.

She imagined the universe not in male terms—the conquered and conqueror—but in female imagery, an organism born out of love. The universe is vaginal, all elements organized around an egg at the center of the cosmos. For Hildegard, "love" is the basic symbolic image that engenders all things, and to her, love meant compassion. She did not emphasize evil or original sin. In her view, there was no fall from grace. In ten of her drawings, Hildegard shows how Satan was crushed from the start, how the cosmos—with humanity as its midpoint—was born from the womb of love. She depicts how human beings cultivate the earth and how a divine fire burns through humanity and purifies it. The world, the city of God, is built to enthrone "love."

Hildegard valued the spark of life that is present in all living things. She blended her interest in science and the natural world together with art and religion. To Hildegard, the missing link between science and spirituality was art. She taught that only through trust in the expression of our own creativity could the models and paradigms of science live in the souls of people. She thought that art "wakes us from our sluggishness." She felt that art overcomes apathy, that art makes cold hearts warm, and dry consciences moist again. Creativity was the only way to express the cosmic experience. She painted many mandalas depicting this vision. Humans become the musical instruments of God. Divine energy plays its tunes through our music making, our poetry, and our painting.

Hildegard was an ecologist in the largest sense of the word. She grasped not only the interconnection of art and science but the interconnections of the universe. And she comprehended the intrinsic holiness of all parts of the cosmos. She wrote:

> "I, the fiery life of divine wisdom, I ignite the beauty of the plains, I sparkle the waters, I burn in the sun, and the moon, and the stars.... There is no creation that does not have a radiance. Be it greenness or seed, blossom or beauty, it could not be creation without it.... The world is living, being, spirit, all verdant greening, all creativity. All creation awakened, called by the resounding melody of God's invocation of the word."

In my convent school, not a single word was ever mentioned about Hildegard. In a place filled with girls who were pushed to develop their talents in the arts and sciences, this role model was forgotten. While I sat for hours practicing scales on the piano, while I identified plants and dissected frogs in the biology lab, while I mixed paint and drew pictures in the art room, Hildegard was kept under wraps. Officially, Hildegard has never been declared a saint, although three popes tried to canonize her.

I looked back at my childhood schooling and understood how important Hildegard could have been to the shaping of my consciousness. If I had learned about people like her, I would have had a different sense of the possibilities of life for a woman in this world. If I had been given female role models like Hildegard—not just the ideal of the Virgin Mary—I would have internalized a sense of feminine strength. Hildegard's works could have helped me find a launching pad for the development of my talents in my early life.

Yet perhaps I would have had to wait until middle age anyway to comprehend Hildegard's mandalas. Perhaps it took a crisis of faith to explore the ways that other women confronted their faith. Perhaps it took a crisis of faith to examine the ways that other women open up alternate visions of spirituality. Thinkers like Hildegard presented an answer to theologians like Thomas Aquinas. Through her creation-centered theology, Hildegard presented a new myth, a new structure, and a new balance for gender relations. She challenged women to be their full selves, to influence the "outside world" as well as home life, to express and experience and not hold back. She viewed life as an adventurous journey where women and men alike share their wisdom with mutual respect.

"Like the billowing clouds, / Like the incessant gurgle of the brook / The longing of the spirit can never be stilled," Hildegard wrote, and the voices on the CD singing her words rose and fell through the air, the medieval harp and fiddle filling in behind the ensemble. Softer, louder, quietly now, the voices chanted their rhythms. I envisioned Hildegard and the other Benedictine nuns swishing down through the cloister toward the chapel, their hands disappearing into their long sleeves. I saw a whole line of women gliding along through that convent, through the ages, their strategies for survival tucked up under their long habits. Teresa of Avila followed Hildegard. She found a very different way to hold up to the pressures of her time.

21

I imagine St. Teresa of Avila as a tall, willowy woman with dark bushy eyebrows, fluid movements, a flowing, steady walk, her head held high, her speech articulate but reserved. Today, Teresa, like Hildegard, would probably be medicated for her "mental condition." A sixteenth-century Spanish Carmelite nun, Teresa levitated, had ecstatic visions, heard voices, suffered with bouts of fatigue, had seizures, became paralyzed, lapsed into a coma, and was given up for dead. She is thought to have suffered everything from a somatoform, or psychosomatic, disorder to schizophrenia, but now evidence suggests that she was probably an epileptic.

Unlike my experience with Hildegard, I was introduced to Teresa of Avila in my childhood. Statues of St. Teresa graced the convent school chapel, a staff in her hand, her white habit accented by a long black veil reaching all the way to her feet. Our parish church contained a replica of Bernini's famous representation of St. Teresa in one of her ecstasies: Her face was serene and otherworldly, her experience of God's love symbolized by an arrow piercing her heart. My teenage eyes took in the complete privacy, abandonment, and sexuality of the moment. I was captivated by this nun who rose so high off the ground when she prayed that her fellow sisters had to hold her down.

In a college theology course that profiled famous people, religious and secular, who had the "courage of their convictions," I became engrossed in Teresa's family history that read like a movie script.

Teresa was born in 1515 to a cultured and merchant-class *converso* family in Avila, Spain. Around 1480, when the Inquisition began heating up its scapegoating of the Jews, Teresa's grandfather, a Christian convert, was rooted out and accused of being a "hidden" Jew and harboring a secret religion. If he remained in Spain and practiced his Jewish faith, he and his whole family were in danger of expulsion or death. If he was accused and maintained his innocence, his whole family might be burned at the stake.

So in 1485, to save his family, Juan Sanchez stood before the Inquisition and confessed: "I have committed the 'crime' of reversion." The Inquisition forced the Sanchezes to do penance for their sins, ordering them to don yellow tunics, "garments of shame," with large green crosses on the front and back. Every Friday for seven weeks, Sanchez and his children walked slowly through the streets of Toledo in a penitential procession, heads down, arms at their sides. They tramped through the busy city streets from one church to the next, asking forgiveness. Townspeople lined their path, cursing them, throwing stones, and spitting in their faces.

Juan Sanchez recovered from this trauma with amazing resilience. He changed his name to Cepeda and moved his family to the more tolerant town of Avila, where a close relation was carrying on a flourishing trade in silk and woolen cloth. Teresa's grandfather became a thriving entrepreneur. Whether the family continued to practice Judaism in secret is unknown. To the outside world they were Catholics. Juan Sanchez's son, Don Alonso, as he was now called, married well, although after a few years his bride died, leaving him with two children. Alonso then married Doña Beatriz de Ahumada, another well-to-do woman, who bore him more children, including Teresa.

When Teresa was only thirteen, her mother died. Teresa soon grew into a typical teenage girl, caring about clothes and boys. At sixteen, her strict father packed her off to the Carmelite Convent of the Incarnation. Her seven conquistador brothers sailed off to the Americas. Teresa hated the nunnery and over the course of the next few years fell ill, left, and returned home. Then she joined the Carmelites again, only to be plagued with chronic illnesses the rest of her days.

Teresa's illnesses threw her spiritual life into further turmoil. For years she waffled back and forth in her religious commitment. Finally, at twenty-three years old, while convalescing from yet another sickness, Teresa read Francisco de Osuna's *The Third Spiritual Alphabet*, a manual on mental prayer, a book that eventually launched Teresa into a life of contemplation and deep interior pilgrimage. She later called this process "the prayer of quiet," and it became her great talent and spiritual strength, catapulting her to sainthood.

But mental prayer did not help her physical heath. In her twenties and thirties, she remained caught in a web of spiritual chaos and doubt. In 1539, Teresa became desperately ill. After a severe seizure, she lapsed into a coma. Her fellow sisters thought that she was near death and dug her grave. She regained consciousness, but for three years she was paralyzed, the nuns carrying her around in a sheet. After she recovered her mobility, which was considered miraculous, she was never totally well.

At the same time, Teresa was a charming, outgoing, beautiful young woman, attracting many men who visited the convent parlor. In this era in Spain, convents often served as crowded dumping grounds for superfluous daughters of the wealthy. The novices and nuns were encouraged to venture out of the convent to visit family and friends. To the mother superior these visits always meant one less mouth to feed. The young women were expected to enter with large dowries, and the nunneries functioned as salons. Young men came to the convents to while away the afternoons, unashamedly flirting. Teresa enjoyed many of these attentions.

With one foot in and the other out of the contemplative life, Teresa continued to be tormented by her spirituality. "It is one of the most painful lives, I think, that one can imagine," she wrote in her *Autobiography*, "for neither did I enjoy God nor did I find happiness in the world. When I was experiencing the enjoyments of the world, I felt sorrow when I recalled what I owed to God. When I was with God, my attachments to the world disturbed me. This is a war so troublesome that I don't know how I was able to suffer it even a month, much less for so many years."

After reading St. Teresa's autobiography in college, I tried to push further and read her other writings. I bought a copy of *The Way of Perfection* and *The Interior Castle*, but the texts seemed abstract. A couple of months later, I encountered the *Playboy*-waving priest in the sweltering church and left Catholicism altogether. I put Teresa's books back on my shelf, packing them up and carrying them around with me while I moved from apartment to apartment, keeping alive the dim hope that someday her words would resonate with me. In my forties, I was willing to struggle with her ideas again.

In 1559, when Teresa was forty-four years old, she walked past an image of the crucified Christ, and suddenly she was on her knees, sobbing and repenting for her sins and her twenty years of indifference. She begged God to open her heart and soul for good. Teresa began having raptures, deep meditative states that transcended "normal" experience. In complete union with God, she romantically described being swept up into his arms as if she were a bride. Sometimes she levitated. At last she had established the intimacy that she so longed for, her heart fully open to another being, the love flowing freely between them. Now her whole essence was turned toward the heavens and away from the parlor. In her first rapture, she reported that Christ said to her, "No longer do I want you to converse with men, but with angels."

Eventually, the raptures ended of their own accord. "I've found a better way to pray," Teresa said, delving even further into mental prayer. But she was always grateful to the raptures because they provided a guiding principle of her life. She learned detachment. Detachment from all people and things allowed her to reach a higher consciousness of the Divine. Never again did she look to the outside world, to the pleasures of the parlor, for her strength and security. Instead she looked within.

The idea of detachment was alluring to me. I'd lived a life of clinging to this person or that place or thing in an attempt to fill up my own vacancies. The short period of time I'd spent with Lu and Father Sergei had taught me a lot about letting go of dependencies. Both of them were actively engaged in life but retained a detachment from the emotional ruts that keep most of us stuck in negativity. I was beginning to see that these two role models epitomized the biblical command to "be in the world but not of the world." Detachment was alluring but scary. It's hard to give up the very things you think will offer you stability. At the same time, through reading the works of St. Teresa, I saw that detachment was the only route to serenity, a deepening of spirituality, and a union with the Divine. Detachment might just release me from the perpetual hockey game of life. Paradoxically, for St. Teresa the practice of detachment merged her identity with Christ's to create a deep sense of serenity.

"Who are you?" Teresa of Avila's Beloved asked one afternoon when she was in interior prayer.

"I am Teresa of Jesus," she replied. "And who are you?"

"I am Jesus of Teresa," came the answer.

St. Teresa's serenity, however, was short-lived. A flying nun of *converso* stock who engaged in meditation was highly suspect by the Inquisition. The Church emphasized attendance at Mass, the most holy moment the elevation and consecration of the Host. Spirituality was to be mediated by the clergy. Any kind of prayer that claimed direct connection with God smacked of the newly emerging Protestant movement. The Inquisition was quick to attempt to quell any of these "heretics." Teresa's own sisters thought she was possessed. The Inquisition ordered Teresa to write her autobiography to explain her spiritual practices and experiences.

Has a beginning writer ever been given a more difficult task? Or had a more hostile audience? But Teresa embarked on the job even though she didn't know Latin. She couldn't meet the Dominicans on their own ground and couldn't have written an academic text if she'd wanted to. Instead, she wrote in the vernacular, an almost stream-of-conscious, down-to-earth but spirited prose with an imaginative use of metaphor. At times, she took on an "aw-shucks" tone, emphasizing her sinfulness and her ignorance as a woman. The Inquisition was disarmed by her book. How could they arrest her when she had already proclaimed herself a sinner?

Twenty years after my first attempts at deciphering St. Teresa's ideas, *The Way of Perfection* began to intrigue me again. In that book, Teresa reminds her readers that everything in the Carmelite daily life must reinforce the idea of constant prayer, of "prayer without ceasing." Peace, Teresa reasoned, is indispensable to prayer, and peace could be brought about by three things: love for one another, detachment from all created things, and humility. These three virtues provide the basis of a harmonious community. At the same time, they allow individuals to advance in their spiritual pursuits.

Written later in Teresa's life, *The Interior Castle* records her reflections on mental prayer in more detail and with a freer voice than she used in her *Autobiography*. She likens the soul to the inside of a castle. You move through the stages of prayer as if they were rooms in such a place. When you become more adept at mental prayer, you experience the "death" of the soul and new life in Christ. To illustrate this renewal, Teresa created her famous metaphor of the silkworm, comparing the death of the soul to a silkworm transforming itself in the cocoon. When it emerges, it is reborn as a white butterfly.

In middle age, Teresa found the strength and courage to emerge as a Church leader, embarking on a reformation of the Carmelite order. Joining with her friend St. John, the two urged the Carmelites, both male and female, to restore the original strictures of their order. Teresa asked the nuns to return to the veil and the grille, to break away from the temptations of the world and the bidding of wealthy patrons, and turn toward their own interiors. It wasn't long before Teresa faced stiff opposition, however. Her own sisters didn't want to be torn away from their lives of pleasures, while the townspeople wanted to continue to have some control over the nuns. The town of Avila started legal proceedings against Teresa. That didn't stop her. She went on to travel throughout Spain, braving burning sun, ice and snow, thieves and rat-infested inns to found dozens more convents. She was called by a papal nuncio a "restless disobedient gadabout who has gone about teaching as though she were a professor."

When she was voted prioress of her convent, the leader of the Carmelite order excommunicated the nuns. A vicar-general stationed an officer of the law outside the convent door to bar her entrance. Other religious orders opposed her wherever she went. Often, she was forced to sneak into a town secretly in the middle of the night to avoid causing a riot. As extroverted as she was, hiding became the theme of her life. She was forced to conceal her Jewishness, her early peccadilloes, the raptures that became a turning point in her life, and, of course, her extraordinary intellect.

In 1582, Teresa set out on a journey in obedience to a call from a duchess who wanted her present at the birth of her grandson. Teresa had a horrible trip. She was subjected to filthy accommodations, little or no food, and the intense hostility of one of her own prioresses along the way. Near the end, word came that the baby had been born on its own. "God be praised!" Teresa said. "They won't need the saint after all." She died a few days later, on October 4.

I sat down on the kitchen chair and poured a few tablespoons of the herbal mixture into a cup. I crossed myself again and drank the liquid down, wondering about my talents, about my secrets, about where my pilgrimage was taking me. I was beginning to connect with women who had struggled to find their own grounding, women who had probed their own inner beings to find their centers and had transformed the limitations of their illnesses to find peace. Both Hildegard and Teresa had taken possession of the secret part of themselves and transcended the structures of their societies.

But could I put their lessons into action? Could I find my own voice? I knew I had to do more than chant and boil herbs to find my grounding and regain my spirit. A year before, in wintry Iowa, ill, alone, and unable to move, I had grasped the interconnectedness of all things. But the realization was fleeting. How could I hang on to this vision? Did it take a trauma to open me up to mystical thought? Did it take repeated traumas to enable me to sustain that thought? Could I truly practice love and humility and find my way in an interior pilgrimage? Could I hold on to detachment and let go of desire as I'd tried so hard to do in the beginning of my journey?

My limbs were moving more fluidly. Normal motion was returning to my body. But I wanted my spirit back. I could detach and let go of almost all material strivings, but I couldn't detach from my wish to heal. I doubted Hildegard or Teresa would have given up that desire.

I crossed myself and drank the herbal liquid down.

22

"We start with the cross," Lu said one morning when I visited her at her desk in her drugstore, a huge plastic container of beads beside her. She held a pair of pliers in her hand. She threaded a thin piece of wire through a small metal cross, twisting it around in a loop, and pinching it together to form a closure. Lu was making rosaries that she would sell in her store and donate to her church in Albuquerque.

"I don't advertise," she said. "People just know I make rosaries and come in to buy them." With tiny wire cutters she snipped off two minuscule links of chain from a longer strand that rested on her desk. "Here, you have to have two links and two links only after the cross," Lu said, pointing to the beginning of her beads. "With rosary making, the spacing—each step—is very important. You can't mess around."

Nimble and lithe, her hands worked effortlessly, holding the beads between her thumb and index finger, rolling them around to assess their size and shape. Lu didn't even have to look down at her work. She guided the chain through the wire as if she were reading Braille. She selected a turquoise bead from the box, a shiny polished stone, smooth to the touch.

The box contained an array of beads, from the turquoise to orange and black baubles that looked as if they had once hung from some grandma's earlobes, to hard little raw berries called Job's Tears. Lu's daughter, who lived in Hawaii, had sent her the berries, which are found there in reeds in freshwater.

"They're hard, and the shine is enhanced by the oil from the owner's hands," Lu said. "Perfect for rosaries."

Lu had learned to make rosaries in Hawaii when she was stationed there with her husband on an air force base. She apprenticed herself to a Christian Brother who taught her the intricacies of counting out links of chain, of snipping off pieces of wire to exact lengths, of bending and shaping them into uniform segments. Lu sat with the brother under a banyan tree, watching his hands, stiff with arthritis, still able to make the most delicate movements. Link after link, the wire looped and twisted together to form one strong, unbroken unit.

The rosary is made up of five clusters of beads, with ten beads per group and one bead dividing each set, or "decade." Ten Hail Mary prayers are recited successively, and the Our Father is prayed between sets. The owner meditates on a different mystery in the life of Christ on each decade, and the rosary is composed of fifteen mysteries of three subsets: joyful, sorrowful, and glorious.

"Each decade holds together like a family," Lu said. "Sometimes I think of them as my original family. There were ten children. I had nine brothers and sisters. Then my mother died when I was only seven years old, and we were left with our father."

"That must've been tough."

Lu said nothing, her fingers working even faster, gripping the pliers, looping the wire.

"Did your father raise you then?"

"Sí, and my stepmother."

"Your father remarried?"

"Sí," Lu whispered, almost to herself, her head down now, concentrating on her beads, but her thoughts far away. Then Lu told me the story of how she had grown up south of Albuquerque in the country on a farm. One day her mother was scraped by a nail sticking out of a gate. She was five months pregnant at the time. She thought the scrape was nothing and went about her work. But soon an infection set in, and before anything could be done about it, she was dying. She delivered the baby and died seven days later.

"Just that quick," Lu said. "We took the baby and put it under a light in an incubator, and it lived."

"How old was the next youngest child?" I asked.

"Just a babe, a babe in arms. I raised her."

"And the stepmother?"

The stepmother had been a hired girl on the place when Lu's mother was alive. She was a neighbor who arrived every day to help with the cooking, cleaning, and child care. She was very envious of Lu's mother and all her children. She told Lu's mother that she wanted children very badly.

One day, with ten children playing underfoot, Lu's mother looked up from her stove and said to the hired girl, "You don't need to worry. One day all these children will be yours."

"Just a few months after that, my mother was scratched by that nail and died," Lu said. "The hired girl continued to come over and help out, and soon my father married her."

"How did that work out?"

"She was very different from my mother," Lu said, then twisted the wire on the last bead of the first decade back toward herself, her eyes riveted on her pliers, never leaving her work. "I have her in a nursing home near here now. This afternoon I need to go and see her." Lu threaded the wire through the bead that would become the Our Father.

"But you know something?" she said. "It wasn't meant to be. My life with my real mother wasn't meant to be."

"No?"

"What about your mother? Is she still alive?" Lu asked me.

"No. She died when I was twenty-three. That was bad enough. I can't imagine going through something like that at age seven."

"We can live our lives thinking this shouldn't have happened and that should have happened. If only I'd had this or that. But this and that did happen, and you weren't meant to have this or that. And there you have it."

"So you've reached a point of acceptance?"

"*Sí.* Sometimes it takes a while, but the sooner you get to acceptance, the better."

Lu explained that she lived her life trying to fulfill her gifts, looking forward, not looking back at past disappointments.

"You see, God has a plan for all of us. I've felt gifted all my life, but it wasn't until a few years ago when I set up practice in this drugstore that I felt my talents come to fruition. See, I had these pliers for years before I ever learned to make rosaries. I held on to them. I didn't know why. Now I find great peace and serenity in my craft, just as you can find great peace and serenity in saying the rosary itself. People say the Church gave the poor peasants these prayer beads so that they could have something to do at Mass since they couldn't understand the Latin. But prayer beads are very ancient, very powerful. Saying the rosary is a pilgrimage, a quiet pilgrimage into the self. And you don't have to go off and spend money.

"My gift had been there all the time, and I had hints of it, but it took me this long to realize my talent, to pick up these pliers. And to gather my herbs. If we could all just step back and see God's plan for us—this is what we need to meditate on and pray for."

Did a personal God have a personal plan for me? This is where I got stuck on my faith quest. I could believe in a universal life force, a power that united all living things, the mystical source of creativity that Hildegard understood, the deep sense of union with the Divine that St. Teresa explored, but the "personal plan" idea brought up old questions and doubts. Did the Divine have that kind of control over every thought, word, and deed in our lives, every pair of pliers that we might carry hither and yon? On a more symbolic level, I could understand what Lu was saying to me. Lu was echoing Hildegard's life and example. Both women understood that you're born with a certain set of talents, and they will always be there with you. It's your job to discover them and put them to use.

I could accept the idea that events happen the way they're going to happen in life, and one event catapults you into the next, each shaping your personality, each shaping your soul in ways that you never had expected. Both Lu and I had lost our mothers young, but that loss pushed our lives forward in positive ways. If I hadn't been in a car accident, I might have made a trip to New Mexico, but it wouldn't have been a pilgrimage. I wouldn't have met this *curandera*. If the medical model had helped me, I wouldn't have been willing to examine women's ancient healing traditions or realized the link to my grandmother's use of herbs and poultices.

If I couldn't agree to an exact plan with every detail charted and plotted, I could agree that each of us has an unfolding of our life. And the routes we travel are never the roads we thought we were going to take. In our youth, we may map out a couple of main freeways for our journey. In middle age, we may find that we veered off onto side roads, paths that were much more interesting to travel. Perhaps it is only in old age that we understand the purpose of our trip and the location. Perhaps we will never know our final destination and can only tolerate the hardships of the trip, can only wonder at the surprises and delights we encounter along the way.

"Here, now, this rosary will be yours," Lu said at last.

She pushed the wire through the next turquoise bead and went on to the second decade.

23

"Yes, you have to pick up your cross," Father Sergei said a week later when I visited him in his garden. "The carrying of the cross is a sorrowful mystery. But you must always remember that after the cross comes the Resurrection, a glorious mystery. You must never forget the Resurrection."

We sat on the bench together, my hat on my head, my cane leaning against the rose trellis. The sun shone brightly on Father Sergei's face, his cheeks a bit more sallow than usual, though his mouth quickly arched into a smile when a goose sashayed across the yard, chased by a gander.

"I got those geese for protection," the monk said. "They're good watchdogs. Sometimes the nuns are here all alone."

I nodded, knowing that the pack of Chihuahuas scampering about the garden was not exactly the equivalent of an attack dog, although they did send up their yipping alarm when anyone arrived at the gate.

"Geese will bite when threatened," Father Sergei said. "But otherwise they are the most exquisite animals. They lay eggs. They provide us with down for our comforters. They weed the garden. They fertilize. They're beautiful to look at. And in the end, they make delicious soup. See, all things have their purpose under heaven. And we humans are just like these geese. We have a purpose but may not always understand it. Only a higher being can know, but we must trust that we have a job to do and we are carrying it out for a reason—even if that reason is merely being part of the cycle of nature. Have you read the mystics?"

I explained that I studied them when I was much younger but had just recently delved deeper into Hildegard and St. Teresa of Avila.

"Excellent!" the monk said. "Then you must read the male mystics, too. Always balance things out—the female and male, the yin and the yang. You must read and reread these writers. Hildegard, St. Teresa, St. Francis, St. John of the Cross—they were counterculture Zen warriors. They understood true healing. They stood up against the oppressive power structures of the times. They understood the cycle of nature and never lost sight of the larger whole."

The whole of Father Sergei's garden lay before us, reflecting different facets of his personality—his love for nature combined with his delight in humor. Vegetable patches bursting with tall, sturdy stalks lined the winding paths, the plants scattered here and there, tucked under the flowering dwarf apricot and apple trees, bright yellow squash blossoms snaking out under the green leaves. Small white crosses graced the vegetable plots, each wooden marker bearing the name of a different human flaw, as if identifying its final resting place. SLOTH was plunked down among the onions.

"These emotions are part of all of us," Father Sergei said, pointing to the wooden markers. "They are involuntary passions that come and go in ourselves all the time. We must be aware of them to be free of them. I placed sloth in the onion patch because the more you watch onions, the slower they seem to grow. You might think them lazy if you didn't know what's happening underground."

AVARICE was staked in the middle of the broccoli patch.

"Ah, broccoli knows how valuable it is, how rich are its glistening buds and stems."

LUST poked up out of the zucchini.

"Well, that's for obvious reasons. To put it kindly, zucchini has a *joie de vivre*."

The monk leaned back on the bench, cabbage moths and sparrows dipping and diving around him, landing on the grapes that wound up and around an arbor.

"My monastic family, the other nuns and monks who live here with me, has no income, so we eat what we grow or what is given to us," Father Sergei said. "Sometimes we eat the same thing day after day. We're given a lot of zucchini when it's in season, believe me. But the Lord provides."

Father Sergei paused, then began chanting a prayer of gratitude in Italian. His voice, deep and resonant, drifted over the carrots and beets, the garlic and green beans.

"I try to imitate St. Francis of Assisi. He became a monk but didn't just hole up by himself. He went out among the people. He became one with his ministry. He put his mysticism where his mouth was." Father Sergei threw back his head and laughed his boisterous laugh, his stomach rising and falling with his exhalations. He placed his hand on his chest, fingers spread apart.

"We must discard our birdbath view of St. Francis and recognize what a revolutionary he was, how he grasped the connection of all living things. He, like you, began his spiritual quest on a pilgrimage."

Francis was born in a wealthy merchant family, Father Sergei explained. His father dreamed that Francis would one day take over the family business. Francis had other dreams. He was a romantic and wanted to be a gallant knight or troubadour wandering through

France, playing his lute, singing his poetry. A charming, good-looking young man, he loved parties, drinking, carousing. He didn't start to find his spirituality until he fell very ill.

"So illness was a turning point for Francis as it was for Hildegard and St. Teresa?" I asked.

"Oh, yes, you must honor illness. It gives us time for reflection. As hard as it is, it helps us sort out our priorities. I know there's nothing worse than someone telling you, 'This illness of yours is a gift.' No, it's painful and discouraging. It's not a gift, but it is a time to pull back and take a closer look at one's life."

Before Francis became ill, Father Sergei continued, the young saint fought in several local wars, marching off in his suit of armor, his flag waving, his piercing dark eyes squinting into the sun. All of Assisi came to the town square to cheer him on, the young women looking up longingly into his handsome face. But he was taken hostage in Perugia and thrown in a dungeon for a year. There he became ill—some say with tuberculosis. There his ideas about life began to change.

When he was released from prison, he longed to watch a butterfly light on a flower, longed to watch a wave pound on the shore, longed to see a rock jut out from a cliff. The dungeon was torture for a man who so loved the pleasures of nature. He tried to resume his old life of debauchery. He tried to ride off to the Crusades, only to turn back a day later. Francis knew that something was wrong, and he retreated to a cave in the hills to meditate and pray.

"When Francis came out of his cave," Father Sergei said, "he thought he had a calling to care for the sick. But sickness and disease had always repulsed him. So he devised a test for himself. If Francis was truly a follower of Christ, he knew he would have to face the most repulsive person he could imagine: the leper."

Father Sergei leaned forward on the bench, his arm resting on his leg, his thumb and index finger pinching together. "*Clickety-clack.* The leper held his clicker in his gloved hand, the sound of the instrument a warning for all to keep away. The symbol of sin, the embodiment of evil, the leper with his missing nose and rotting flesh was forbidden from entering the city gates. He was forbidden to talk to anyone and forced to place himself downwind of passersby.

"The dashing young Francis rode up on horseback, a silk cloak wrapped around his chest. He wanted to gallop away, to run from the spot, never to look back, never to return. Yet Francis knew that if he didn't confront the leper, he would never confront the deepest part of himself. A voice inside Francis said, 'Confront the leper, and all that was once beautiful and alluring will seem bitter, and all that once seemed ugly and unbearable will be transformed into joy.'

"Francis jumped off his horse and approached the leper. He dug into his purse for a gold coin, but when he gave the leper the money, he picked up the diseased man's hand and pressed it to his lips, kissing it.

"After that, Francis's life turned upside down."

"But was the incident with the leper a mere act of charity or a moment in his growing spirituality?" I asked.

"Both. Acts of charity became his spirituality. Francis gave up his riches and took up the life and cause of the poor. More than anything else, Francis himself could finally see the leper as a symbol. You see, Francis was a very literal-minded fellow. Once, Francis heard Christ tell him, 'Francis, rebuild my church,' and he went off and sold a bolt of his father's expensive cloth to buy mortar and stones to renovate the crumbling San Damiano Church near Assisi. Another time, he went to Rome unannounced to have a conference with the Pope. When he showed up in a dirty tunic with a long straggly beard, the Pope said, 'Go and speak what you have to say to the pigs.' And Francis did! He spent the morning in the sty communing with the hogs.

"Of course, there was something rewarding in his literal-mindedness. The Pope was so impressed by his obedience that he gave Francis a conference and let him establish the little order of ragtag beggars he called the Friars Minor. Francis's own wealthy father thought his son was nuts and disowned him. The people in Assisi thought Francis was loco, too."

Father Sergei twirled his finger near his temple. "Plum loco." The Chihuahuas chased around and around our bench in a circle, their speed picking up with every lap. "Okay," the monk commanded, "stop." The dogs halted and dropped to the ground, panting, mouths open, tongues out. "No. You see, most of our holy people, our prophets, go against the grain of society and are considered crazy. They have a different vision than the rest of us—a symbolic vision—that may threaten ours, so we dismiss our holy ones and make them outcasts.

"Everything in this garden is symbolic," the monk said, "as is every event—whether joy or pain—that we experience in life. The vegetables represent our flaws, and the flowers have their own meanings. Those yellow roses say that they are jealous, jealous for life. The pink ones remind us to lighten up. And the red show us how to live with full passion."

I sat on the bench, the dogs at my feet, and tried to pull back my lens to view life from a wider, more symbolic perspective. I was beginning to understand this mystical slant on the world. I had grown up with a family of farmers and had had my own garden for twenty years. I valued and readily understood that nature needed to cycle, that plants needed to bear fruit and seeds to allow life to come again. I'd learned the rhythm of vegetables, how peas needed the cool rainy days of spring and tomatoes needed the heat and humidity of midsummer to ripen, how crops could be planted in succession, one after another in the same row during the same growing season. I even came to understand harsh, frigid, snowy winters, how we needed them to kill pests and to provide cover and moisture. Yet even as a practiced gardener, it's easy to ignore the symbolism of the garden plot. It's easy to remove yourself, your own death and the death of your loved ones, from this larger framework of nature.

One day, when I was taking care of my mother at the Blue Top Motel and fighting the very idea of death, I picked up my biology textbook. The author posed this question: What would become of the world if we didn't have death? He said that humans would quickly multiply and use up all the natural resources. Overpopulation would go hand in hand with disease and poverty. Great suffering would spread all over the map. Death, to this biologist, was a kind of conservation of our collective energy and integrity. Death, he wrote, was a layering of one generation living on top of the decaying other, of one generation providing the compost, the instigation for growth, evolution, and change for the next. This recycling made complete sense to me at the time and was more comforting than any myths of sin, fallen souls, and redemption.

Sitting there in Father Sergei's garden, I could once again embrace the cycle of nature. It felt a little like embracing my old faith in science. After all, the natural world provided the basis for science.

The natural world felt concrete and specific, more defined than an elusive deity. Yes, I could have faith in the cycles of nature that were here before my eyes—the climbing red roses arching over our heads on the trellis, the pink and yellow rosebushes near our bench in bloom. Yet I wasn't completely satisfied. Okay, death I could grasp, but why suffering? Why does the world have to go through so much pain and grief?

"Aha!" Father Sergei scooted closer to me on the bench, as if he were reading my thoughts. "You must study St. Francis's idea of harmony to better comprehend pain and suffering."

Francis found harmony in all things, Father Sergei explained. He sensed the connections among humans, plants, animals, mountains, oceans, and the heavenly bodies. Humans were just part of the whole and not the center of the universe. Francis was said to have tamed wild wolves, to have sent birds flying away in flocks. He considered and addressed all natural phenomena—fire, night, day, and even death—as his brothers and sisters. He saw the harshness and cruelty of the world intricately connected to its gentleness and beauty.

Maybe suffering allows us to fully realize the opposing seasons of the cycle of nature, I thought. Suffering highlights the gentleness and beauty of our lives and enables us to live life more passionately.

"Now you're beginning to get it," the monk said as if he were dipping down inside my head again. "When we stop fighting our pain, we reach some peace. Maybe the pain will go away, maybe it won't. But when you think of pain as just another one of the connected threads of the universe, you'll have a different experience of it.

"And even with your suffering, you must always live in a state of gratitude," the monk said. "Gratitude and hope. That's the message of Francis. See, this Hispanic community here in the barrio has a fatalistic attitude. Here, we were once the oppressor. Now we are the oppressed. See what I mean about playing out your part in the cycle of history? And my people, the Spanish Jews, how ironic how they fit into the whole scenario. The kind of pain and suffering Francis identified arises through nature. Other suffering arises through the power structure. Oh, yes, the mystics understood the power structure, but they transcended it."

The monk stroked his beard, his fingers intertwining with the curly, coarse gray hairs. "My people here fall into despair, feeling like no one cares. They take drugs, shoot heroin. I think of this as a sort of cry in the wilderness. People ask me why I don't have my monastery out in the desert someplace. This is the desert, I tell them. I've tried to make an oasis in the desert, to become a kind of desert father. I try to provide hope for the despair. I give money to the homeless for their meals. I take in those who have been shunned and beaten up. I try in every way to live my religion. Today, most people practice what I call 'microwave Christianity.' They practice it for a few minutes when it's convenient, then dump it.

"See, Francis used to sink into depressions, but he struggled to maintain hope. Francis lived out his faith through good deeds. He never wrote down his principles, leaving no records for the Inquisition to seize and label heretical. He didn't want a conflict with the Church, and he looked beyond its decadence. Instead, Francis wanted a brotherhood, not a religious order. People from all walks of life, all ages, all races and religions gathered around him.

Everyone was welcome—whatever his marital status, religion, or ethnicity. His good friend Clare set up a similar group for women."

Father Sergei explained that Francis and Clare ministered to the poor, the sick, the outcast and ostracized. They didn't try to just donate money to the poor but attempted to return to them their self-respect. They didn't believe that material things were necessarily bad, but that everyone received all things from the Creator and, in that, all are equal. When criticized by his bishop for living too austere a life, Francis replied, "If we had possessions, we should need weapons and laws to defend them. What could you do to a man who owns nothing? You can't starve a fasting man, you can't steal from someone who has no money, you can't ruin someone who hates prestige."

In 1226, Francis fell ill, plummeting into another deep depression, and nearly went blind. He went to the Poor Clares, and these sisters set up a hut for him near their quarters. In his misery, Francis wrote one of his most beautiful poems, "The Canticle of Brother Sun," addressing Brother Sun, Sister Moon, Brother Wind, Sister Water, and Bother Fire. In the poem, Francis praises even the negative forces of nature—Sister Bodily Death. All are part of the inevitable. All sing the song of the glory of God. All things are placed in existence for reasons we don't know.

"God's ways are past finding out," Father Sergei said, the sparrows coming to light on the branches of the apricot tree, the branch giving a little with their weight. "The more we know of the world through science and our sophisticated technology, the more we know of mystery. We are so uncomfortable with mystery. We want to know things for facts, to nail things down. I'm here to tell you to embrace mystery and let it be. True mystics understand this.

God is the emblem of love. We can be one with him through being one of his creatures. We may never completely understand this unity, for God will always remain mysterious."

24

"**B**ut what if you can't hang on to hope?" I asked Father Sergei. "What if you sink down into depression like St. Francis and stay in that state?"

One of the younger monks appeared at the back door of the monastery, his brown habit flowing to his sandaled feet, his long blond hair cascading to his shoulders, bagpipes in hand. The goose and gander charged toward him, necks extended, hissing.

"Shush now. It's okay," the younger monk said to the geese, then turned toward Father Sergei. "Is it all right if I practice my pipes?"

"Of course!" Father Sergei waved him on, then explained, "I encourage all my monks to develop whatever talents they have when they enter the monastery. That monk is musical, so here we are in the middle of the barrio dancing to—what else?—Scottish bagpipe music."

The younger monk stood close to the fence near the alley, the geese trailing at his feet. He blew into his reed, emitting a low, mournful drone, a note that sent the geese into alert, their eyes opening wide, heads turning toward the sound.

"So what if you sink into a deep depression and stay there?" Father Sergei repeated. "So what if?"

"How do you pull yourself out?"

"Why force yourself out? Why not just stay there?"

"Oh, because it feels awful."

"So are we talking about despair?"

"Yes."

"A despair that's so black that you feel like you've been abandoned by everyone including God?"

"You've got it."

"Aha! Then we're no longer talking about mere depression. We're talking about the 'dark night of the soul,' as St. John of the Cross called it. St. John was one of us. He was of *converso* stock. A small guy—just four feet eleven—but full of big ideas. He became a Carmelite and friends with St. Teresa of Avila. Together they set out to reform their order. John's fellow Carmelites arrested him and dumped him in prison for nine months."

"His own monks put him in prison?"

"*Sí.* Reformers are never very popular among their own. He was stashed in a six-by-ten cell. There was little light. Fray John was repeatedly beaten, and his body bore the marks the rest of his life. Just like St. Francis, St. John suffered horribly in solitary confinement, but it also launched him into mysticism. He went with the experience and began some of his famous poems there."

The rhythm of the younger monk's music kept up a steady tempo, the slow wail of a dirge breathing out and breathing in from the bags of skin, the notes rising up from the cluster of pipes strapped on his back. The monk tapped his foot and swayed slightly with the beat. I pictured St. John, alone, disheveled, despondent in his filthy cell, penning those lines, "One dark night … O guiding light! / O night more lovely than the dawn," to the musical accompaniment of the bagpipes.

"But how quickly fortunes turn," Father Sergei said, his fingers tapping time to the music against his leg. "John finally escaped from prison and became a head honcho in the Carmelites. But here's the important thing: He didn't become stuck-up and let his power go to his head. He continued to work like a real person, scrubbing the abbey floors and tiles, doing carpentry, and working in the garden. He showed solidarity with the worker and compassion toward the ill. He knew how to care for the sick, comfort them, and give them hope.

"But unlike St. Francis," Father Sergei continued, "St. John's fame didn't arise from his acts of charity. He founded another kind of healing ministry—an exploration of the interior of the soul. And what did the dark night of the soul mean to St. John? It was a metaphor for his experience of solitary confinement. His physical imprisonment became the symbolic walls of a deep depression—that despair we were talking about. There, you can see only darkness and experience nothingness, no joy or hope. Life no longer has passion, mission, or direction. Prayer becomes a burden. In the blackness, you renounce all desire, all grounding in previous securities, ideas of religion, concepts of God, even of mysticism. It is as if you have to open a void and fall into it to obtain higher consciousness."

"But how can you move to higher consciousness in solitary confinement? I'd be so pissed at the people who put me there."

Father Sergei paused, wincing and holding his side in pain. The bagpipe music stopped, and the geese ceased their weed eating, craning their necks toward the older monk.

"I told you I have liver and kidney damage from my beatings," Father Sergei said. "Lu across the street gives me herbs. Sí, her herbs have kept me alive for many years. But what has really been my salvation is forgiveness. I let go of my anger. I don't hold on to fury. I don't even let it enter my system. I forgive from the start. Every time I was beaten, I forgave. That's what the Gospel means when it says that we must forgive our enemies. We must literally forgive and not go down the path of hate in the first place. St. John forgave his tormentors even while they imprisoned him. He is a model for all of us."

"Does forgiveness carry you through the dark night?"

"Forgiveness allows you to fall deeper into the dark night."

"Deeper?"

"I told you that you want to sink down into the dark night and stay there," Father Sergei said. "You are fighting so hard to get out. You must enter into that void, because then you make the great discovery that God is the void, God is the dark night."

"How could God be the dark night?"

"How could you be listening to bagpipe music in the middle of the Albuquerque barrio?" Father Sergei laughed. "You'll find the Divine in paradox, in contradictions, in the moment of surprise. You're not going to find the Divine in some safe, cozy little apartment where everything moves along at a predictable pace."

The bagpipe music picked up its beat, the dirge shifting into a faster reel. The younger monk's face was red with exertion, his cheeks puffed, breath blowing into the reed. I tapped my foot, and the geese scattered to either side of the apricot tree.

"You can get through the morass," Father Sergei reassured me. "St. John understood that God is the abyss, the dry desert. When you abandon yourself to this dark presence, this inner guide, you are led to the other side. You persevere. The sufferer finds comfort in knowing that all pain contains the hand of God. Suffering is a purification process, clearing away the debris of attachment and making way for the Divine light. For St. John, pain was not a misfortune but a value when endured with and for Christ. Not that

St. John advocated suffering. Oh, no. During this time there were monks who whipped and beat themselves in an attempt to purify themselves. The Penitentes, we called them in New Mexico. Fray John referred to these acts as the 'penance of beasts.'"

"So, you mustn't beat up on yourself."

"Never. Never physically nor emotionally. No. St. John, like St. Teresa and all the other mystics, learned to detach. We might think of the practice of detachment as watching life go by as if it were a movie. It's there to view, to enjoy, but we mustn't become embroiled in its anxieties. You see, it's another contradiction. The soul must leave all things by denying its appetite for them. The soul advances by abandonment, finding truth in God. When all has been strained away, our emptiness will be filled with a new presence, a union with God. Appetites interfere with this union. You must let the union happen. You must allow yourself to be carried along by God as a child does before it learns to walk.

"St. John viewed the world from a different perspective. Literally, in his writings and sketches, he imagines himself gazing down at the world from the top of a summit. He detaches himself to merge with God, body and soul, becoming one. St. John described this merging in terms of courtly love—the imagery of his day. The soul is the bride. Christ is the groom. Their union is permanent. The soul 'breathes in God just as God breathes in her. Of me are the heavens and of me is the earth.' Oh, St. John was a *harto santo*—a real saint. That's what St. Teresa called him when he became her confessor."

"But should we always live like St. John in such sanctity?" I asked Father Sergei. "Shouldn't we ever fight back?"

"Oh, I didn't say that."

"But you let the gangs beat you up ..."

"Have you never heard of nonviolent passive resistance? Of Gandhi? One of the first tenets of Buddhism is that you are the center of the world—not in an egocentric way, not in the way that St. Francis objected to, but in a way that allows you to realize that your small actions, whether good or bad, have an effect on the universe. You see, that's St. John's example with his tormentors. Who knows which of those gang members will absorb my message of love—maybe none of them. But at least it gave them pause. It made them become aware for one small moment of their own lives. Perhaps they were one tiny step closer to what Buddha said about life, that it is neither brown, black, nor white, that it is neither tall nor short, fat nor thin. That life just is."

Perhaps pain and suffering just are, I thought. A part of life, a part of the whole. Sister Death, Brother Pain. If I thought of them in more intimate, integral terms, they could take on personas, different faces, different personalities. What if we didn't have suffering? I asked myself. Imagine that world. How would the human psyche change? I came back to St. Teresa and St. John's idea of detachment. In the Divine light, detached, free of the bonds of attachment, humans could live at a higher, deeper level—one with more compassion, awareness, and gratitude. One with more passion and even more humor.

The younger monk trilled the final bar of his reel, the notes carrying far in the dry air, up and over the barrio, through the traffic, up Route 66. He bowed to us, bowed to the geese, and disappeared back into the house, his set of pipes clacking on his back. The Chihuahuas settled down under the birdbath. The two geese waddled up to us, pulling out weeds as they went, making way for the bounty of vegetables at our feet, opening their beaks wide, their orange tongues wagging, the color reflecting the shade of the brilliant sun just beginning to set on the other side of the monastery fence.

25

our A.M. I drove out into the dark night, a still, blue-black inky night in New Mexico, a third-quarter moon hanging high in the sky. My cane at my side and Ernesto's map on the car seat beside me, I nosed my way south of Soccoro to the Bosque del Apache, a wildlife refuge and oasis of swampy marshland in the middle of the dry desert. Ernesto's notes told me that more than seven hundred years ago the Piro Indians had settled in the Bosque area. Attracted by the fertile soil and rich animal and plant life, the tribe flourished until European diseases and the Apache raids decimated their population.

In 1939, the area was established as a sanctuary for migratory birds whose populations had also been decimated. In 1941, only seventeen sandhill cranes used the refuge. Sixty years later, the sandhills number more than seventeen thousand. I hoped to catch the last of the cranes and snow geese before they launched their northern journey, so I followed the dirt road into the Bosque, slowing the Trooper down to a crawl, careful not to make too much noise for fear of disturbing the wildlife. In the thin moonlight, I could make out the outline of a great blue heron on the bank in front of me, its black crown feathers abandoning themselves to the darkness of the night.

I turned into a pull-off, snapped off the ignition, and rolled down the window. The *yip, yip, yip* of a coyote call carried toward me on the dry air. Marsh grasses shot up in front of the car, their pointed, rigid tips reaching toward the sky. Beyond the grasses, I recognized the sounds of a body of water, the gentle lap of a small wave, the *plunk* and *plop* of a bird standing in a slough. Beyond the marsh, I imagined the meanderings of the Rio Grande, the river snaking through the region, the current building and subsiding with every twist and turn. In the Trooper's rearview mirror, I took in the long expanse of the desert behind me, the flat bareness stretching for miles to the outline of the Magdalena Mountains, their peaks a gray blip on the horizon.

I pushed open the car door with my cane, slid out of the seat, and stood alone in the darkness. I waited quietly without moving. I waited and watched. During the past weeks, my physical pain had decreased and my body continued to heal, but my psyche still felt as if it were drifting somewhere above the marsh, receding into the clouds. The deep despair I'd carried since the paralysis hung on, seemingly pressing tighter into my skin like the thumbscrews used to torture the witches, like the nooses slipped around their necks. Up, up, up my mind drifted over the marsh grasses. Down, down, down I sank into the darkness and stayed there. For some brief moments every day my attention remained in the present, and I'd focus on the antics of a goat, the flash of a comet through the sky, or the silhouette of a great blue heron on the bank. These were moments of great relief and clarity. I struggled to hold them in my consciousness at all times. But I failed. Instead, I tumbled into the void.

After my mother's funeral in Iowa in the early 1970s, I failed to pack up her bedroom. I had returned to the Blue Top Motel, the October sun going down on the freshly combined cornfields, the stalks reduced to stubble. I curled up on the couch and fell asleep, sinking down in the dark night of grief. I slept there, as I had for almost three years, every evening for the next couple of months. I told myself that this was silly, that I could now sleep in the one bed in the apartment. But my mother's bathrobe was still hanging on a hook behind the bedroom door. Her pen, her stationery, and her journal were still next to her rosary on the bedside stand, her sweaters in the dresser drawer. The Audubon prints of sandhill cranes and great blue herons hung askew on the wall. The yellow chair sat empty in the tiny room.

I busied myself with schoolwork and teaching. I swam laps in the indoor pool. I had dinner with friends. I went to movies and stayed out late, coming home to the penthouse to crash on the couch. My sleep was restless and fitful, my dreams fragmented and scary— falling off cliffs, animals charging toward me, being boiled alive in burning oil. Some days I would rise early, determined to move back into the bedroom, determined to gather up my mother's rosary beads and put them back in their case. Then, instead, I would tumble down the stairs to get the paper, put a pot of coffee on the stove, and sit in front of the TV until it was time to catch the bus to the university. October passed this way and bled its way into November. I told myself, you have to clean up the bedroom, sort through your mother's things. I'll get up tomorrow and start in on the job. I'll start tomorrow. I'll start first thing in the morning.

I began to fear that the bedroom was going to turn into something from a gothic novel: the deceased person's room left exactly the way it had been on the day she'd died, the books on the shelves and the clock on the wall collecting dust for decades. I'd read too much Edgar Allan Poe, too much Faulkner, not to know how creepy this could become. It was just a very small bedroom, after all. I remember how my mother had to tackle my grandmother's house after her death—thirteen rooms and eighty-two years of pack-rat behavior.

The day Boo died, my mother rolled up her sleeves, and she and I gave the entire downstairs of the house a top-to-bottom scouring before the wake that evening. Then my mother spent a month in that house, cleaning, sorting through items, giving things away, and storing the most treasured keepsakes. She worked with tireless energy even though the task was very tough going. I remember her opening my grandmother's flour bin in the kitchen, a bin that held the main ingredients of all her cakes, cookies, and doughnuts—the foods that had meant celebration and love to us. My mother burst into tears and collapsed into her own hands at the counter. She sobbed until the whole empty house quaked. Then she stopped. When she was finished with the kitchen, she moved on to the dining room.

I stood in the Bosque, the flat desert surrounding me, and knew I had to roll up my sleeves and move from one spiritual room to the next. I couldn't remain in darkness forever. I realized that my journey from Iowa to New Mexico had become a pilgrimage from one wide-open horizon to another, one level plain to the next, one colder, the other drier. But here in New Mexico I was getting the chance to find an anchor, to find bearings, to find moorings. I tried to imitate what Lu had shown me through example—to reach inner peace through acceptance. Still, I knew that the peace I was seeking, the loosening of the rope, the widening of the thumbscrews of the dark night, could only be achieved through fearless confrontation.

I walked into the dark night of New Mexico knowing that the only way out of this desert was through it, knowing the only way out of despair was through a kind of death of the self. That was the true journey, the true pilgrimage. I needed to find the kind of detachment that both St. Teresa of Avila and St. John of the Cross advocated. I needed to step away from my own ego and personal situation. I needed to step away from my needs, worries, and concerns and walk into the spiritual realm. Here on the edge of the water, I needed to surrender to the essence of the void—the knowledge that, yes, I am alone and ultimately unattached to all but one thing: the abyss, the dry desert.

I leaned on my cane. I let the sadness, the anger, and the grief attached to my injury bubble up inside me. I let myself think about all the what-ifs of the situation, all the questions that I wanted to avoid. What if I hadn't gotten back on my feet? What if I had remained in the wheelchair? Where would I be now? Would my darkness have become a darkness of walls rather than birds? What if I never fully regained the use of my limbs? What if I relapse and become paralyzed again? What is down the line? What will happen in old age? What will bring about my death?

I let the questions wash over me and sink into my consciousness. I stood perfectly still and allowed the questions to remain with me, breathing them in with the night. I was so close to the heron that I could have stretched out my arm and touched the bird, yet it did not move. It rested perfectly still on the bank, blinking its eyes at me. For almost five whole minutes it stood there on one leg, its neck curled in. A mule deer doe appeared in the marsh grass, a buck with a full set of antlers trailing behind her. The two emerged in front of me, unprotected by brush or trees, without expectation of harm.

The heron and the deer had surrendered themselves to the night. St. Teresa and St. John, Hildegard and St. Francis had all surrendered themselves to the night. Could I? Spirituality meant the ability to withstand imprisonment, to stand up to the Inquisition, to hold yourself at the water's edge, helping others across the waves without going under yourself. No matter which way the water flowed. No matter how the current pulled and tugged. In chaos I hoped to find inner stillness. In chaos I hoped to face my own aloneness and connect the threads of my existence. In chaos I hoped to connect so profoundly to a higher force that I would never again question its reality. "O guiding night! O night more lovely than the dawn!" St. John had written from his prison cell.

Two months after my mother's death, I was still sleeping on the couch. I never went into the bedroom, so the small apartment became even smaller, shrinking in my mind to the size of a prison cell. By December I knew I had to address my problem. I looked for sales and bought a new bedspread, sheets, and blanket. I took down the old curtains, bought a remnant, and sewed a newer, brighter pair. I sorted through my mother's clothes and took them to Goodwill and a resale shop. I bought a small palm tree in a pot and placed it on a stand under the window. I sifted through and paid all the old hospital bills and filed the insurance forms. I still couldn't bear going through the bedside stand, so I slipped the rosary inside and taped the drawers shut and left that job for a couple of years later.

In December, I finally crawled between the new sheets in the bed. The crisp, cold air blew through the cracks in the window, and I sank down under the covers. I woke on Sunday morning and in robe and slippers shuffled out to the kitchen area and brewed a pot of coffee. With a thermos and one of my schoolbooks in hand, I crept back into bed and luxuriated in diving into the reading material, savoring every word with every drop of the warm liquid that slithered down my throat.

By noon I was dressed and off to the library for an afternoon of research. I returned at a reasonable hour, fixed myself supper, and then loved collapsing back into my bed and drifting off to a restful sleep. My dreams continued, but now it was as if they were sent from heaven. I was sleeping in the bed, and my mother was sitting in the yellow chair. She sat there with me as I had with her. Ella Fitzgerald sang on the little radio, the deep resonance of her voice filling and warming the tiny bedroom. My mother asked me questions about my day, and we chatted as we had during her dying, talking about *The Grapes of Wrath* and the Joads' journey down Route 66, the intrigue of Watergate, the downy woodpeckers at the feeder.

Night after night for months my mother took up residence in the yellow chair and when I had a problem, she helped me talk it through, lending her advice when she could. We talked about death, about dying, about what it feels like to be alone in one's illness, even with someone sitting there beside you in the yellow chair. We talked about what it means to have your strength broken, to be at the end of your rope. We spoke about large things—my plans for the future, my philosophy of living, how one continues on in the face of suffering. We spoke of small things—how I had been searching for the safety deposit key and how she'd left it on a ring wrapped in a napkin tucked into the corner of her purse.

We spoke more freely than when she'd been alive. In the dream, I knew that she was a ghost, a presence only. I knew that I was dreaming. Yet the whole event seemed very real, very concrete. I looked forward to going to sleep and asking her counsel. She helped me through the coldest days of winter when the snow piled up in drifts and the only guests at the Blue Top were the National Guard troops who had been called in to clear the highway.

Then one day in the spring, the crocuses in bloom, the forsythia just about to burst forth in blossom, my mother sat in the chair beside me in my dream and said, "I'm getting tired."

"I'll sit in the chair for a while, and you can lie down on the bed," I said. "Would you like to trade places?"

"I wouldn't trade places for the world," she said.

"Would you like a cup of coffee then?" I asked, and from somewhere under the covers I produced the thermos.

"No, thank you," she said. "I'll be going home now."

And with that, she stood and quietly, ever so silently, without a wave or a glance over her shoulder, walked down the narrow stairs and out the door, never to return again.

I was alone in the dark night.

The dark night began to recede. The sun began its slow rise toward dawn over the marsh, its beams bleeding a deep magenta across the water. The deer leaped across the ditch and back into the brush. The heron lifted off, its head thrust out, its wings open wide. I followed its flight with my binoculars—out over the grasses and reeds—and suddenly my lenses were filled with birds, literally thousands of overwintering snow geese circling the water. The geese landed, their wings flapping, their beaks opening, honking with a cacophony of a string of cars caught in a traffic jam. Their feet alighted on the red sand, the whole bank turning white with the vast numbers of birds.

I drove on down the road another mile and then a woman unexpectedly appeared in my headlights. She stood by the side of the road, waving a bandana, flagging me down.

"I was so excited about the birds that I jumped out of my car to take a picture," she said, "and I locked my keys in my car."

There in front of the snow geese, wading in the water, were the sandhill cranes, their gray bodies blending with the color of the dawn. A muskrat swam past and into its house. Grebes paddled in and out of the reeds. Heads down, mallards dove for fish, their feet and tail feathers bobbing in the water like buoys.

I searched for any tools I might have in the Trooper that could help the woman with her car. Just when we had exhausted the possibilities, two park rangers pulled up beside us. They happened to be carrying a kit for opening locked vehicles.

"I'm Navajo," the woman said, "and my people don't like to have their pictures taken. They say it takes away the spirit. I think the birds were trying to tell me something."

I thought the woman was trying to tell *me* something. I wanted my spirit back. I wanted to move among these birds—the ten bald eagles perched on a stump and the one whooping crane mingling among the sandhills—and feel grounded again. I wanted to go home now to the center of my very being and crawl in between clean, new sheets. Yes, come home now, come home, I begged my spirit. Another heron lighted down in front of me, and the sandhills poked their beaks into the water, hunting for food. I imagined all the birds who had hunted the marsh before them, all the icons of my ancestors who had shown bravery in the face of adversity, all the saints who had dealt with suffering and illness, cycling back generation after generation. In this ever-changing place, this land of wings and flight, I was reminded that life's only permanence is its transience.

Soon, the temperature would change, the wind currents would shift, and the sky would transform the landscape. The snow geese, sandhill cranes, and eagles would all migrate to other environments. What once was would never be again. At the same time, these fleeting moments—the flap of the wings, the click of the beaks—would be replayed next year and the year after. Soon, I would stand in the light, the sun's rays turning to a golden yellow, the full weight of the dark night internalized within me. Soon, I assured myself, I would comprehend the cycle of nature, the cycle of human events, and I would make more sense of my existence. Soon—tomorrow or first thing the next morning—I would come to a better understanding. Soon, I would surrender.

26

"It's a witch! Like me. I want this one!" Lu said, grinning, picking up a Beanie Baby from a table at the Albuquerque Flea Market. Lu was my guide, leading me through this underworld of rickety tables and booths, showing me the underpinnings of her calling, showing me the passionate engagement of a woman who had thrown off the rope and thumbscrews. I had come through the dark night of the Bosque, but I was still searching for my spirit, that spontaneous part of myself that delighted in adventure and sensory experience. I wanted to laugh again, to connect with people again, to be swept up in the fun of the moment. I wanted to move forward with courage and awareness.

Lu fingered a small beanbag doll, a woman riding a broomstick, her nose long and dotted with a mole, a babushka tied around her head. Lu handed the owner of the booth a ten-dollar bill, stuffing the doll down into her purse, the witch's head peeking out over the clasp.

"I'll buy you one, too," Lu said and gave me a small chimp, its tail long and twisted, its head fringed with white fur. I stuck it in my backpack with my turquoise rosary and St. Christopher's medal.

I poked along the flea market with my cane, my legs carrying me past the Beanie Baby booth to one filled with old Wonder Woman comic books, to another crammed full of old hardware—brass doorknobs and hinges taken from once elegant houses. We walked by the next booth full of old china, mismatched and chipped sets of

Haviland. We found a stack of old Mexican phonograph records, the album covers pinned to the back display drape. We took in a table filled with towels and sheets, another piled high with garden trowels, old rusty rakes and hoes propped up against the edge of a board suspended between two sawhorses.

Finally, we came to a table chock-full of old costume jewelry: necklaces and earrings, bracelets and brooches. Lu examined an old necklace made from fake crystal beads. She blew off a coating of dust from the necklace and held the beads up to the light. "*Bueno,*" she said, then rummaged around on the table until she discovered another necklace with similar beads. "Okay, now I would have enough."

"For what?"

"A rosary, silly," she said. "I'll take these apart, shine them up, and make something beautiful. But they're asking way too much money for these old necklaces."

Each string of beads had a price: $5.

"I'll give you two dollars for each of these," Lu said to the owner. She held the beads in her hands and stuck out a five-dollar bill.

The owner, a heavyset man with a pointed nose, shook his head, no.

"Well, they're dirty, and I'll have to clean them up …"

"They're already priced to sell," the man said.

"Well, then, I'll leave them," Lu said, and returned the necklaces to the table.

"How about I just take your five-dollar bill for both of them?" the man asked.

Lu handed him the money and slipped the necklaces in her purse next to her witch.

"Now I want to see if there are any little tins for sale. I need some for my salves," Lu said, and soon we were bent over a table filled with old bottles, jars, and little round tins, their lids decorated with white peonies, clusters of grapes, or sunflowers. Lu opened the lids of the tins, holding them up to her nose, and when she was certain of their freshness, she paid for them and added them to the collection in her purse.

"You see," Lu said, walking away from the booth, "I am quite well known for my treatment of Bell's palsy. I have a certain combination of herbs that I make into a salve, then I have my clients rub it on their cheeks both morning and night. And chew gum. It exercises their jaws. After a few weeks, the condition usually clears up."

Lu was not only famous for curing Bell's palsy but for healing other, difficult conditions. A few weeks earlier I had been asked to give a writing workshop to some physicians at a conference for internal medicine and the arts in Santa Fe. I talked about the components of nonfiction writing, introduced several models, and then asked the participants to free-write the opening of a piece. After about thirty minutes, we regrouped and read the short essays out loud to one another.

One young doctor who worked at the veteran's hospital in Albuquerque began his piece describing the sign that hung on the refrigerator door of one of his patients: DNR—DO NOT RESUSCITATE. The physician had diagnosed his patient with liver cancer and told him that he had just a short time to live—maybe six weeks. The doctor set up hospice care for the patient and sent him home to die. A few months later, the patient returned.

"What in the world happened to you?" the doctor asked. "You're supposed to be dead."

"I'm all better now. I don't have liver cancer," the man said.

"That's impossible," the doctor replied, and repeated his diagnostic tests. To his astonishment, he found no trace of liver cancer.

"But what did you do?" the doctor asked.

The man told him he'd gone to an herbalist who said he didn't have liver cancer in the first place but a severe case of ulcers. She gave him an herbal remedy that healed him within a matter of weeks.

"And that herbalist was you, right?" I asked Lu.

"Oh, yes. That was just one of my cases. I gave him yerba del manzo, and he was fine."

"But how did you know he didn't have cancer?"

"I know. I've had a lot of experience with this sort of thing. And—" Lu paused and said in a quiet voice—"I'm in direct communication with God." She looked up at me, almost apologetically. "That's not to say that the doctor wasn't—"

"I understand."

"I'm not bragging. I just know where my gifts come from."

Lu's gifts came not only from a direct dialogue with a higher consciousness but from a long Hispanic tradition of herbal cures and remedies. Lu's step-grandmother had been a *curandera*. As a child, Lu had watched the older woman minister to neighbors and friends.

"I saw her heal many people," Lu said.

Lu cautioned about *curanderas* whose gifts weren't used properly, those who she felt abused their powers to cast spells and do harm instead of good.

"No, I don't mess around," Lu said. "I get a feeling, a certain feeling about people. I know who are good and bad. Some other *curanderas* are honoring other gods, and when you call down other spirits, you're going to get nasty stuff come into your life. But when you call on the Holy Spirit, things will be well."

Lu told me about Father Sergei and a book he had once given her. The book sat on her counter next to her desk for months, then suddenly it disappeared. Someone had stolen it.

"It was gone for about five years," Lu said. "Then one day a man walked in, a complete stranger, and handed me the book. 'I thought you might like this,' he said. And there it was, my exact copy— Yerbas medicinales by Dr. Peero Alvarez Gonzáles. You see, God makes things possible when he wants to, not when I want to," Lu said.

"And for you, is that the meaning of faith?"

"Sí. To go with the flow of God's will. Not to stop the flow or leap ahead with worry."

I could understand the concept of going with the flow. I could also grasp the damage I often did by fighting the flow. But should I just accept everything? Didn't humans have will? What if I hadn't had the will to get myself up out of that wheelchair and onto the walker? To get myself off the walker and onto the cane? Where did my will stop and Divine will begin? Did surrendering to the Divine mean abandoning my will? Or did it simply mean acknowledging a will stronger than my own?

Lu hurried down to the south side of the flea market where people were selling baked goods and vegetables.

"We need to see if there is any local honey," she said. "If you take local honey, it desensitizes you to local pollens. This is what they did, you see, before allergy shots. Now, I give my people this honey for several months before the pollens fly, and they don't cough and sneeze like before. Before, they were up all night. Never got any sleep. Oh, it can be horrible."

Lu bent over a table of jars of honey. She lifted the jars to the light. She unscrewed the lids and took a tiny taste on her finger.

"Ah," she said. "This says local honey, but I don't feel it is. It has the taste of something too far away."

Lu moved down the line, from table to table, until she found a stack of raw honeycombs, the local owner there to answer her questions.

"Yes," she said, taking one in her hands. "These look like they are right." Lu gathered up five or six combs and stuffed them down around her witch in her purse. "*Bueno.*" She patted the witch on the head. "Sweet dreams."

Witches and chimps, honeycombs, tins and beads all stashed in Lu's Chevy van, we sped away from the flea market, down I-25 through the heart of Albuquerque. We passed the airport, planes circling for landing over our heads.

"Where are we going?" I asked.

"We're going on a desert pilgrimage," she said. "I'll show you where I grew up in Belen. But first we have to make a stop." Lu careened down an exit ramp, the van taking the curve gracefully, the tires hugging the pavement. We pulled up in front of a high-rise retirement home, and Lu hopped out, slamming the door shut. "I just have to drop off a few things for my stepmother," she said.

I leaned my head back on the seat, the warm sun pouring through the window. On the floor next to my feet was a bucket with a few clumps of yerba del manzo, or swamp root, in the bottom. Lu had dug them from the banks of the Rio Grande earlier in the week. I had strolled into her store that day to find her quilting a large brown wall hanging that read: HERBS OF THE RIO GRANDE. She had pushed aside a couple of racks that held the hot water bottles and glow-in-the-dark Jesus statues to make way for her quilting frame. When I went into the shop, she was bent over her material, embroidering a replica of the small gnarled root of yerba del manzo.

"See, I've been invited to the Smithsonian Folklife Festival," she said. "Next summer I'm going to hang this quilt behind me, then set up a huge cauldron of herbs and stand there stirring it. You know, 'Double, double, toil and trouble,'" she said with a laugh.

There was little trouble ahead when Lu came back to the wheel and steered us south, away from the city and out into the desert. In just a few minutes, the vista opened before us, and the tall buildings and traffic vanished into the vastness of the dry landscape. The flatness spread out all around us, the earth tones of the desert—mocha to mauve—creating a graduated blend of colors, a dip of muted, melting Neapolitan ice cream, the chocolate swirling and dripping into the strawberry. The sky reclaimed its presence, the blue backdrop taking up half of the horizon. A single white cloud drifted before our vision. Tumbleweed blew across the road, and on either side of us, sagebrush scattered itself across the expanses.

"Ah, there's silver sage," Lu said. "And there's chaparral." The van veered off the freeway and onto the shoulder of the road. Lu jumped down from her seat and produced a large shears, a small shovel, and a basket from the back of the vehicle. "Come on," she called, and began walking straight into the desert toward a large shrub sticking out of the sand. I tagged along after her, the wind picking up my hair and blowing it away from my face, the cars whipping by on I-25 just a few feet away. Lu snipped off part of the shrub and placed the resinous leaves in her basket. "The Mormons used chaparral—or creosote, some call it greasewood—for cancer treatment. The jury is still out on its effectiveness for that, but it is an antiinflammatory," Lu said.

"And here's rue," Lu said, spotting a small woody shrub. "See, rue is very good for my Bell's palsy people. You smoke it and blow it into their inner ear. During the plague, thieves drank a brew of rue and red wine vinegar, and it was said to protect them while they stole from corpses. So, we'll just steal a little rue."

Lu took a sprig of rue and placed it in her basket. "And we'll dig some yucca, too," she said, her foot braced against the top of the blade, forcing the shovel down into the sand near a clump of the sharp-leafed succulent. "I'll take these roots back to the store and make soap and shampoo with them."

Back in the van, we trundled down the freeway to the Belen exit and got off onto a two-lane, lesser-traveled back road that took us straight into the farming and railroad town. Belen was originally called Belem, or Bethlehem, by the twenty-four founding Spanish families who had fanned out to farm the fertile Rio Grande valley. Once a thriving center of trade, trains whizzed in and out of Belen, delivering passengers and supplies and picking up hides and produce to be shipped throughout the country. Now small adobe houses straggled along the one main street, a rusty tricycle in one yard, a rusty beer can in another.

The van rumbled through town and carried us to the cemetery. We grabbed the basket and shears, and walked among the sand-covered graves.

"Oh, I see mimosa there, just ahead," Lu said.

No marble mow-over tombstones marked these gravesites. No life-size angels or mausoleums memorialized these dead. Instead, two pieces of rotten wood tacked together to form a cross marked one plot. An old upended railroad tie pounded into the ground graced another. Bouquets of plastic flowers—red roses, yellow daffodils—were stuck into the sand. Other graves were simply set off by piles of rocks arranged around the edges of the plot.

"Over here is my family," Lu said, pointing to a cluster of graves near the fence. "See, here's my grandfather and step-grandmother."

We walked around the mounds that had long since been leveled by the winds and blended back into the surrounding sand.

"And this is my mother." Lu stopped in front of a grave wedged in beside her grandparents. She crossed herself and bowed her head.

"Her funeral must've been a sad day," I said.

"*Sí*," Lu nodded. "My mother was a native Indian from Mexico. I look like her side of the family. We have the brown eyes, darker skin. My father's family was from Spain. They had the green eyes, lighter skin."

We stood before the graves for several moments in silence, taking in the desert stillness, letting it circle around us and penetrate our very beings. The smell of the herbs, the feel of the sand working its way into my shoes and lodging between my toes, focused me on this spot, on this grave and what it must mean to my friend.

"But you know something?" Lu said. "My mother's death was the thing that made me what I am today. I had to jump in and be strong. Take care of my younger brothers and sisters." Lu stared straight into my eyes, her own eyes knowing and reassuring. She didn't have to say anything more. Instead, in a moment of unspoken communication, I understood all that she was telling me about the larger pilgrimage of life, the will of the Divine and the shape of human character.

Then Lu's mood brightened. "Here, take my picture." She handed me a small camera. She stood at the foot of her mother's grave, grinning, her hands resting on the wooden cross.

I snapped the photo.

"*Gracias,*" she said, then pointed at a clump of foliage in the distance. "Look, there's orange mallow. And blanket flower."

We took a few snips of each on our way back to the van, then rambled along the outskirts of town and out into the countryside until we came to Lu's old farm. The low-slung, boxy adobe house that once was surrounded by strawberry fields still stood its ground at the center of the homestead. Nestled next to the house, an outdoor brick oven where Lu's mother once baked bread was still intact. An old windmill, its metal blades squeaking and spinning in the spring breeze, still pumped water from underground. Next to the red-handled pump, a catalpa tree unfurled its white blossoms and large heart-shaped leaves over a garage where Lu's brothers once slept. In the distance, cottonwoods and aspens shot up along a drainage ditch that ran water to the Rio Grande and almost claimed the life of Lu's sister who once fell in and couldn't fight the swiftness of the currents. We bounced over a set of railroad tracks.

"I used to lie awake at night and listen to that train whistle blow, and I'd cry," Lu said. "I'd wail right along with the train."

I held the two images in my mind—one of the small girl crying in desperation, and the other of the older woman who healed the desperate wounds of her people. I could easily understand how the threads of this *curandera's* life had come together and created coherence.

Lu pulled the van over to the side of the road. "Look, horsetail!" she called. "*Cola de caballo. Vamos, vamos.*"

We gathered up an armful of the reeds, long hollow stems that rose up out of the ditch in a shower of green.

"The early settlers used horsetail for cleaning and sanding," Lu said, "to scour their pots and the like. But I make a horsetail tea. It builds the blood, hardens the fingernails, makes your hair grow. It's also a diuretic. And an astringent. Good for treating bladder and prostate problems, and kidney stones. It contains silica. Good for the connective tissues."

Once we'd loaded the truck with horsetail, we walked down to the drainage ditch to wash our hands. The clear, cool liquid ran over our fingers, the water reflecting the pinkish color of the soil. We knelt there and enjoyed the feel of the coldness on our fingertips. Tome Hill, a sacred site, loomed behind us.

A few weeks before, I had come to Tome on Good Friday when every year thousands of pilgrims climb El Cerro, the hill that rises 250 feet above Valencia County. People had lined the sides of the roads, old people with walking sticks, young people with baby strollers, and groups of teenagers, their arms swinging, backpacks slung over their shoulders, water bottles and cellular phones hanging from their belts.

At the foot of the hill, a Schwan's truck and a family Kool-Aid stand fortified the worshipers before their long climb. A fifty-year-old woman, sun visor pulled down over her eyes, squatted on a rock, licking an ice-cream cone. Children in shorts and T-shirts slurped the sugary Kool-Aid from paper cups. An old man stood ready to make the ascent, a wooden cross in his hand. A group of five or six young men, fellow pilgrims, each with a pit bull on a leash, pooled together on a rock, their faces turned toward the jagged path, their pets sitting obediently at their feet. Then with a mixture of joyous camaraderie and solemn piety, we were all swept up in the climb, one foot finding its bearing on the lava rock, another slipping on a piece of shale, the sagebrush zigzagging all around, the sun shining on our backs.

Once, centuries ago, the Anasazis, an ancient tribe of American Indians, had climbed the hill. Then the Penitentes. After World War II, Lu's cousin returned to his hometown to build a memorial to fallen soldiers. He worked for a year on three 15-foot-tall crosses of railroad lumber and sheet metal that he finally erected on top of El Cerro.

"For decades my cousin led the procession up the hill," Lu had told me on Holy Thursday. "But this year a stroke landed him in a nursing home. So his son will lead the way."

Almost to the top of the hill, I had stepped off the path for a brief rest and let the pit bulls race past me, their mouths open, paws flying. I leaned back against a boulder and listened to Lu's cousin, a young man in jeans and a cotton sweater who looked more like a real estate salesman than a devout believer, lead the pilgrims in song. I pushed on and reached the top of the hill. The melodies of the Spanish hymns carried down the hillside to the flat valley below, where a single tractor crisscrossed the alfalfa field that was just beginning to turn green.

"We must learn to confront our suffering," a Franciscan monk said, addressing the crowd that was milling around, happily shaking hands with old friends, throwing their arms around relatives, visiting, and laughing. The monk pressed on through the Stations of the Cross and passed around a loaf of bread for communion. A man in a cowboy hat played taps on a bugle. Lu's cousin placed his hand on his heart. We all joined in a chorus of "God Bless America." A moment of silence followed, the sun shining so brightly now that its beams seemed to ricochet off the Monzano Mountains in the distance and bounce back, penetrating my skin with a burning warmth that was at once comforting and painful.

The old man with the cross began picking his way downward, his eyes fixed on the ground. Then, panting and barking, the pit bulls catapulted over the rocks, and the teenagers raced down the sacred hill toward the ice-cream truck and the Kool-Aid stand.

"*Bueno*," Lu said. "El Cerro is steep. In your pilgrimage up that hill a few weeks ago, you learned to take small steps, one after another. In your larger journey, you must assume this same pace. It may seem like you are going nowhere and will never arrive at your destination, but if you are steadfast, you will find your place. Now you've seen where I grew up, how I've come to be who I am, what steps I've taken. Someday you will discover yourself, what purpose you have on earth."

We flicked our hands through the water once more, our spread fingers making rivulets in the stream. Then we dried our hands on our jeans and headed home.

27

"Who *are* you?" Father Sergei asked, staring at me as if I were an apparition, a wondrous but strange thing before his eyes. During the months that we'd been meeting, he had never even asked my name. I had said little about my background or myself. We sat and talked together, and no matter where his mind went, it gave me insight and solace.

"I am a pilgrim seeking healing," I said.

"Oh, you're looking for miracles from God on high!" The monk laughed, a tender but slightly sarcastic chuckle.

"I'm sure everyone comes here wanting something from you," I said by way of apology.

"No, no," he said. "It's a sign of faith."

It had been raining, one of the few rainy afternoons I'd experienced in New Mexico, the sky suddenly darkening, the water falling down in thick sheets, pounding the pavement. Without break or letup, the rain had fallen relentlessly in a steady downpour, as if trying to make up for the past few months of dryness. The wind had driven the rain into the windshields of passing cars, their wipers furiously pumping back and forth. The wind had blown up, catching beneath my umbrella, the umbrella I'd been carrying around uselessly for months, a fixture at the bottom of my Iowa briefcase. It had been difficult to navigate, my cane in one hand, my umbrella in the other. I'd ducked under the awning of the hardware store to shelter myself from the torrent. Then, with water plastering my hair to my ears, I'd tottered to Father Sergei's.

The monk had shown me into his little garage-church, the windowless room dark and still. He lit a couple of the votive candles at the entrance to the sanctuary, then eased himself down cross-legged on the floor, the shadowy light illuminating his face. He sat in the lotus position, his body moving stiffly and slowly, his legs folding underneath him.

Water trickled down onto my blouse. The rain pounded on the roof and swirled through the gutters in the streets outside. I stared up at a sheep's skull tacked to the wall.

"My people here love the visual," Father Sergei said, "the auditory, the olfactory—the things of the senses. That's why I have this chapel filled with so many colors and smells—to stimulate the body to pull the exterior journey of the world into the interior world of the soul. Here, smell this." The monk reached over and pressed into my hand one of the damp cotton balls from the statue of the weeping Virgin Mary. Rosaries were draped over a small wooden scaffolding surrounding the statue. The monk grabbed another cotton ball and offered it to me. "Smell it," he said. "The tears always smell fragrant—like roses."

I held up the cotton ball, its perfume enveloping my nose.

"My people come here and take these cotton balls home and place them on their ill loved ones, and the sick become healed," the monk said. "Then they return and bring pictures of their cured." Curling and cracked Polaroids secured by straight pins hung from the scaffolding encasing the Virgin. The photos created a collage of images from the parishioners' lives: a small child riding a bicycle, a middle-aged mail carrier toting his bag, an old woman stepping out of bed, her walker left behind.

"My people don't need these cotton balls," the monk said. "They can be cured without them. But the cotton balls provide a symbol for them, and the sick are healed."

Well, I thought, I suppose if you believe enough in anything, miracles will happen. In my imagination, I was still standing on the edge of the marsh, unable to surrender to the idea of the Divine.

"Ah." The monk shook his head at me as if he were reading my mind again. "That attitude will get you nowhere. You could be cured right now, at this very minute, if you would only stand firm in your faith," Father Sergei said, turning around, his eyes meeting mine, their darkness riveting through me with the precision of an electric drill. "See, people come here and want miracles but don't really believe. It doesn't work that way. I don't perform the miracles. I do nothing but guide you along your pilgrimage. And you must remember that all of life is one big pilgrimage—not just your little hike up El Cerro or even your trip to New Mexico. Those are mini-pilgrimages in the grand scale of things. Your life has a route it follows, a path that carries you where you need to go. You have to realize you're on that path, and you need to stop taking detours this way and that, stop wishing you were on the freeway instead of Route 66."

"But how do you know you're on the right road?" I asked, wondering how Father Sergei knew about my pilgrimage up El Cerro or my metaphorical detours along my longer route.

"When you're on the spiritual path, you're on the right road. Have faith you're on the right road," Father Sergei said. "Listen, there was a mother who brought her young daughter here the other day. The daughter was deaf. The mother had taken her to the doctors, but they could do nothing. 'Oh, *Papa*, won't you help my daughter!' the woman begged. 'I can help your daughter, and I will,' I said. I sat her down on the bench right where you are. I spit on my two fingers and placed them in the daughter's ears. The girl closed her eyes, and I began to chant a prayer of healing in Russian.

"'But what if it doesn't work?' the mother cried. 'What if it doesn't work?'

"'And it's not going to work with you asking that question,' I said. 'You of little faith, go on out of this room right now. Immediately.' I kicked her out. I returned to the daughter, the girl who had perfect faith. I spit on my fingers again and placed them in her ears. I chanted. I asked that God's healing powers come down upon her. We joined together in our prayer, and after a few minutes the girl said that she could hear my voice. She raced outside and found her mother and told her that her deafness was gone!

"So that's the kind of faith you have to have," the monk said, "the faith of a little child. You must come to the kingdom of God like an innocent."

"I used to have that kind of faith," I said.

"*Sí.* And as we grow older, our own sophistication blocks us."

"I had faith in the miracles of science then, too. Now I have less faith in the mastery of humans and more in the Divine."

"Good. You see, the failure of science in your life released you to have more faith in God. You have to understand these paradoxes. The incidents, the events, the disappointments in your life you thought were truly sad, frustrating, and sorrowful were really joyful. You cannot label an experience good or bad. You never know how it's going to ultimately turn out. Then once you learn to stop making judgments, you totally surrender to the Divine."

"But how does that surrender happen?"

"Through prayer."

"I'm not sure I even know how to pray anymore. Teach me the best way."

"You journey down the sacred hill of deep mystical pilgrimage through the practice and the recitation of the Jesus prayer or meditation. You practice inner stillness," Father Sergei said, tossing a pebble in the air and clasping it in his hand on its descent. "And to understand the Jesus prayer, you must know that the Western church developed along the lines of rationalism, but the East stuck with a mystical theology, a desert spirituality."

Desert spirituality had a long tradition in Judaism, Father Sergei explained. Many of the prophets received their visions in the desert. The Covenant was forged in the wilderness of Sinai. During the time of Christ, a monastic group called the Essenes lived in isolation in the desert. Both Jesus and John the Baptist may have been connected to the Essenes. They retreated to the desert outside Jerusalem to pray and purge themselves of evil before they began their ministries.

The early Christians carried on the desert tradition by setting up monasteries in Egypt—an outgrowth of a movement begun by St. Anthony of Egypt, one of the first Desert Fathers. He organized his followers into small communities in the desert early in the fourth century. These holy men and women denounced worldly goods, sexual relations, and family ties, taking up a life of poverty, seclusion, and prayer. The monks who went into the desert as hermits thought they were answering the call of Christ: "If you would be perfect, go, sell what you possess, and give to the poor, and you will have treasure in heaven; and come, follow me." The hermits lived an austere life, devoting themselves to poverty, service, self-denial, work, and prayer.

"I don't exactly get it," I said. "Everyone who lives in the desert and practices an austere life is practicing desert spirituality?"

"The desert is often a physical reality, yes," Father Sergei said. "I've tried to show you that there's a long tradition of people going out into the desert to pray. The desert usually strips you of distraction and creates a harsh environment that more easily focuses your attention on the task at hand. But the desert is also a symbol for what's going on inside you. You are stripped of attachments. You become detached and stare yourself in the face. You confront your own foibles. You give up your self-centeredness and realize you have to rely on your faith in God."

"So you don't need the physical desert to go through this process?" I asked.

"No, you can face down your demons anywhere."

"Even in Iowa?"

"Even in Iowa." The monk laughed, his beard bobbing against his chest. He shifted his weight on the floor, stretching his back, his toes wiggling in his sandals. The votive candles burned lower, the melted wax—liquid and hot—filling the glass holders and spilling over the edge. The rain splashed against the window in the door.

"The Jesus prayer is the seed of desert spirituality," Father Sergei said. "It's a quiet prayer. You say the name of Jesus over and over in faith and love. Some repeat the phrase, 'Lord Jesus Christ, Son of God, have mercy on me.'"

"That's it?"

"That's it," the monk said. "Seemingly so simple, but so very powerful. It's like a mantra. It takes you to another place, a place where you concentrate body and spirit on the energy of God. You see, the stark, open landscape became the perfect backdrop for the meditation. The desert became the void for those early monks. The Western Church with its mind-body split could never understand this kind of prayer. They liked linear, spoken prayers. The Eastern Church went in another direction with this unifying silent prayer. It comes from the heart. The whole person is involved—mind, body, and soul."

"Show me how it works," I said.

"Okay," Father Sergei said. "Watch me. Just sit there and watch. I breathe deeply." The monk straightened himself, his backbone stiffening. He inhaled from his diaphragm, the air trickling out his nose slowly, his lungs emptying. "Now, first, you enter a state of quiet," the monk said. "Don't try to think things out. Don't call any images to mind. Don't read or recite anything. Just stay calm. Then concentrate, say the name of Jesus. Say the name of Jesus with devotion. Say it to yourself. Repeat the word over and over while you keep up your breathing until your breathing becomes rhythmical."

In, out, in, the monk's breathing flowed; in out, in, his whole chest expanding, contracting, his eyes closed.

"Now I let my mind sink back into the unifying concept: All is One. All my energies join together—mental, spiritual, physical. All is One. A sense of warmth comes over me as if there is a fire in my heart. God's heart is on fire. My heart and God's heart are one. I feel the fire move through my whole body. I feel the energy moving."

The monk's breath became shallower. Slowly, blinking, his lashes fluttering, he opened his eyes, his whole face relaxed, refreshed. He stretched his arms and yawned. "Now that I've taught you how to pray, forget it."

"Forget it?"

"That's right. There is no right way to pray. There are traditions, but there are no exact formulas. Pray the way that feels good to you."

"What about this idea of praying without ceasing?" I asked. "How is that possible?"

"Let's get that straight," Father Sergei said. "That doesn't mean you walk around in a trance all day saying the Jesus prayer. If you do that, you'll just bump into things and stub your toes. You can't do two things at once. Praying without ceasing simply means to be mindful, to do everything that you do with an awareness that you are doing God's work."

"Everything is God's work?" I asked. "Everything that happens to us is blessed by God?"

"Okay, look. You've been in a car accident, right? That's my guess." Father Sergei said.

"Yes," I said, realizing that the monk had great intuitive powers. He seemed to know my story without my having verbalized it.

"Well, sometimes we're given those challenges to rally our systems." Father Sergei rocked back on his haunches, stroking his beard, his eyes scanning the red oriental carpet on the floor. "See, I was in an accident as a boy. I was on my bicycle and run over by a car. Broke every bone in my body. I was in traction, too, strung up everywhere. My legs, my arms were in casts. Only my little toe was sticking out. I was in so much pain, I wanted to die. I wanted to give up. My family was there and didn't know how to help me. Finally, early one morning on rounds, the doctor came in and tweaked my big toe.

"'*Chico*,' he said, 'you have to rally. You have to get up and out of this bed.' That was good for me."

"So God's tweaking my toe?"

"Okay, you've already had one healing, right? You were paralyzed and never supposed to walk again. *Correcto?*"

"*Sí.*" Again, I was astonished by the accuracy of the monk's perceptions.

"You picked up your pallet and walked. And now you want another miracle?"

"*Sí.*"

"You're a glutton!" Father Sergei joked, his eyes shifting out of the power drill mode and now sparkling with playfulness.

"I'd like to get out of pain and off this cane."

"You don't need that cane."

"Easy for you to say."

"The great mystic Hildegard said she'd noticed that God does not enter totally well bodies. So you're in a crisis. You have to have a crisis to find your faith. It doesn't work any other way. I had to be run over by a car and almost killed as a child to become a healer. How else would I know what it feels like to have pain? It's my archetype, my role that I'm fulfilling in life, my script that's come down to me from generation to generation, my history, the healing of my own people, the healing of my history that has made me whole.

"You have a similar mission. You not only have to heal your own wounds but, by doing so, you will heal the wounds of your ancestors—injuries that go back for centuries. All the broken necks, all the broken hearts. Call it karma, or what have you. You must return to your icons and let them be your guides. You can't stay in your bed and let your heavy casts from the past weigh you down. You must straighten your limbs. You are all bent and crooked now like one of the junipers in the mountains, blown over by the wind. You right yourself and you will right all those around you."

"How?"

"You will block the wind! Then they will no longer be broken. Look, you must take the teaching of the mystics to heart. You must take up a practice of some kind of meditation and find inner stillness. To do so you must live the spiritual life, not necessarily the religious life. There's a difference."

"And that is?"

"To be religious means that you engage in a certain ritual toward a certain deity. And that's fine. We need to pray together in groups, and it doesn't really matter how we conceptualize God. That's cultural. But to be spiritual means that you connect with the energy that holds you to the earth. But you already know that. You've done it before, and you can do it again—whether you are paralyzed flat on your back or up and walking on your feet."

"But how do you hold that center?"

"You cultivate it in your prayer life. That's what I've been trying to teach you. Now stand and I'll give you my blessing of healing."

Father Sergei placed his hands on my head, his fingers pressed down firmly on my wet hair. He closed his eyes. He began to sway, his body moving back and forth, back and forth, his lips parting in chant and his voice whispering "El Paso del Mar Rojo," the prayer of the Jews as they sailed toward Turkey after their expulsion from

Spain, the chant of a people trying to combat despair, trying to reach a long-lost promise of safety.

> When the people of Israel
> fled from Egypt singing,
> the women and the children
> left singing the Song of Songs ...
>
> Moses saw Pharaoh pursuing them
> with a red flag.
> "Where have you brought us, Moses,
> to die in these sands
>
> to die with no graves
> or to be drowned in the sea?"
> "Do not be afraid, my people,
> do not despair ..."
>
> Let us remember the miracles
> of God on high.
> He is One, there is no other,
> he is Master of all the world.

"Go now," Father Sergei said, the votive candles flickering. He threw open the door of the church. The rain had stopped, and the sun was trying to break through the cloudy sky. "Go now out of this darkness, into the light."

28

After my mother's spirit had exited my dreams at the Blue Top Motel, insomnia entered my nights again. I lay there in bed, the clock ticking away, knowing that I needed to sleep, knowing that I didn't function well without it. Oh, no, I'd think to myself, now it's only six hours before dawn. That's not enough sleep, and I have an exam at nine in the morning. Oh, no, now it's only five hours before dawn. Now four, now three.

Worries flooded my mind. What was I going to do after I graduated? Where was I going to get a job? Where was I going to live? How was I going to get my belongings there by myself? Would I have to drive my own U-Haul? Anxieties spun around and around in my mind until I heard the clock strike out its notes, and then my thoughts only accelerated.

Finally, one night, I thought, enough of this. I randomly selected a letter of the alphabet—Z—and blew the image up very big in my mind. When I closed my eyes, I only saw Z and nothing but Z. I didn't articulate anything. I just visualized the letter Z. Thoughts charged in and tried to usurp Z's place, but I would insist on its presence, letting the intruders drift away.

Soon my mind quieted, my anxieties calmed. My breathing slowed into a steady, rhythmical pace. I would hold the image in my mind for as long as it took to fall asleep. And it worked every time. I became better and better at my method, and over the course of a few months, I was lessening the time it took to induce sleep. Soon, I was dropping off five or ten minutes after my head hit the pillow. I seemed to have conquered my insomnia. Whenever it reappeared, I took up the practice again, sometimes for variation selecting another letter of the alphabet, whatever came to mind.

It wasn't until I was in my thirties that I realized I'd taught myself to meditate. Meditation had become a popular movement at the time. Among my friends there were transcendental, Zen Buddhist, and Eckankar meditators. Just seventy-five miles away was Maharishi University, or Guru U., as we called it. Many people I knew drove there for a series of lessons in meditation. At their final class they paid $500 to receive their mantras.

"And what is a mantra?" I asked.

"A word or phrase that you center on while you're meditating."

Oh. I realized I'd saved myself a bunch of money. Yet many of these people were doing interesting things with their discipline. They developed better self-confidence and felt more attuned to the world. They became successful entrepreneurs. And some of them who practiced meditation three times a day even levitated—actually hopping up into the air a few inches.

Meditation was not an unfamiliar concept to me. When I was a child, no one in my family, neighborhood, or circle of friends ever mentioned it. But the Visitation nuns who taught me and kept those relics of St. Jeanne de Chantal in their deep pockets were a cloistered order with a foundation in French mysticism. The nuns frequently spoke of meditation but offered few specifics. From what I could gather, you went into the chapel, knelt down, and had a conversation with God, letting your inner voice guide you in reply. Or you thought about a Gospel passage carefully and deeply, inserting yourself somewhere in the scene, empathizing with the other characters in the drama. Both of these ideas appealed to me. They seemed like a kind of intimate, personal prayer.

What I loved most was to go into the school chapel early in the morning and hear the nuns chant the Divine Office. Behind the wooden grille, a massive screen of crisscrossed pieces of lathe, sixty black figures, half on one side of the aisle, half on the other, swiveled around and bowed to each other, then turned again and bowed to the altar. They sang the Psalms in Latin, their voices, sometimes deep and melodious, sometimes high and squeaky, floating up toward the ceiling. They took turns in the role of the cantor, the person who stood and sang the antiphon in solo, the rest of the community responding in kind. Some of the nuns had beautiful, clear voices. Others could not hit a note. But it didn't seem to matter. The momentum of the chant carried the prayer along, the errors and flaws of the moment all part of the event.

I knew enough Latin to pick out a few words here and there, but mostly the chants were coming toward me as if sung in some deep, primitive tribal language. In its slow, hypnotic way, the Divine Office touched the cord that alters consciousness, lifting me out of my ordinary schoolgirl existence into something more ethereal. I knew little about the Psalms, but I could grasp enough to understand that as the calendar moved through the liturgical cycle, the prayers journeyed through the cycle of emotions of humankind: anger, grief, sadness, longing, revenge, comfort, relief, victory, joy, happiness.

Here was a time when all other thoughts cleared my mind, and I could sit on the hard wooden pew just feeling the pure sensation of that particular hour of that particular day. It was a perception of being surrounded by an abstraction, an idea, without the need to tack that spirit down to a human form. At that point I didn't need all the statues that filled the chapel, the beautiful cloths and crucifixes that adorned the altar. I could close my eyes and be transported, transformed.

It took me years to connect my insomnia cure with the chanting of the Office. One seemed like a simple mind trick, the other a truly spiritual experience. And during those decades when I thought I'd given up the silliness of religion, the shadowy image of nuns behind the spaces of a wooden grille came back to me, figures that I could hear but not see, only the outlines of their forms visible, figures who sang with one voice, a voice composed of many resonances. The sight, sound, and texture of that scene held me in its grip.

In my mid-thirties, I embarked on a study of hypnosis. It led me to realize that there are many ways to induce trance, many ways to contact the subconscious. Holding a number or letter in mind was one. Listening to chants in a foreign language was another. While in trance, a positive suggestion often resulted in a positive result in the so-called waking world. Or even without suggestion, the trance state itself was relaxing, restorative. I realized how it might be used to enhance relief of back pain or insomnia, and how it might also be conducive to prayer. I realized how the state was the basis of shamanism. True shamans made trancelike pilgrimages of the spirit, seeking to contact the supernatural world and bringing back healing cures for their tribes to better serve the community. Visualization, meditation, and prayer were processes mere moments away from one another.

I have kept up my alphabet meditation most of my life. It has been there for me in times of extreme stress, providing me with more control and more effectiveness than any sleeping pill. I also learned to use the imagery of hypnosis, to create and work with the icons of my own inner world. Like the inside of Father Sergei's garage-church, my mind filled with pictures—concrete, specific representations of people, places, or events—which then became metaphors. If I wanted to do well in a job interview, I imagined myself the winner of the Tour de France, my bicycle wheel spinning over the finish line, the crowd cheering. If I wanted to lose weight, I imagined myself a sleek gazelle bounding across the plains.

I was a poet. These mind pictures and bodily sensations were not difficult to harness. In one discipline, I recorded them on paper, and in another, I recorded them on the screen behind my eyes. I learned enough about the Chinese system of acupuncture points that I didn't have to go to an acupuncturist but could simply visualize the placement of a couple of needles and relieve headaches and minor aches and pains. I carried all this knowledge in my head, and even though meditation, hypnosis, and acupuncture weren't the subjects of the classical education my grandfather had in mind, I slowly began to understand the significance of his remarks: Education is the only thing that they can't take away from you.

The knowledge of these simple ways to focus the mind in order to enhance the body gave me the power to change my life. If nothing else, they freed me from a lifetime dependency on the pharmaceutical companies and perhaps an addiction to prescription drugs. I practiced my alphabet meditation. I practiced hypnosis, and long after the Catholic Mass had switched from Latin to English, long after the Gregorian chants were replaced with guitar Masses, I bought tapes and CDs of medieval sacred music, the voices of the singers sweeping me up, carrying me to a place deep inside my subconscious.

"To pray without ceasing, you must be mindful that your whole life is a prayer," Father Sergei had told me.

"You must begin the day with prayer," Lu had said.

Soon I found myself substituting the image of Jesus or Mary for the letter in my alphabetical meditation. I fingered Lu's turquoise rosary, placing just one word, one image on each bead. Then I let myself drift into the sensation of goodness, of the love or warmth that I had felt in my school days in the chapel. I let myself drift into the love and warmth I'd felt as a child from my ancestors, the mothers of all the mothers who had mothered me. I took long, deep breaths, falling into a rhythm, letting the rising and falling of my diaphragm and chest carry me along. Physically, I never left the ground, nor did I want to, but mentally, I was elevated into another sphere.

During these moments I could understand levitation—both at Guru U. and at St. Teresa's Convent of the Incarnation. I could understand shamanlike flights of imagination. I could understand the healing powers of both a *curandera* and a *converso* monk. I pulled the strength of those energies into myself—both female and male—searching for the safety of my desert stillness, of my path toward home. But more than anything else I felt I was on my way to a higher consciousness. I ferried myself across the waters to a place where the scapegoating and the suffering imposed by human power structures was alleviated. I ferried myself across the waters and found safety.

I prayed over and over again each night before I went to sleep, my fingers moving across the beads, my mind blanking, my mind concentrating, releasing, fixated on healing. Finally, one morning I bent my knee, and the pain was there but tempered, its voice modulated. It had given up its fear, its usual snarling articulations. My joints moved more easily. I could raise my leg without wincing. I bent my other knee and experienced the same sensation. Not a total cure but a waning, a lessening of the fullness of the pain. When I had arrived in New Mexico, my pain was ripe and full. Now it hung there above me like the morning moon, an outline of what it had been.

I lifted my right arm and it seemed to glide through the air by itself, recognizing its proper arc and function. No longer did I have to command its path, its journey across the water. No longer did I have to trick it to do its work, prod it to sail forth with the wind at its back, to beg it to function for just one hour before it could rest. That morning, my arm still had its doubts about its journey, but it pushed on. The mutiny was over. My arm wanted to cooperate with the rest of my body, to actively engage in the voyage.

My mind joined my body. Slowly, I sensed my spirit was returning to me. I no longer felt as if my psyche were flying off somewhere over the marsh. Now my flights of imagination were internal. I still experienced flashbacks, with their continually spinning slide-tray of past traumas, but now I could watch those slices of life with interest rather than horror as they clicked by. I tried to take Lu's larger view that all events—good and bad—ultimately shape our character and will play out later in life. Patience, I told myself, have patience. In time these events may look different to you. I tried to take Father Sergei's view that one healing could affect others. "All the broken necks. All the broken hearts," he'd told me. Still, I didn't feel that I could gather up all the threads of my life and make sense of them. I called on my icons—my mother and grandmother, Hildegard, St. Teresa, St. Francis, and St. John of the Cross—for help.

At last I felt as if I was pushing on toward a state of stronger courage and wider vision. And I had finally found the guts to return to the transverse myelitis support group Website. Methodically, I clicked my way through the stories of those who had posted their photos on the site. All had spent long months in hospitals and physical therapy facilities. Some were permanently living in rehab units. None were able to walk on their own. A young woman of eighteen who was able to get herself up on crutches wrote, "Push yourself to try to get out of that wheelchair. Connect with the deepest strength you have inside yourself and try, at least try, to put weight on your leg and take that first step."

29

I n mid-April, I found myself in the barrio church parking lot, hat on my head, facing the intense morning sun and standing unaided without my cane. Father Corazón, the Catholic parish priest, was shaking hands with the mayor of Albuquerque. The local alderwoman milled through the gathering crowd, smiling and nodding to the greetings from her constituents. A band of mariachis was warming up their instruments, the guitar player tuning his strings, the trumpet player sounding a few bars, their sombreros bobbing, shading their eyes.

It was the morning of a street festival, the blessing of the new bus stop shelters and the plaza, a celebration complete with dancers from Carmen and Rafael's troupe and Mexican food in recognition of the cleanup effort in the barrio. Months before, the neighbors had banded together to counteract the drugs and crimes in the area. Neighbors had loaded into pickup trucks with megaphones and pulled up in front of the crack houses. "Get out of our neighborhood!" they had shouted at the drug dealers. "We take back our street!"

The city had funded a grant for an architect to design the bus shelters. He had completed the project, decorating every bus stop shelter on the street with tiles made by local schoolchildren. Etched into the clay were the pictures children had drawn of local businesses—both old and new—that lined the boulevard. Now the whole neighborhood took on a different feel. The street was swept, the gutters cleared of litter. In addition to the café, a couple of new businesses had received a fresh coat of paint before opening their doors for business. People were sitting on the porches of their houses, holding babies. Others were walking down the street, chatting with one another. Grandsons and granddaughters pulled and tugged at the hands of their grandparents, attempting to move them along faster down the sidewalk.

"Tomorrow is the street festival," Lu said to a customer when I had visited her in her store the day before. "You're coming, aren't you?"

The customer, a large woman with jet-black eyes, smiled and nodded.

"And you come, too," Lu said to me.

The customer glared at me, her look taking me in, from the top of my head all the way down to my shoes. She glanced back at Lu.

"She's blond-haired and blue-eyed," Lu told the woman, "but she's okay."

With that endorsement I knew I had to show at the festival. The next day I arose early, my arms and legs moving with greater ease than I had previously known. The healing forces of New Mexico—from the sun and dirt to my work with Lu and Father Sergei—had all continued to have a slow but powerful effect. Meditation, prayer, and the inclusion in a circle of friendship in the barrio had helped me still more. I'd pulled myself out of the pit of loneliness and rediscovered both my sense of connection with others and my love of solitude. Gradually, I'd reached the point where I was ready to try to walk alone without the cane in the middle of a crowd—at least for one morning.

I gobbled down a quick breakfast then drove the six blocks to the barrio, but when I pulled my car into the parking lot, I suddenly decided to leave my cane in the car. The pain in my legs was still there, but less severe. I thought I could let go of the cane for this one morning and pick it up again if I needed to that afternoon. I was the only *gringa* in this crowd. I already called attention to myself. I didn't want the double difference of an appendage.

I locked my cane in the trunk and took my first few steps in public without an aid in more than a year. At home I'd scooted around my apartment without the cane, grabbing the kitchen counter, the chair, and then the bureau for balance. I had these pieces of furniture lined up strategically, stringing them out across the room to form a kind of railing of their own. Like a blind person, I knew where they were by touch and could get myself to the bathroom in the middle of the night without even having to turn on the light. But in public the cane gave me the necessary support I needed to raise one foot in front of the other and keep me from tottering over on the sidewalk when my knees buckled. The cane gave me the strength I required to rise from a seated position.

I stepped into the parking lot, both arms free, feeling nimble and light. The mayor reached over and shook my hand, the alderwoman right behind him. They both treated me like an honored guest and directed me to the front of the procession, right behind Father Corazón and the mariachis.

"*Buenos días,*" I said to the mayor and alderwoman. "*Mucho gusto.*" What I really wanted to say was: This is all a mistake. I'm really a *gringa* gimp from Iowa who walks with a cane. You don't want me at the front of the parade. I'll just slow you down.

But it was too late. The mariachis had assembled, guitar players at the head of the procession, horn players falling in behind, their white suits reflecting the brilliant sun. The band began playing, the music loud and joyful, the sound of the brass and strings echoing down the street, the soft sides of the pink and brown adobe storefronts absorbing the noise. Father Corazón, dressed in pink vestments, followed behind the band, a cutting of a juniper bough in one hand and an altar boy in a long white cassock and hood carrying a bucket of holy water beside him.

We moved forward, the crowd pressing in around us, several hundred people singing, swaying to the music, their hips rotating, their hands clapping. My legs seemed to have a mind of their own, falling in with the beat of the band, each step easier than the last, each step transporting me to a place where the act of walking was once again natural and unconscious, the essence of being human— standing up on your own two feet, alone, unaided, in front of the masses. Father Corazón dipped the juniper bough in the bucket and with a flick of his wrist sprinkled holy water on the first bus stop shelter. He bowed to the bench. The crowd bowed to the bench. Father Corazón crossed himself. We crossed ourselves. The children who had made the tiles for that shelter stood in front of the bus stop bench and beamed, their parents behind them with hands on their shoulders, smiles wide across their faces. A reporter for the Albuquerque paper snapped a photo.

We marched on, down to the next corner, to the next bus stop just opposite the door of Father Sergei's church. Lu stood in front of her drugstore, smiling and waving a red scarf, her hand moving up and down, bending at the wrist. My feet moved up and down, bending at the ankles, my legs carrying me along with the flow of the crowd, going with the flow. Father Corazón shook hands with Father Sergei, who appeared in his black cassock with a heavy silver-chained crucifix around his neck. They bowed to each other. They bowed to the bus stop. Holy water sprinkled down on my forehead, ran down my cheek.

Father Corazón blessed the doorway of every storefront—the drugstore, the hardware store, the refurbished café, the old boarded-up store that once sold wool and hides—the holy water falling down, down, evaporating in an instant in the hot sun. The crowd paused with each blessing, the neighbors halting their chatter long enough to cross themselves and catch a few droplets of water. At the end of the business district, we flooded into the plaza, the mariachis booming out their melodies, the children's folk dance troupe swirling round and round in their red vests and skirts, the puffed sleeves of their white blouses billowing out from their arms. Antonio wore a large sombrero and kept the beat for all, his feet flying over the paving stones. The boy in the wheelchair pivoted around Antonio, his head nodding toward his left shoulder then toward his right.

The mariachis belted out another tune. Long banquet tables were unfolded in the plaza and loaded down with tacos and burritos, soda pop, chips and dip. The neighbors circled around the food, balancing a paper plate, cup, and plastic silverware in their hands.

The daughter of the owner of the former tortilla factory stepped up to the microphone. "Today, we celebrate our neighborhood," she said, "a neighborhood that once made us proud, a neighborhood that is making us proud once again."

One by one, the children who had made the ceramic tiles came forward and told of how they had researched the history of the street, how it had once been prosperous, how now they feared for their lives here, how they wanted things to change, how most of all they wanted to be rid of drugs and crime.

One by one, older people told how this street used to be the *camino real*, the main path through New Mexico, how the street used to be Route 66, the main path through the United States. The elders told of how they went out at Christmas and begged for treats, reciting a verse:

> *Angelitos somos, del cielo*
> *venimos, pidiendo regolos*
> *y Sí no cumplen ventanas*
> *y puertas quebraremos y*
> *castigos les desearemos.*

> *We are angels from Heaven,*
> *we come, asking for gifts.*
> *If you don't comply, windows*
> *and doors we shall break and*
> *wish punishment upon you.*

The elders never thought they would see a day when the windows and doors of the area would be broken. As children, the biggest threat came from gypsies, not drugs. Every year for at least a month the gypsies camped in the woods down by the river. Everyone hurried home to hide anything of value. Pieces of gold were tucked under floorboards, and chickens were stashed down the holes in the outhouses. At night, the children of the neighborhood crept down to the camp and watched the gypsies singing and dancing, beating their drums and tambourines, and feasting on everything they had looted from the local grocery stores. Some of the locals secretly had their palms read and fortunes told by the gypsies, but eventually they confessed their sins to the parish priest, who gave them a tongue-lashing and a long rosary to recite for their penance.

But penance was far from these neighbors' minds now. The smell of chili peppers filled the air. More paper plates and cups were produced. Paper napkins in hand, mothers wiped off smudges of melted cheese from toddlers' mouths. Cans of Coke popped open with a *whoosh* and a *fizz*. The sun shone high in the sky above us, my neck turning red with sunburn. Women pushed babies in strollers. Men stood together in clumps, smoking, laughing, and slapping their thighs. The mariachis resumed their tunes, groups of young schoolchildren showcasing their steps on the stage.

My foot tapped to the music, up, down, up, down, my legs— longing to join in the dance—on solid ground.

30

The next time I found Father Sergei at home, it was early May. He was sitting in a folding chair in his garden under his dwarf fig tree, sparrows flitting from its branches to his shoulder and back, his prayer book spread open on his lap. The little dogs had greeted me at the gate, but the monk hadn't risen to meet me.

"Come on back to the garden," he called.

The monk was alone, looking thinner, both his hair and the garden having taken on a look of wildness and disarray. For the first time, Father Sergei's beard appeared ungroomed, and weeds popped up here and there in the midst of the broccoli and squash.

"I'm dying," the monk said.

I sank down on the bench. "Oh, no," I said. "No …"

"Oh, stop," Father Sergei said. "It's fine. I've accepted it. It's part of the cycle of nature. My liver has been bad for a long time, and now it's filled with cancer. Tumors are growing on my spinal cord. It won't be long."

"But—"

"No, there are no buts. You're just like my monks and nuns. They are so sad. They are crying and mourning. But they should be happy for me. I'm being released from this life and jettisoned on into the next!"

"It's just that a few weeks ago you were so vigorous."

"Ah, but St. Paul said, 'God has chosen the weak things of the world to confound the things that are mighty.'" Father Sergei tilted back his head, the sunlight bouncing off the gold crown on his tooth. One of the Chihuahuas jumped up on his lap and licked his face. Another one of the brown pooches—no bigger than my foot—clawed at my pant leg. I picked him up and petted his head, his eyes, black and beady, peering up at me.

"How long have you known you've had cancer?"

"It doesn't matter. I've had cancer before. Thirty-five years ago. When I was a younger man, I took the chemo and radiation treatments. I lost all my hair. I was weak and totally debilitated. Since then, Lu has given me herbs, and they have kept me alive for years. Oh, the doctors say they can give me a liver transplant, but I'd rather they save that for some younger person. Now it's time to go. My community asks me why I don't pray for a miracle, why I don't heal myself. Well, I've lived a miracle all these years, but it's over."

"How about just another year?"

"Ah-ha! You can't pray bargains," Father Sergei said.

The monk's dog curled up and settled down in Father Sergei's lap, its head resting on his knee. The dog in my lap yawned, then licked my hand.

"No, death is a natural act," the monk said. "Show me the person who hasn't died, and I'll show you one who hasn't lived."

"Yes."

"No one wants to admit that, but once you do, once you give up control over your own mortality, once you give up your preconceived notions of how you think things should be, you can finally transcend this world."

"You have to surrender?"

"Sí. And through prayer you stay in touch with what Hildegard called the spark of life. But you have done this… . You see, I noticed that you are off your cane."

"It's the most amazing thing," I said. "Little by little, my walking has been improving."

"I told you, you didn't need that cane. You see, you have to look at life with a bigger lens. You must practice a paradigm shift. You must move from your thoughts of 'This life that is happening to me' to 'This life that is happening.' Life contains pain. That's a fact. Buddhism teaches us to retrain our minds and stop fretting over the pain. Fretting is a mind habit. You see, it's all a matter of looking toward the vista. It's all a matter of balance. You are healing. I am dying. You are going up. I am going down."

"I have to admit, I didn't feel anything when you did your laying on of hands."

"Ah, you wanted healing on your own schedule. It doesn't work like that."

"It may be too soon to tell. I mean, I'm doing a lot of other things to help myself."

"You feel less pain, no?" Father Sergei leaned back in his folding chair, his head tilting to one side. The spring wind blew his beard up and away from his chest. The whirligigs spun around and around. The Tibetan prayer bells tinkled their one-note chant. Another Chihuahua tugged at the monk's cassock, his jaws anchored around the black material. The geese, first one, then the other, scurried toward us, heads thrown back, honking at the little dog. The pooch in my lap leaped into the fray, baring his teeth at the geese, charging toward their orange feet, barking his high-pitched yap.

"Hey!" Father Sergei said with a smile, breaking up the fracas, holding up his index and third fingers in the peace sign.

"How do I know what faith is?" I asked.

"You need to pull back and look at the world from a more distant perspective. The point of view is from above, not smack up close, eyeball to eyeball. St. John of the Cross made a little sketch of Christ from a vastly different perspective, as if looking down at the Savior from the heavens. You know Salvador Dali's famous painting of the crucified Christ?"

"Yes, of course."

"That painting is based on St. John's sketch. It teaches us detachment. Look, if we're to learn anything from mysticism, it's the lesson of symbolism. I've tried to tell you this before. You have to look at things as part of the whole, the way Hildegard depicted her mandalas. No one event stands on its own. It has wider resonances. Your neck injury has wider implications, although you may or may not ever understand them. What matters is that you know that all things are part of a bigger pattern, that we carry certain energies with us, certain roles from one generation to the next. We fit into the cycle of nature. You must realize this and then and only then will you be fully healed.

"See, every family, every culture has its stories. In my family—the hidden Jews—the stories became so secret that we didn't even realize that we were carrying them around anymore. You must understand that we're all playing out our parts in certain myths. You can dismiss myth as mere fabrication. You can dismiss religion as mere myth. But myths are integral to our existence. That's why I insisted on opening that woman's crucifix that day—the one that hid little scraps of the Torah from Seville, the one that revealed to her her Jewishness, her heritage. We must look inside ourselves, confront what's there, and realize how it's still operating in our own lives."

"So we must all pick up our crosses and pry them open?"

"You must look inside your own cross. You must look inside your own heart and draw strength from what you find. There you will confront the void. There you will find God. St. Teresa of Avila understood the void. When she was an old woman, her inner voice told her to go and establish a new convent a long distance away. She was tired and didn't really want to do it. Her friend St. John of the Cross was against the plan. They quarreled over it. Teresa set out on her mission with a heavy heart. She had to cross a cold river on a mule. Ice floated by and hit her, knocked her off her mule, and threw her into the water. She was rescued and lay down in a little hut near the riverbank. She looked down at the crucifix around her neck and said, 'Dear God, if you can do this to an old woman, where should I look for you?'

"'In your own heart' came the reply."

"St. Teresa invented interior prayer, *correcto?*" I asked.

"*Sí*. She rediscovered it for her own time and place," Father Sergei said. "She taught that we must have constant contact with God. It's like building up your spiritual bank account. Most people put nothing in their accounts, then when a crisis hits, they panic. And, you see, it took a crisis for you to really start to pray, to ask for Divine intervention."

Father Sergei uncrossed his legs, the Chihuahuas quiet now, slumped down around his chair, napping. The monk yawned, visibly tired himself, his eyelids beginning to droop.

"See, when you meet your maker on the Judgment Day, God's not going to ask you how many times you fornicated or anything like that. God's going to ask you what you did with this life that was given to you. That's the question you must be prepared to answer.

"And what you make of your life depends on your lens, finding that wide angle, looking through the camera symbolically. I sit in my garden," Father Sergei said. "I sit here in my garden in the spring, like today, and in the summer and fall, but also in the winter when it's all gray and brown. My monks think I'm crazy. My monks ask me what possible pleasure I get from sitting in the garden in January. They see only dead sticks and still earth, but I see flowers and trees in bloom. I see the Resurrection."

31

The plaza in the middle of the university campus was quiet. No whacking hockey sticks, no whirling roller-blades, no bouncing balls were in sight. A few students sauntered by on their way to class, but the vendors and political candidates hadn't set up their carts and megaphones yet. In the distance, the traffic rolled by on Central Avenue, but its noise seemed miles away, removed to some other planet. I sat alone on a wooden bench outside the Zimmerman library and let the early Wednesday morning light wash over me. I hadn't used my cane since Saturday, the day of the street festival, and my limbs still felt as if they were capable of operating on their own without help of aids or props. Aimlessly, a brown-and-white short-haired dog wandered toward the Humanities building. A chicken pecked at an insect near the library steps.

I loved those chickens that wandered Albuquerque, seemingly belonging to no one, surviving by their own wits. Even though chickens are domesticated birds, there was something wild, rural, and untamed about their appearance on a university campus. I watched the chicken amble around the plaza, then head toward the university museum, its eyes alert, beak ready to strike at any food along its path. I watched a cluster of men in suits pass the chicken on the sidewalk. The men chuckled, then hustled on to their meeting. New Mexico: Land of Eccentrics. The chicken reminded me of Iowa and how I would be leaving Albuquerque soon, how my time here was almost at an end.

I thought about Lu and what a fine example she had provided me, how she spread good works and cheer throughout the whole barrio with selflessness and compassion, how she was truly a holy woman, how she was a mystic and healer. When she gathered her herbs, when she talked to her statues, she entered a different realm, a kingdom of cultural heritage, family strength, and wisdom that few of us ever tap. I was learning to tap into my heritage in the same way. Lu lived in a world of possibilities. Some might call it a childlike world. Some might call it a superstitious world. I called it a devout world, one that exemplified a deep connection to the Divine. I wanted to follow a similar path.

I thought about Father Sergei and how these last days might be my final precious moments with him. What grace had brought me to him at this time. Perhaps there was a plan, a larger vision that connected us to one another. Yes, perhaps we were all players in a larger myth. What a strange and wondrous thing it was that Father Sergei and I intersected in this time and place. What gratitude I felt toward this man who had taken all the time in the world to sit under a rose trellis and counsel a stranger, a *gringa*. At our first meeting, the monk spoke in riddles. At our last, he urged me to accept the riddle of my life. At our first meeting, I thought he might be crazy. I didn't realize the depth of his wisdom until months later.

Out of the corner of my eye I caught sight of Ernesto near the Union, a backpack slung over his shoulder. I raised my arm, the arm that had been so hard to raise just a few months ago, and waved a full-fledged wave, a gesture filled with friendliness and thanks for his help and many kindnesses. He waved back and scooted on through the heavy Union doors. I tilted my head up, let the sun flood my face, and followed the trail of a plane leaving a jet stream, a white streak in the blue sky.

Robert appeared in front of me. "I noticed you across the plaza and just had to come over and say hello," he said. "And now I see you're without your cane." His face widened into a grin, and he clapped his hands together.

"I am!" I said. "For the past couple of days I've been walking on my own."

"I'm so happy for you," Robert said. "This is a happy, happy day."

It was a very happy day, but a mood of melancholy spread over me, a feeling that all pilgrims must experience once their journey is nearing completion. Yes, my mission was becoming more and more successful. Yes, I was looking forward to returning to my life in Iowa. I had already written the hatchery to order the chicks for my coop. But I was going to miss my friends in New Mexico. I was going to miss all those I'd come to know as healers, from Lu and Father Sergei to Ernesto, Robert, and Cookie. I was going to miss the desert with its many-faceted variations, its dry heat, its mountains, its wide-open plains.

I decided to let my paper grading and class preparation go for the day. I slipped into the Trooper and drove down to the South Valley, to the drugstore. When I pushed open the heavy door, Lu was nowhere in sight.

"She's taken the day off," Lu's sister said. "Try again tomorrow."

I nodded, browsed through the store, and bought a newspaper.

A car honked in front of the door. I glanced out the plate glass window, and there was Lu in her Chevy van, waving to me to come outside. "*Vamos, vamos,*" she called through the open window.

"Where are we going?" I asked, crawling into the front seat of the van.

"To the casino."

"At this time in the morning?"

"Sí. Confront your suffering, sí. Pick up your cross, sí. Serve with humility. You need to do all that, but you must also have fun!" Lu said.

Just south of Albuquerque, Lu pulled the van into the casino on the Native American pueblo, her herbs rattling around in baskets and buckets in the back. A huge building sprawled out in front of us, a structure that looked like a warehouse but was loaded with neon flashing lights and signs, arrows pointing toward the doors. The cheesiness of the casino stood in stark contrast to the pueblo next to it, an ancient, austere cluster of white adobe dwellings, boxy and windswept, that had stood up to centuries of poverty and exploitation.

"We're going in the casino?" I asked.

"Sí," Lu said, striding toward the front door. "We're going in here, and we're going to win!"

We left the natural world, the beauty of the desert stillness, the landscape of wild herbs and wild memories, and entered the world of chance, the world of bright lights, noise, and ringing bells. Clouds of cigarette smoke pooled near the ceiling, turning the air a murky gray. Old men in suspenders shuffled their way toward the blackjack table. Young women in shorts and tank tops bet on horse races shown on large video screens mounted on the wall. Lu led me through the maze of games, her pace focused and direct. We steered around the roulette wheel and made our way to the back of the building, a building that had the feel of Kmart on a busy Saturday afternoon, people crowding the aisles, their voices echoing off the walls, the blue lights blinking.

Lu slapped down a ten-dollar bill at the cashier's booth, and the attendant gave her several rolls of nickels. I changed a ten of my own, and we wound our way back through the crowd to the slot machines, past the dollar slots, past the quarter slots, to the nickel machines that lined up in rows, their tiny windows filled with apples, oranges, and grapes spinning round and round. Lu slipped onto a stool, and I plopped down next to her. A man in a Stetson hat and cowboy boots played the machine beside us. A woman with a ring through her nose and a rose tattooed on her bicep stationed herself beside him.

"*Bueno*," Lu said. "Now watch this. Here we go." She dropped a nickel into the slot and pressed the button. The apples, oranges, and grapes whirled.

"Is this what it means to have faith?" I laughed.

"No, this is luck. *La suerte*," Lu said. "There's a difference."

I put my nickel in my slot and pressed the button. "Here's to la suerte, then," I said.

Lu's fruits landed on one orange, one lemon, and one apple. Mine landed on an apple, an orange, and a sprig of grapes.

"Oh-oh," I said. "This is going to be my *suerte*."

"You don't know. You can't say that. You have to keep playing. Plugging away, no?"

"*Sí*," I said. I dropped in another nickel, and the fruits spun round. *Chink, chink, chink.* This time they landed on a grape, a lemon, and an orange.

The cowboy leaned forward intently toward his machine, straddling his stool as if it were a steed, rocking a little at his hips. Nose 'n' Rose spit on her nickel before plunging it into the slot. Lu pressed her button, and a huge grin swept across her face when $5 worth of nickels crashed down in the tray, spilling out of the sides of the machine, a few stray coins slipping onto the floor. "I told you we were going to win!" she said.

I dropped my nickels in faster now, thinking that speed might give me an advantage. My fruits spun around and around and around, looking for their mates, my eyes glued on their progress, dizzy from the motion. I pressed the button with greater force. I crossed my fingers. I banged my fist on the machine. A sprig of grapes, an orange, an apple. My tray empty.

The cowboy opened a new roll of coins, taking off his hat for a moment to wipe the sweat from his forehead with the cuff of his shirtsleeve. Nose 'n' Rose slipped a stick of bubble gum in her mouth and worked it up and over her tongue, her jaws opening and closing with a rhythm that matched the beat of the rock music blaring from the speakers above our heads.

"Ho, hooo," Lu said, scooping up another $10 worth of nickels from her machine. "I told you we'd have fun!"

I plugged away again. No matches, not even close. I plugged some more, my roll of nickels dwindling in my hand.

The cowboy lit a cigarette, his face frozen next to the whirling windows. Smoke curled up into my nostrils. I became nauseated. Nose 'n' Rose blew a bubble. It popped. She lapped up the gum from her lips with her tongue.

Another $5 crashed out of Lu's machine.

"You have the touch!" I said.

"You know what they say. I'm tuned in," Lu smiled, another nickel clicking through the machine. The windows twirled.

"Then this *is* faith," I said.

"No, I told you, *la suerte*," Lu said. "*Muy* confusing for people. Faith doesn't mean that everything will always be good in life. That's luck. Faith means you'll always be connected no matter where life takes you."

Life took me nearly to the bottom of my nickel wrapper.

"Okay. *Vamos*," Lu said. "Time to go back to the store. I've won twenty dollars."

"In such a short time," I said.

"Yes, but last week I won a hundred," Lu said.

The cowboy reared back on his stool and chugged a gulp from a beer bottle. Nose 'n' Rose blew another, larger bubble, one that almost covered her entire face.

I squeezed my last nickel in the palm of my hand, and we headed back down the path home toward the barrio, wherever life was taking us.

32

Be not perplexed,
Be not afraid,
Everything passes,
God does not change.
Patience wins all things.
He who has God lacks nothing;
God alone suffices.
   —St. Teresa of Avila

Be not perplexed.

I lay back down on my pallet on the floor that night in my apartment. My herbs boiled, the steam trickling down the walls, the stars outside the window brightening my room, the din of traffic roaring down the freeway in the distance, the freeway that had replaced Route 66. My breathing slowed, rising and falling, rising and falling. I picked up the turquoise rosary again and began—one line of St. Teresa's prayer on each bead, the beads moving through my fingers, fat and slick, each stone assuming its own unique shape.

Be not afraid.

The beads fit together like my family, Lu had said. The beads fit together like all our families, like the larger family that we are, each link in the chain entwined with the next, each link strong and tightly clasped. For what is fear but the lack of faith that the links will hold. I let go of one bead and moved to the next.

Just one nickel left in my purse, I realized that I'd placed my bets and won—perhaps not in the smaller, practical moment of the slot machine in the casino, but in the larger, more illusive scheme of my life. I'd arrived in New Mexico in the dark night of the soul, looking for healing, looking for a way to bring myself back into the light. I'd lost all faith in human order and had grave doubts about Divine order. It left me nowhere, with no center, no grounding.

The long-loved solitude of my youth had collapsed into loneliness. My long-loved belief in the sacredness of life had fizzled into alienation. Yet I'd entered Albuquerque in the middle of the cold winter and was returning to Iowa in the middle of the spring, the desert in bloom. I'd entered Albuquerque full of fear that I would grow into old age hobbling around on my cane, and I was returning to Iowa without the cane.

And what is suffering but fear, fear that there will be further loss? Past loss can be mourned, but real suffering comes from the unknown. We must confront our suffering. We must have a model for suffering. We must accept our fate with a more cosmic view and hold on to hope, hold on to our belief in ourselves, even in the face of disaster. Like St. Christopher, like the *conversos*, embarking upon the waters. Like St. Francis who understood that good and evil, enjoyment and suffering—even the most extreme hardships that one could experience—were all part of the same package. The real challenge comes not in striving for the things we all desire: wealth, love, status. All of these states can easily vanish. The mystics purposefully abolished them for themselves. The real challenge comes in facing suffering with courage and dignity. That act alone allows one to grow spiritually, to make a victory of the challenge. Like St. Teresa, we must look into our own hearts to find that courage. We must look inside our own crucifixes, inside our own families' histories, to give us that strength.

Everything passes.

Sometimes beads do unravel, and sometimes bodies do fall and scatter—into the ocean, into the river, across an icy road. And we carry the bodies, the children, the crosses on our confounded shoulders forever. We ferry them across the water. And the way we take up those crosses becomes the most important, the most meaningful thing we will ever do. We ferry them across the water, and then we deposit them on the other shore. We release them. We let go of desire. We begin to practice gratitude for what we do have.

Was I pain-free? No. Would I ever be lonely again? Yes. Would I ever again fall into the dark night of the soul? Yes. For if I'd learned anything from Father Sergei and Lu, my guides, my teachers, my healers, I'd learned to recognize the rising and falling patterns in my physical health, in my emotional and spiritual well-being. I had learned to recognize the patterns as they churned back in history in my own family, in the family we call humankind.

God does not change.

Only our stories do—the stories we invent to shape our lives, each story assuming its own unique shape. I once learned that the origins of religion were mythological. Now I wonder what we would do without myth to answer our questions. Stories become our histories, and our histories, our stories. I am a good witch with a garden full of herbs, a chicken living under the porch, and a corn knife in my hand. I am a witch, good or bad, my neck pulled this way and that. I am a wise woman, Fabiola and Jacoba Felicie. I am a shaman, flying through the air. I am Isaac Abravenal and Abraham Seneor terrorized by Tomás de Torquemada. I am a crypto-Jew carrying my secret inside my head. I am a woman in the South Valley carrying her secret inside her crucifix. I piece together the scraps of paper, pieces of the Torah. I piece together the story of my life and pick up my cross. When we discover our histories—the real links, the true threads—our lives change. We move through the cycle of nature. We move toward the Resurrection.

What changed my perspective? What moved my thoughts from suffering to detachment? What moved my energies from alienation to engagement? Historical and present models. First, the great mystics, the Teresas and Hildegards, the Francises and Johns, the saints who had once intrigued me but had seemed so incomprehensible. Now they seemed so pragmatic, with their wisdom and compassionate ways of living, their gentleness and force, their more expansive worldviews. Second, the everyday mystics, the monks and *curanderas*, the people who had once intrigued me but had seemed so frightening. Now they seemed so exemplary, with their lives lived in a neighborhood that most would shun. Third, the family mystics, the ancestors and icons, the women who had gone before me, who had taught me how to live with pleasure and fun, and to suffer with courage and dignity. "Mother, Grandmother," I called, "carry me across the water. Let me go into the dark night and come out on the other shore."

If your whole life was designed carefully and lovingly to change you, to teach you a lesson, I asked myself again, what would it be? To learn the teachings of the mystics. To learn to strip my life down to the essentials. To live the lesson or else—or else my life would be stripped down for me. To live through the chaos and hold steady and firm. To learn that there is only one stable thing in a life of chaos. There is only one stable thing, and all is one. Stripped of all connections, it was only then that I could experience the interconnectedness of all things. It was only then that I could reach forgiveness.

Patience wins all things.

Despair loses everything, and fear fuels despair. As I grasped that bead of the rosary, I prayed to let go of my own fear, of my own hopelessness. When I am attacked, I prayed, let hatred never even enter my heart. Let me remember the words of St. Francis:

> *Lord, make me an instrument of your peace.*
> *Where there is hatred, let me sow love;*
> *Where there is injury, pardon;*
> *where there is doubt, faith;*
> *where there is despair, hope;*
> *where there is darkness, light;*
> *and where there is sadness, joy.*
>
> *O Lord, grant that I may not so much*
> *seek to be consoled as to console;*
> *to be understood as to understand;*
> *to be loved as to love;*
> *for it is in giving that we receive;*
> *it is in pardoning that we are pardoned;*
> *and it is in dying*
> *that we are born to eternal life.*

Let me remember the words of Father Sergei: I forgive you for attempting to murder a servant of God. I hold up my cross, and I forgive all who have tortured others in the name of this cross. I forgive you and release you to the universe. I forgive. I pull back and detach.

Before I came to New Mexico, I realized that investment in human institutions was as chancy as dropping nickels in a slot machine. More than ever before, I could grasp the problem of power, how one group merely tries to usurp another. Yet through my work with Father Sergei and Lu, I had reclaimed faith in human friendship—that on an individual level, one human could bond with another. I understood that that bond might not be perfect, but I reclaimed faith in the preciousness of its existence in the moment. I found connection and pleasure in friendship in a backyard garden, in a drugstore, in a café and plaza.

Once I reclaimed human friendship, I could once again acknowledge Divine order and surrender my will to it. I learned that Divine order has no order. I learned that the Divine, or the higher vision of nature, works in opposites. I had to release myself to irony, to paradox. I had to learn to think in symbols. I had to abandon myself to the idea that things are neither "good" nor "bad," that one simply has to go with the flow of events.

He who has God lacks nothing.

I had a pair of pliers, a pair of pliers that I'd carried with me all these years. I prayed: Let me find fulfillment in their creative activity. Like St. John's poems, like Hildegard's musical compositions, like St. Francis's dialogues, like Teresa's books, let them have their say. Let them do their work. Art transforms life, pushing us forward with hope despite the pain, pushing us forward, connected wholly and intimately with both the female and male, the yin and yang, the good and bad witch, the light and dark sides of the self.

Healing is a process of looking back, of finding the things in the past that have been significant to you. That mean the most. That give you the buoyancy to risk the future. Healing must also be a process of looking forward, no matter how uncertain the future may be. Some healings are instant, spontaneous. There is a prayer, a laying on of hands. There is a pill or an operation, and, *poof*, everything is changed. These healings have a sudden dramatic impact on the psyche. Healing from the wounds of chronic illness or injury is more amorphous. The only certainty is that it will surely flood again. We ferry ourselves across the water. I cross a cold river on a mule. I ride the waves.

I learned to have faith in the unfolding of these events, the unwinding of lives. All forces, all of nature became closer to my consciousness: Brother Sun, Sister Moon, Sister Water, Brother Fire, Sister Mother Earth, Sister Bodily Death. I tried to forgive, and I learned to play—to realize the spark of life in the rosebush, the zucchini plant, the horsetail herb. To recognize the joy of marching down the street with friends, walking without a cane for the first time in months, the mariachis' music echoing in my ears. To recognize the joy of going to the casino, of venturing off to the unknown.

I had a pair of pliers, a pair of pliers I'd carried with me all these years. At last, I knew what to do with them. I used them to mend all the broken necks, all the broken hearts. I prayed: I surrender. I surrender and stand tall in the wind, joining one link to another, one to another, until all things are connected again, and both the ceiling fan and the earth spin round and round, the sun in the heavens above us.

God alone suffices.

My pilgrimage was coming to an end. In a few days, I would pack up my clothes, my books, my traction rig, and stuff them all back into the Trooper. I would drive myself home, traveling through the mountain pass, past the roadside motels with their flashing VACANCY signs, past herds of antelope dancing across the plains. I would return home to the lush green of the midwestern summer where the leaves were unfurled on the maple trees, the gardens were in bloom, the roses climbing up the trellises. And if some nights I still lay awake in the dark, I would know that it is the job of the pilgrim to return from a journey with the lessons she has learned and to see all things differently again.

Epilogue

Father Sergei's little congregation squeezes together on the one pew along the far wall of his church. It is time for the Gospel, and the lot of us—the odd lot that we are—wait patiently. The older woman in the long veil sits next to me, her lips moving in her own private prayer, her thigh pressed against mine, my St. Christopher medal and turquoise rosary hidden in the pocket of my dress. The suburban couple crunches in next to her, their Down's syndrome son left standing next to the lectern, his glasses slipping down on his face. He continues to rock and sway even though the chanting has come to a temporary halt. The younger couple plops down on the floor, their babies corralled in the web of their crossed legs.

Then one of the young monks, the bagpiper—his hair long, blond, and flowing around his shoulders—comes out from the sanctuary. Everything ceases. We rise. The congregants abandon their prayers and stand motionless, attentive. The young monk stands at the pulpit, opens the Bible, its thick pages crackling with the movement, and reads the day's Gospel:

> At that time, it came to pass on one of the days, that Jesus sat teaching. And there were Pharisees and teachers of the Law sitting by, who had come out of every village of Galilee and Judea and out of Jerusalem. And the power of the Lord was present to heal them. And behold, some men were carrying upon a pallet a man who was paralyzed, and they were trying to bring him in and to lay him before Him. And as they found

no way to bring him in, because of the crowd, they went up onto the roof and lowered him through the tiles, with his pallet, into the midst before Jesus. And seeing their faith, He said, "Man, thy sins are forgiven thee." And the Scribes and Pharisees began to argue, saying, "Who is this Man who speaks blasphemies? Who can forgive sins, but God only?" But Jesus, knowing their thoughts, answered and said to them, "Why are you arguing in your hearts? Which is easier to say, 'Thy sins are forgiven thee,' or to say, 'Arise and walk'? But that you may know that the Son of Man has power on earth to forgive sins"—He said to the paralytic—"I say to thee, arise, take up thy pallet and go to thy house." And immediately he rose before them, took up what he had been lying on, and went away to his house, glorifying God. And astonishment seized upon them all, and they glorified God and were filled with fear, saying, "We have seen wonderful things today."

The nuns at the lectern chant and bow and bow and chant:
Praise the Lord, O my soul: in my life I will praise the Lord:
I will sing to my God as long as I shall be, Alleluia.

Next, Father Sergei appears from the sanctuary, his face pale and wan. He seems tired, as if the opening of the service has consumed all his energy, as if he doesn't have the strength to even lift his arms under the weight of the vestments. His hair, still jet-black but lacking its normal sheen, flows down around his shoulders, softening the curve of his stooped demeanor. He winces in pain, forehead wrinkled, his hand holding his lower back. He straightens himself as best he can and takes three shuffling steps toward us.

"My friends," the monk begins. "Today's Gospel tells us that we are all paralyzed, we are all lame—if not in our physical bodies, then in our hearts. We must seek reconciliation for our sins, but we must also push forward with our lives.

"So many of us are frozen, paralyzed with fear. It's up to each of us to let go of our fears, to abide in the stream of God's graces, to live in that place. Fear holds you down, straps you to the pallet like the man in the Gospel. And what are we afraid of? Afraid of being alone. Yes, of being by ourselves so that we can no longer block out the sound of God's voice. That's what loneliness is really about—no longer being able to find a diversion from your path.

"And fear of death? We have such a terrible fear of death. In my dying, my fellow brothers and sisters have been coming to me crying, saying that they just won't be able to stand it when I'm gone. Instead, they should be happy for me! It's the natural cycle of life. We rejoice when babies are born. In death, that baby has come full circle. We should rejoice when the adult dies and makes room for another baby to be born. It's the cycle, the cycle that we must become attuned to, that we must never forget we are an integral part of. When we comprehend the cycle, there is pain, yes, but no real suffering, because we understand that we are merely part of the whole. We remove suffering through our acceptance of God's greater plan."

Father Sergei stops to clear his throat, coughing into a handkerchief, his chest rising and falling in spasms. The three small children struggle free from their parents' embrace, crawling and tottering across the floor. The six-month-old baby, the clasp of his diaper pin protruding from his pants, wriggles into a tight, dark space under the pew. The Down's syndrome man keeps up his rocking, creating a silent, steady rhythm—back and forth and back and forth—that we all follow from the corners of our eyes.

"There was a woman who came here many months ago," Father Sergei says, taking up the thread again. "She was suffering horribly. She had been paralyzed. She was up walking on a cane but was still crippled, in so much pain."

Wow, I thought to myself. That sounds a lot like me.

"See, she had been hit in an automobile accident."

A lot like me.

"She was raised a Roman Catholic and had lost her faith."

Could he be talking about me? No, I never told him I left the Church. He'd have no way of knowing that.

"She was afraid.

"She came to me, and I laid my hands on her. She wanted a healing, but nothing happened right away. She still had that little part of herself that was doubting and questioning."

That was true.

"And then she surrendered. She got herself through the dark night of the soul. She had to go through that to get to the other side. She ferried herself across the water."

Right.

"And then she found her faith."

I did.

"Her faith was there all along, but it took a crisis to discover it again. Just as Christopher Columbus 'discovered' America. The continent had been there all the time, but it took a mission of faith to find what had always been. She found her faith was wider than just one church. She connected with the real current of love, the reason for being, the reason why all things are connected and valuable in this life. She opened her heart. She contacted the source of mysticism that was inside her, the source of miracles. She'd had a lot of bad luck and an equal amount of good faith. And she found her faith in spite of herself."

That's a good way of putting it.

"She faced her cross with dignity. She looked inside her own family crosses and discovered her archetypal patterns. She learned that we must all open our crucifixes and pull out the bits of Torah inside."

And read what's printed there.

"We think miracles come from some outside source, some big, powerful male God on high swooping down to transform us. But Jesus said, 'The kingdom of God is within you.'"

Sí.

"Even though we may never completely understand our role in the universe, we must believe in the connection of all things, how one act links to another, one bead to another—like the rosary. I can trace my family back to the twelve tribes of Israel. We've lived a life of exile. That was our destiny—just as it was our job to leave Spain and 'discover' America, just as it was my job to 'rediscover' my Jewishness. We are all on a voyage of discovery. Our job is to steady the course, to resist our natural urge to mutiny."

Right.

"And, oh, this woman followed all her doctor's courses and did everything that she was supposed to do. That helped. That helped a great deal, I'm sure. The doubting Thomases among you will always say that the doctors cured her. Or you may think that she was destined to get better anyway on her own. But she was never supposed to walk again. The bottom line is, she was supposed to be in heavy leg braces the rest of her life. Gradually, little by little, she let go of the walker. She let go of the cane. Like one of the junipers in the mountains, she righted herself. She learned to pray again. She drew strength from her icons. She healed. Inside and out. She healed emotionally and spiritually—even more important than the physical. She read history. She studied the mystics and integrated their teachings into her life. We have seen wonderful things today.

"And she will go on healing. On the pilgrimage, it is the journey, not the destination, that counts. We who had lived on Route 66 saw this phenomenon over and over again. Every car, every driver was so focused on getting to California that they zoomed right by the important stops along the way. She has stopped and lingered a while in those old motor courts. She has taken the time to search out and see what she must see.

"Sí, we have seen wonderful things today. But it wasn't me who healed her."

Yes, it was. Now he's being too modest.

"No, you mustn't assume that it was me who healed her. I've never healed anyone. The seeds were already there."

What?

Father Sergei looked up, his dark eyes focused, intense, piercing mine through the haze of the incense.

"It was her faith that healed her," he said. "It was her faith that healed her."

Afterword

I returned from New Mexico to Iowa and saw all things differently again. I unpacked the wooden crucifix and rosary I had received from Lu. I hung the cross on the living room wall and draped the rosary from a hook near my bed. These objects helped guide me through several weeks of meditation upon my journey. Home from my pilgrimage, the green grass, the moist air, and the cardinals at the bird feeder, all seemed wondrous, rediscovered. I had moved away from the dry dessert, the sand, the roadrunner outside my door and had found the Midwestern spring bursting out around me. I was happy to see my neighbors and friends once again, to be reunited with my cats and pet goats. I was happy to purchase my goslings and nurture their young lives along safely in my coop. Even though my legs were still unsteady, and occasionally I had to pick up the cane once again, my relapses were infrequent. I tried to move forward unperplexed and unafraid.

Day after day throughout that first summer home from New Mexico, I gave thanks for the mysticism and miracles I had experienced in Albuquerque. Some days, I would sit in my easy chair sipping a cup of tea brewed from Lu's herbs. I'd stare at the shining turquoise stones of Lu's rosary and think to myself: What, oh, what happened to me? Then I'd remember the red and yellow roses winding up Father Sergei's arbor. I'd feel the paws of his Chihuahua dogs scratching at my legs, and visualize the sign he had painted on his garden gate. In my life there were many thorns—but what roses!

I planted my own garden. Bending over, crouching toward the ground, I made long furrows in the soil and reached down to slip bulbs, seeds, and seedlings into the ground. The carrot seeds spilled from my fingers directly into their furrow. I spread a thin layer of compost on top of them, doused them with seaweed and fish emulsion, then covered them with dirt, my back curling, my arms pushing the hoe across the ground with easy, steady strokes. I chuckled and thought of sloth in my row of onion sets. Avarice came to mind near my row of broccoli plants. How rich you are, how valuable. I pulled a floating row cover over my zucchini squash and just shook my head. Lust, lust, lust. What more could I say?

My New Mexico experience took some time and energy to digest, but finally I sat down at my computer and began the manuscript. Once again my days became extremely busy teaching at Iowa State University, raising my food, addressing my medical conditions and trying to write a new book. I put my head down and wrote during any of the free moments I could find during the day, getting up early in the morning before I went into work, returning to my desk again after dinner. I intentionally isolated myself while I felt my way through the story of *The Desert Pilgrim*. My admiration for my healers grew even stronger as I dramatized their abilities on the page.

Sadness washed over me, though, when I thought of Father Sergei. I assumed that he had died. Liver cancer is a quick death sentence. I kept in touch with Lu through postcards and a few quick phone calls to the store. After a couple of years—that went by in a blur—the book was finished and published. When I received my first advance copies I signed one and sent it right off to Lu. A few days later she called me on the phone.

"Oh, I love this book," she said. "Now you must send one to Father Sergei."

"Send one to Father Sergei?" I asked and thought to myself: "Send one to Father Sergei? What's the postage on that going to be?"

"No, he's alive!"

"Alive? How could that be?"

On the Sunday morning that was supposed to have been Father Sergei's last service he spoke of Jesus' healing of the paralyzed man. He spoke of my healing but didn't mention his own impending death. His fellow monks had already built his coffin. I assumed that he would, as he had wished, be buried in his own garden. I took solace in the thought that he would return to the soil and complete the cycle of nature in his own backyard. The next morning—the morning of my departure—Lu crossed the street to the monastery with a special blend of herbs. She gave them to Father Sergei then held her hand high over his body and gave him a special blessing from the Holy Spirit.

"And he lived!" Lu said. "He lived!"

On my book tour in Albuquerque I drove to the barrio, then pulled open the door of the drugstore, the chime still jingling against the glass. I ran behind the counter and threw my arms around Lu. Everything was still in its place—the boxes and Mason jars filled with herbs, the smaller packets of herbs hanging on the wall (Raspberry, Ruda, Romero), the counter filled with jars of candy and the copies of El Hispano News near the cash register. Lu was bright and cheerful, making tins of salve for Bells palsy, helping a customer suffering from asthma, another with stomach problems.

She had copies of *The Desert Pilgrim* propped up and proudly displayed on the counter.

At one o'clock we waited for the pharmacist to come in and watch the store. He no longer wore his official white smock and had given up on filling prescriptions, but he still arrived every day to do paper work and to wait on customers. He helped them with herbs and occasionally fielded a query about a toothbrush.

"Now we'll go to the Hispanic Cultural Center," Lu said. "Father Sergei will join us."

I stepped out the door of the drugstore and spotted Father Sergei on the sidewalk next to the gate to his monastery. An icon of the Blessed Virgin graced the gate, her red robes and golden halo bright and shining in the desert sun. A large Russian spire—white spine supporting a blue bulb and golden cross—rose from the roof of the chapel. The adobe walls of the monastery had been repainted. St. Michael the Archangel stood even taller now than he had in years past, his arm arching his sword toward the chapel door, his golden wings spread, his breastplate glistening.

Father Sergei stood on the sidewalk, leaning into a cane. He was even thinner than the last time I had seen him, his hair grayer, his cheeks leathery and sunken. He walked with more hesitation, one brown Birkenstock sandal in front of the other. Yet, there he stood—alive—his spirit never wavering. I ran across the street and he opened his arms for my hug.

"I'm so, so happy to see you!" I said.

"Blessings on you, my daughter."

Together, Father Sergei, Lu and I walked down old Route 66, *El Camino Real*.

"Where are we having lunch?" I asked.

"You'll see," Lu replied.

With each step, I saw a different barrio stretch out before me. Yes, I knew that an undertow was still present in the neighborhood, but old Route 66 had dramatically changed. The old-boarded up businesses had been reopened, their signs repainted, the buildings refurbished. The café, the grocery store, the flower shop. Gone were the litter and homeless from the gutters. In their place were bus stops decorated by students in fancy ceramic tile. *La Comunidad.* The bus stops depicted life—old and new—in the barrio. One displayed the people: men, women and children, at work, at home, at school, brown skin, brown and black hair, mustaches and dreadlocks. *Us.* Another displayed a mariachi playing a guitar, a woman dancing in a long, flowing purple skirt, two native dancers with feathered headdresses, a man in a large sombrero singing. *Musica, Baile, Y Danza.*

Our dance took us past the doors of the Catholic Church, once a down at-the-heal school gymnasium used as a chapel. Father Corazón had moved on to another parish, but the old kneelers and pews had remained in a space that had been transformed into a traditional southwestern church. What was once just a makeshift altar plopped down under a basketball hoop, was suddenly a church that rivaled Chimayo for its authentic Hispanic feel and artistic beauty. The walls were no longer bare and rough cut, smudged and dented from the assaults of basketballs and kickballs over many decades. The walls had become earth-toned, adobe-like panels that narrowed the focal point to the main altar in the front of the church. In the rear of the church, a small chapel memorialized those who had died in the 9/11 attacks in New York City. A beam recovered from the rubble of the World Trade Center ran through the middle of the small room, creating a bald, bold line. The names of the dead were carved into stone on the walls.

The National Hispanic Cultural Center stood tall and proud at the end of the street. When I was living in Albuquerque and visiting the barrio regularly, I often drove by this space—a dry, dusty lot. Now, a large complex filled the corner, boasting a performing space, classrooms, visual art galleries, a bookstore, a plaza for traditional dancing and a restaurant with traditional food. The Center was a whirl of activity sponsoring everything from an exhibit of New Mexican hand painted *retablos*, Spanish language lessons, a celebration of *Dia Del Libro* (World Book Day) and even showings of international Spanish films.

We sat down at a table in the restaurant by the window, the bright New Mexican light shining in my eyes, bathing the three of us in its glow. We were all hungry and the aroma of the buffet table filled our nostrils with temptation. Here were two remarkable people, I thought, with strong personalities, but so little real ego. They knew their strengths, their profound abilities, but they didn't advertise them. As St. Theresa of Avila and St. John of the Cross knew so well, mysticism is about surrendering the ego, entering the dry desert, and abandoning all appetites. Only then would you make a connection to the wider whole. Only then would you meet the void, the divine.

As we approached the buffet, I thought about how often in the last two years I'd tried to practice those mystical precepts: humility, love, detachment. I thought about how often I'd failed. The life of the mystic was one of continual practice and learning, of faltering, stopping, picking up your cross and continuing on your pilgrimage again. I asked Father Sergei what had allowed him to continue.

"The cancer is still there, but it's in remission. I've been given more time to do the Lord's work."

Lu, who told me then that she was related to St. Theresa of Avila through her Spanish father, was also continuing her work. Pepe, the homeless man she had fed sandwiches every day from the refrigerator of the drug store, had died. The city cremated him but could find no family members to claim his ashes. They called Lu.

"Yes, I'll claim his ashes," she had said, and gave him a proper burial.

Lu also helped high school students reclaim their heritage. She led high school students on walks along the Rio Grande at the Cultural Center, teaching them the ancient healing properties of the Hispanic healing tradition.

The next day, Lu agreed to accompany me to my reading at the University of New Mexico bookstore. Just a little over a mile away from the barrio, once again, I was struck by how separate the two worlds are from each other. I stood at the podium, and read to an eclectic audience filled with ex-nuns, true believers, hippies who had lived by their wits in the desert, New Age practitioners, alternative medicine advocates, nurses and M.D.'s, anthropology students, and curious book lovers. Then Lu took the stage, and as if she had been a university professor all her life, lectured on the history of the Hispanic herbal healing tradition—facts, dates, people and places at her fingertips. She was deluged with questions ranging from bee stings to AIDS.

My book tour took me off on a flurry of activities to other bookstores, other towns and cities, giving readings, leading retreats and teaching workshops. My life took me back to my home, my teaching and writing schedules, yet every year or two, I try to finish up my work, hunt for a cheap plane ticket, and sneak off to New Mexico for spiritual renewal. During these years Father Sergei became a bishop in the Orthodox Church and Lu was honored by the Smithsonian Institution. A miniature replica of the drug store and a display of herbs and religious articles became part of a touring exhibit of the Folklife of the Rio Grande.

A few years ago Lu and I were squeezed into a booth in the café having breakfast when a woman suddenly came up to our table and threw her arms around the *curandera*.

"Thank you so much!" the woman said.

"Who are you and what did I do?" Lu asked.

"You saved my life!" the woman said.

The woman had had a large tumor successfully removed from her abdomen. The problem became the incision that, no matter how hard the doctors tried, just wouldn't heal. Finally, they left her with an open wound, fearful of an infection. In desperation, the woman came to the drug store. Lu brewed up a concoction of herbs and applied them to the wound.

"In about a week, the wound healed right up!" the woman said. "It healed right up!" She kissed Lu on the forehead, hugged her again, then hurried off to work.

"What herbs did you use?" I asked.

"I can't remember," Lu said, nibbling on her tortilla.

Father Sergei, too, has continued his healing tradition.

"I now have a specialty," he told me on a recent visit.

"A healing specialty?" I asked, anxious to hear about this turn of affairs. "What is it?"

"Infertility," he said.

Father Sergei explained that with the publication of *The Desert Pilgrim*, people began to appear at his door seeking guidance. Often these were couples who were having trouble conceiving. He brought the couples into his chapel, lay them down on the rug, then placed relics on their abdomens. He gathered his monks and nuns around the couples, chanting and praying over them.

"And it seemed to work," he said, pulling a small stack of baby pictures from his wallet.

The dynamics of my two healers on their shared corner in Albuquerque seem to work and keep working.

Last summer I sat in the drug store and saw another homeless person—this time a schizophrenic woman. She wore a large cowboy hat on her head and had no front teeth. Lu greeted her cheerfully, opened the refrigerator door, fixed her a sandwich and gave her a bag of chips. The woman said that she was getting her teeth fixed soon, hoped to get off the street and move into an apartment. Lu nodded encouragement.

Another woman entered and brought Lu a packet of greeting cards that she had hand-painted. In Spanish, the woman told Lu that the cards were a gift for helping her have the self-confidence to interview for a good job as a social worker. She got the job and was very grateful for Lu's counsel.

Lu cleaned out the backroom of the drugstore that had once housed her granddaughter's dance studio. Out went racks and racks of costumes and in came a sofa, easy chair, end tables, statues of the saints and icons. Now the room is a meeting place for other healers. A student apprentice busies himself making herbal tinctures.

Across the street, the monks are not idle. They have converted the attic of their bungalow into an arts and crafts workspace. In the natural brightness that beams through skylights in the roof, the monks teach regular classes in icon making.

On my last visit, I examined the small, wooden icons on the worktable, the rounded curves of the faces of the saints and their golden halos. I sat there on a bench, taking in the sheer visual pleasure of the icons and wondered how anyone learned such control over a paintbrush.

"It's better if you have no visual art training," one of the monks told me.

Father Sergei nodded. "It's best to be fresh, taking in the training without any preconceived notions. Just entering into the prayer state."

Next to the icons sat a pile of leather belts and several bags—hand tooled with intricate Celtic symbols. The monk who had once entertained me in the monastery garden with his bagpipe music made the exquisite leather goods. He took them to art fairs and worked steadily to fill orders, providing income for the monastery.

"My Irish grandmother taught me never to buy what you can make yourself," he smiled at me through his long, blond beard. "I learned the craft from her."

One of the nuns had also helped secure extra income. She set up a stand in front of the monastery on Route 66, cars whizzing by with the steady thump-thud of blaring rock music, to sell small jars of jam made from the monastery fruit trees. Surrounding the jars were a selection of hand-painted icons. I stood on the sidewalk and chatted with the nun, the hot summer sun beating down on my back. She had had to deal with severe health problems herself, including several surgeries and hospitalizations.

"I look at the world differently now," the nun said. "My illness helped me get my priorities straight, to value the important things in my life, to live each day with gratitude."

A man pulled over in a long, slick dark blue Buick, a shiny gold chair around his neck. He was a city official and a regular jam customer.

I bought an icon of St. Mary Magdalene.

"She was the first to witness the resurrection of Christ," the nun told me. "She was one of the women who found the empty tomb—a very important Biblical character.

I feel my own emptiness filled, my own longing for spiritual insight satisfied each time I visit New Mexico. From the barrio, I have followed El Camino Real south, revisiting the Bosque de Apache. Once again, I've stood in the marsh, the "Dark Night" becoming the golden morning, and watched the snow geese and sandhill cranes lift off from the water, wings flapping. I've stood there at dusk and watched flight after flight of the birds return to roost near the water.

I've returned to my own roost at Chimayo, sitting in the church, meditating upon my own healing. I've taken students there to experience the site, focus their thoughts and record their impressions of mysticism. I've taken friends who, disappointingly, were not impressed and thought the place like any other tourist stop. Then I took a friend to Chimayo who was battling cancer. She knelt before the hole in the ground and rubbed dirt up and down her arms and legs. Suddenly, she reported feeling tingling all over her body. She was overcome with the sensation.

Mostly, I've returned alone. I've pressed my back against the hard, wooden pew, dropped a coin in the slot, lit a candle and said a prayer of gratitude. I've returned again and again to the teachings of the mystic saints: Hildegard of Bingen, St. Francis of Assisi, St. Theresa of Avila, St. John of the Cross. I've found in them a way to live one's spirituality, a real poetry of transcendence.

Once, I imagined that I would never walk again, that my only travels would be in the imagination of my mind. Once, I imagined that my mind, body and spirit would never find their way out of the abyss. Once, I imagined that healing was similar to slaying an evil giant in a secluded valley. Now, healing feels more like shaking hands with that giant and walking hand-in-hand together up the long mountain road.

—May, 2008

Bibliography

Achterberg, Jeanne, "The Golden Thread" in Imagery in Healing: Shamanism and Modern Medicine. Boston: Shambhala Publications, 1985.

———. "Medieval Christian Cosmology" in Woman as Healer: A Panoramic Survey of the Healing Activities of Women from Prehistoric Times to the Present. Boston: Shambhala Publications, 1990.

Armstrong, Regis J., O.M. Cap., and Ignatius Brady, O.F.M., trans. Francis and Clare: The Complete Works. New York: The Paulist Press, 1982.

Borchert, Bruno. Mysticism: Its History and Challenge. York Beach, Maine: Samuel Weiser, Inc., 1994.

de la Bedoyere, Michael. Francis of Assisi. Manchester, N.H.: Sophia Institute Press, 1999.

Flinders, Carol Lee. Enduring Grace: Living Portraits of Seven Women Mystics. New York: HarperSan Francisco, 1993.

Hildegard of Bingen's Book of Divine Works. Edited by Mathew Fox. Santa Fe, N.M.: Bear and Company, 1987.

Kavanaugh, Kieran, and Otilio Rodriquez, trans. "The Dark Night" in The Collected Works of St. John of the Cross. Washington, D.C.: ICS Publications, 1979.

Kay, Elizabeth. The Chimayó Valley Traditions. Santa Fe, N.M.: Ancient City Press, 1990.

Longford, Lord Frank. Saints. London: Hutchinson, 1987.

Paris, Erna. Chapter 14 in The End of Days: A Story of Tolerance, Tyranny, and the Expulsion of the Jews from Spain. New York: Prometheus Books, 1995.

The Psalms, St. Joseph Catholic Edition. Catholic Book Publishing Co., 1996.

Roth, Norman. Chapter 8 in Conversos, Inquisition, and the Expulsion of the Jews from Spain. Madison, Wisc.: University of Wisconsin Press, 1995.

St. Teresa of Avila. Collected Writings. Edited by Otilio Rodriquez. Washington, D.C.: ICS Publications, 1976.